FURNITURE HOT SPOTS

FURNITURE HOT SPOTS

THE BEST FURNITURE STORES
AND WEB SITES COAST TO COAST

JENNIFER LITWIN

*Dear Michele and Gary,
Enjoy! We miss you.
Love,*

The Lyons Press
Guilford, Connecticut

An imprint of The Globe Pequot Press

Contents

Acknowledgments

Furniture Hot Spots has been quite an undertaking, and I have many people to thank for making this book a reality. First, and most importantly, I want to thank my agent, Linda Loewenthal of the David Black Agency, who deserves a medal for her hard work, smart ideas, and patience in the last year. Her support and belief in the book made it possible. I will be forever grateful to Linda.

I would also like to especially thank Jay Cassell, Ann Treistman, and Christine Duffy at The Lyons Press for not only believing in the project, but for coming up with creative ideas. They had the special gift of staying calm and focused throughout the project.

Thank you also to Robert Lang who helped me come up with ideas for the book and write the book proposal. This process took months! He has been a calming force and was always available to discuss the project.

I also want to thank Cheminne Taylor-Smith and Karl Kunkel of *InFurniture* and Richard Dzierwa of *Consumers Digest* magazines for helping me to understand how consumers approach the furniture industry. Knowing how buyers can be frustrated shopping for furniture made me want to share sources and tips that would help people effectively buy furniture.

I also want to thank my friend, Dorothy Harris, for coming up with many ideas for this book and helping me better understand the trends in the furniture industry. She has been a wonderful store of knowledge.

I need to thank all of the concierges in hotels around the country. What a hard job! I especially want to thank Julian at the Regency Hotel in New York City and Julie at the Four Seasons in Washington, DC, for helping me with directions, drivers, store information and other pertinent city facts. I will never forget the effort that went into helping me make this the best guidebook possible.

Thank you to all the drivers I hired in each city to help me navigate my way to all of the stores. I especially thank the drivers in San Francisco, Los Angeles and New York for taking me to 30 to 70 stores in a really short period of time. This was perhaps the hardest job of all. Learning all of the streets, driving during rush hour, and waiting hours while I reviewed stores took the patience of a saint. I can't thank you enough. It is because of all of you that I was able to get my reviews done efficiently.

Thank you to Ellen Blackman, my publicist, one of the most talented people I know, who worked day and night coming up with thousands of ideas and pursuing every one of them.

I need to thank my team of helpers who worked tirelessly to help me produce this final book and came up with many ideas: Jeff Connell, Cheri Gogo, and of course, Teresa, who never misses a day with the kids. I will never forget how hard you all worked to make this the best project it could be.

I was also lucky to get so many referrals from fellow store owners. I thank them all, because through them I found some wonderful stores that I wouldn't have known existed, especially one little treasure of a store in a small town in Texas.

To my family, Edward (age eight), Bailey (four), and my husband Stuart, thank you for supporting me throughout all of my travels and long hours of work. I know this hasn't been easy, but you all encouraged me from the beginning to pursue my dreams, and for that I am so grateful.

Introduction

"Do you sell anything other than English antiques?" "We don't sell *any* English antiques. We only sell French antiques, dear"—then a long silence. That was the reply I received from an overly affected salesperson at a prominent French (though it obviously wasn't prominent enough to me) antiques showroom in the formerly Kennedy-owned Chicago Merchandise Mart. I was so mortified by my gaffe that I fled the showroom. Here I was, a grown, intelligent woman embarrassed and intimidated.

Have you experienced a similar scenario in your quest to furnish your home? My guess is that you have, whether you are interested in antiques, fine furniture, or any sort of furniture—otherwise, you most likely wouldn't have this book in your hands. Trust me—furniture buying doesn't have to be this way.

The bad experience I had with the salesperson at the Merchandise Mart changed my life in many ways. I had always had a secret passion for furniture, and this embarrassing experience inspired me to follow my heart and a new path. Determined to learn everything I could about furniture, I left the trading floor of a large bank and went to Sotheby's auction house to intern. While at Sotheby's, I realized that many people are intimidated buying furniture (and art), no matter what the price and origin. Even celebrity shoppers often feel overwhelmed and intimidated by the shopping process (as I encountered later in my business).

Obviously, there was a great need for someone to step up to the plate and help others buy furniture. So I left Sotheby's and opened my own store. As I traveled all over the country buying inventory for my store, I began doing what I did best—shopping for customers. Regular customers from all walks of life and budgets, who frequented my store, including many professional interior designers, would describe the pieces or furniture looks they were after, and I would scour stores everywhere, hunting down their requests. Becoming a professional buyer for my store allowed me to learn much about the process of buying furniture (yes, it is a process), but even more importantly, it gave me the opportunity to develop an intimate understanding of this most difficult task from the consumer's point of view.

I have written *Furniture Hot Spots* to demystify the $71 billion furniture industry, to make shopping for furniture simple for buyers in *all* price ranges who might, as I did, feel intimidated or overwhelmed. As a former bank fund analyst turned antiques broker, I understand the value of one's home and everything we put inside it. In this book I have done the legwork so now you can easily find the best stores and Web sites that have the really great furniture you want.

Tired of reading expensive, sleepy coffee table books that gave me little worthwhile information about furnishing my home, I decided to research the industry, and *Furniture Hot Spots* resulted from that effort. When I taught an upscale fine furnishings course, one of my students commented, "Coffee table books are lovely to look at and the decorator shows are interesting to watch, but at the end of every show, I always think I must need a decorator because I would never know where to buy that furniture." Indeed, the designers on the shows never tell us where they get their furniture. Many of the best showrooms are trade-only, doing business only with designers/decorators, which means you can only shop there with a decorator. I do not think you *need* a decorator, especially if you use this book which will give you the resources (both stores and Web sites) you need to know where and how to buy furniture. I have written *Furniture Hot Spots* to serve as the ultimate tool for furniture shopping, a quick, easy-to-use guide for everyone interested in purchasing quality furniture—antique, modern, or contemporary—in a wide range of prices.

I have reviewed stores in 12 cities and the book is categorized by cities, and neighborhoods within cities. Until now, no one has written a national guidebook reviewing furniture stores for shoppers seeking the best furniture. I admit to some subjectivity in my reviews. For example, how was I treated when I went shopping in these stores? Was the dealer friendly? Do I think the furniture was overpriced relative to similar merchandise sold by other dealers? However, these judgment calls, which are based on my many years of experience as a professional buyer, are meant to give shoppers everywhere a heads-up that will help make their furniture shopping experience successful. In order to do these reviews, I traveled hundreds of miles, coast to coast, personally scoping out each and every one of the stores listed in the book. I visited each store incognito, actually pretending to shop for furniture. The reviews are mine, and mine alone.

Using chairs as symbols, I rated each store from five chairs (the best in its class) to one chair (the worst) for price, personnel, ambiance, and quality. Due to limited space in this book, I chose not to include the one and two-chair stores and Web sites, and there were many stores I was unable to visit. The majority of the stores listed here are worth a visit. The overall review is based on level and quality of service, friendliness, price range and buying terms/discounts, quality of merchandise, store ambiance, and Web site. You should know that five chairs for price does not mean that prices are "good", rather that prices are high. If the store is, in my opinion, one of the very best of its kind in the country, I gave it a chair of distinction, placed after the store name in the heading. When it is possible to buy online at these stores, I make a mention of that in the store's listing.

Furniture Hot Spots will provide you with a solid, representative sample of stores in the cities I visited. I have attempted to list stores that are close to one another within neighborhoods, and I didn't go beyond city limits. Thus, suburbs are excluded.

This book will arm you against all those cold shopkeepers out there, strange buying terms, and those "special" relationships store owners have with interior designers. By the way, I found that in more than 85% of cases in which a store says they "only" give discounts to the trade, these stores will also extend the same discount to the public, if you ask! This is valuable information.

With *Furniture Hot Spots* in hand, you will be able to explore the best furniture shopping venues, from auctions to stores to flea markets. Okay, ready for your journey across America to find the best furniture sources? Allow me to be your guide and help you eliminate the hurdles in what should be an enjoyable and productive experience.

Furniture Hot Spots Key

To aid the consumer, *Furniture Hot Spots* uses a chair 🪑 to rate stores on the following categories: Price, Service, Ambiance and Quality. The more chairs a store receives in each category, the higher that store's overall rating.

The ratings are subjective reflecting the author's experience at each store.

By Price*

🪑 Under $100

🪑🪑 Items under $500

🪑🪑🪑 Most items between $500–$1000

🪑🪑🪑🪑 The majority of items between $750–$2,000

🪑🪑🪑🪑🪑 Majority of items above $2,000

* **Price does not necessarily reflect value**

By Service

🪑 Very unpleasant shopping experience

🪑🪑 Minimally attentive/pleasant sales staff

🪑🪑🪑 Pleasant, but unmemorable shopping experience

🪑🪑🪑🪑 Knowledgeable, friendly staff

🪑🪑🪑🪑🪑 Highly knowledgeable and excellent service

By Ambiance

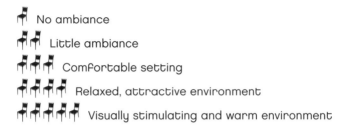

🪑 No ambiance

🪑🪑 Little ambiance

🪑🪑🪑 Comfortable setting

🪑🪑🪑🪑 Relaxed, attractive environment

🪑🪑🪑🪑🪑 Visually stimulating and warm environment

By Quality*

🪑 Below average quality

🪑🪑 Adequate quality

🪑🪑🪑 Majority of the stock is good quality

🪑🪑🪑🪑 Many items are of excellent quality

🪑🪑🪑🪑🪑 Most items are of superior quality

* The quality ratings were comparative. For example, a store carrying Mid-Century Modern furnishings was compared to another store selling similar inventory around the country. A store specializing in 19th-century French furnishings was compared to a store specializing in 19th-century French furnishings.

Chair of Distinction

A chair of distinction represents a store that in my opinion is outstanding in virtually every category. This is a store whose inventory is special, the service is exceptional, the ambiance is wonderful and the quality is superior. A store that receives a chair of distinction is a store that I would highly recommend visiting when in that city and if you are interested in that particular style of furniture.

PART I

HOW TO
SHOP FOR
FURNITURE

CHAPTER 1

Successful Auction Shopping

Making It Easy for the Rest of Us

There is something about an auction that gives it such an irresistible aura of high anticipation and intrigue. Think about all those auction scenes in the flicks where some suave James Bond–type character makes a slight gesture at just the right moment. Bingo! He acquires an undiscovered Van Gogh worth millions for a paltry sum. I suppose whether we like to admit it or not, auctions do conjure up notions of winning the proverbial pot of gold at the end of the rainbow, even for the most sophisticated. I know I was very excited when I went to my very first auction with my husband, Stuart. Newly married and in the market to furnish our first home, we had heard much about auctions and thought we would be the successful winners . . . of what, we didn't know, but we were on a mission to conquer the auction industry.

This first time out was Leslie Hindman's Marketplace auction in Chicago. For those of you unfamiliar with the name, Leslie Hindman Auctioneers, founded in Chicago in 1982, eventually grew into the largest auction house in the Midwest and the fifth largest in the country. Even back in those early days, Leslie Hindman's auctions were well-attended and popular, drawing all age groups, and people from a diverse socioeconomic background.

A friend had suggested Leslie's auction because it seemed to her more like going to a huge party with interesting people than attending some uptight auction populated by a bunch of stodgy snobs. This auction seemed like the perfect one for us to get started. For Stuart and me, it was like heading off to Las Vegas—a little scary, because we didn't know how we would end up. We only knew we were not prepared to lose all of our money.

Being inexperienced auction shoppers, Stuart and I approached our bidding in the same way naïve gamblers approach a gaming table in a Vegas casino. Our goal was to not just win but to win big! With visions of becoming instant veteran auction shoppers, the two of us just dove in and held our breath. Bidding the most on everything without even thinking, we learned, was not the most successful strategy. We ended up with a truckload of some of the worst finds in America, but we could say that we were the "successful" bidders.

To make sure *you* never get sucked in the way we did, let's begin with Auction Shopping 101. First, auctions are comprised of two parts: dealing with buyers, and dealing with sellers. These two different sides of the business are important to understand before attending an auction. Sellers have one goal: to sell their goods for the most money possible. Buyers have one goal: to pay the lowest price possible. Where the buyers and sellers will meet is unknown at the onset of the auction. This uncertainty over the final price makes the auction process both exciting and scary.

Buying at Auction

There isn't just one kind of auction. There are hundreds of kinds of auctions out there to choose from, whether you are in a small town or big city. There are inexpensive furniture auctions, art auctions, fine modern or antiques auctions, estate auctions as well as auctions specializing in various commodities. The one thing all auctions have in common is they are like working the stock market—at an auction, just as with the stock market, the goods or stocks are only worth what someone is willing to pay for them. Antiques dealers often shop at auctions hoping to get a great deal that they can then mark up and sell to the public. These dealers know that they can find great deals here, and they need sources to buy antiques just like you do.

At auction, ***you, the buyer, must beware***. When you are at an auction, *never* assume that the auction house is accurately describing a piece of furniture or artwork. No matter how sophisticated or well-known the auction houses, they can and do periodically make mistakes; some more than others. Keep in mind that auction houses receive thousands of items that they must research to determine a value. All of this work means that the door is left open to human error. There is not always enough time to thoroughly investigate and correctly describe each and every item up for sale. Also, some appraisers are better than others when it comes to accurately appraising an item.

Where Are the Auctions?

In every major city, there are a few reputable auction houses. A good way to find them is through a word-of-mouth referral. If you don't have any friends or family members who are knowledgeable collectors frequenting auctions, ask for the name of one or two from the owner of a well-regarded furniture shop in the area. If you're interested in auction shopping, it is a good idea to put your name on their mailing or e-mail list so that you'll be notified of all upcoming auctions.

Most auction houses put together a catalog with fabulous glossy pictures that beautifully show off the individual pieces (designated by lot number) that will be auctioned. Personally, I find the lot descriptions overly academic with hard-to-grasp terminology for the layperson. It is extremely important that auction houses be consistent in their descriptions of auction items. This is achieved by keeping the description order the same. The piece is described by what period it is from, where it is from, important and unusual dating features, if any, approximate or exact date it was made, and the kinds of materials that were used in production. Again, the correct format for the descriptions is vital.

When I started my internship at Sotheby's, my first assignment (you could tell I was at the bottom of the ladder) was to research and help catalog virtually hundreds of Japanese snuff bottles. I was bored out of my mind, but I learned quickly how to read and understand auction catalogs. You can do the same. After reading enough entries you will be able to decipher the important facts about a piece.

Catalogs are expensive to purchase, sometimes costing more than $20 per copy or $200 for a yearly subscription. The bigger auction houses tend to categorize their catalogs and auctions by style of furniture, like French or English. The small auction houses usually have one catalog covering everything they plan to sell at an auction; they usually do not have specialized auctions because it is too expensive for them to provide the manpower. These days you can save yourself the expense of buying a catalog by viewing lots online or at the auction house, with stickers of descriptions of pieces actually placed on the piece for sale.

How Do Auction Houses Determine the Value of Something?

Understanding how an auction house actually determines the value of an item is a very puzzling area that leaves many people feeling in the dark about the shopping experience. When you want to buy a dozen eggs, you pretty much know what you can expect to pay at the supermarket, more or less. You are familiar with supermarket pricing, and of course in the store, each item's price is marked. This pricing method doesn't apply to auction houses. Auction shopping is far more ambiguous. The catalog may say that a chair has an "estimated sale value" of $400 to $800, a 100% difference in price you could pay! What other industry besides the stock market operates like this?

In the stock market, I might believe a stock is only worth buying if its price is $10 per share; other people may believe the stock is worth buying at $11 or $12 per share. These people are driving up the stock price. Auction houses also try to drive up the prices. Auction houses are ecstatic if they can sell a piece for more than its market value because they want to make the seller happy; not to mention that the house will receive more money for a commission. How does the auction house know how to create an estimate? They *assume*, for example, that a particular lot will sell for between $50 and $100. They base their assumptions on what similar items have sold for in previous auctions. An estimate is based on the condition of the item. If, for example, a piece had been poorly repaired or refinished the estimate would be lower than it would be if the piece was kept in original form or properly refinished or repaired. Removing original fabric can also lower the value of a piece. Keep in mind that auction houses are not always right as far as their estimates go. They are simply playing a guessing game based on what they think supply and demand will be for the item.

What Factors Affect the Sale Price of an Item?

Each item for sale at an auction is assigned an identifying *lot number* used both in the catalog and at the auction. There are many factors that greatly affect the lot's sale price. I once bid on and succeeded in buying a beautiful Scandinavian 1820s bench for very little money because it was the first lot to be auctioned on a Saturday morning at 9 A.M. No one else had shown up for the auction when the lot number was called, because it was early and there was a torrential downpour outside. I was the only crazy one there at that hour. The time of day, weather, demand for a particular piece, supply of that piece in the marketplace, the auctioneer's creative talent used to excite the audience, and the number of and status of those in the audience are all variables that come into play to determine the sale price. Let me tell you, being in a pressure-filled room with everyone you know or don't know can do strange things to you as a buyer.

Consider the effect demand can have on a sale price. A few years ago, a friend called to say she was interested in bidding on a Biedermeier chest that was going to be auctioned off that Saturday. She asked me what she should bid (talk about pressure). Without actually seeing the chest, I asked her what the estimate was in the catalog. She told me $3,000 to $6,000. I told her that if she really loved the chest, she should consider the maximum amount of money she was personally willing to pay for the chest. Without looking at the chest, I said $4,000–$4,500 seemed like the right price. Ultimately, the chest sold for $9,000!

Biedermeier was making a huge comeback a few years ago, and everybody at this auction was sniffing out everything Biedermeier. For me, $9,000 was a huge overpayment for this chest, but you can be sure that this auction house increased its estimated sale price for a similar chest at the next auction because of the higher price that was paid for the Biedermeier chest at this auction. Biedermeier, in particular, fetches higher prices than other styles of furniture at auction because there wasn't a lot of Biedermeier furniture being produced during the fifteen-year period from 1815 to 1830.

On the supply side, the popularity of furniture styles changes constantly and this also influences price. These days, Victorian furniture is just not hot in the antiques world. It seems that whenever Victorian furniture comes up for auction, it doesn't sell for a high price. There is so much of it for sale at auction, and its heavy form is not as desirable as other furniture styles. Think of those big, cumbersome dark-wood, red-velvet-upholstered sofas with uncomfortable springs. People today want more comfortable furniture without hard springs, not to mention other anachronisms like horsehair upholstery fabric! I will say, however, that there are some wonderful Victorian pieces that are both stylish and very reasonably priced when compared with antiques from other periods.

Another factor affecting the final sale price is the auctioneer, the most important employee of the auction house. The goal of an auctioneer is to create a huge level of excitement in the audience, which will drive up the price of the lots. Auctioneers usually go to school to learn the art of being an auctioneer. Very skilled and enthusiastic auctioneers are in high demand. I went to an auction recently where the auctioneer began yelling at various audience members. He was trying to bully them into bidding for pieces that no one in the audience wanted.

So How Can You Bid at an Auction?

Buyers can bid on auction items in several ways. Begin by registering yourself and your bank account with the auction house's business office. Once registered, you will be given a paddle with a number on it. Now you are free to bid away. Note that it is possible nowadays to register online with most auction houses. The bidding starts at a pre-established price and then moves up incrementally.

If you don't have time to come to the auction, you can usually submit a silent bid in person, by fax, or e-mail. The bidder completes a form with all his payment information and then issues a maximum bid on a particular lot. Bidding this way removes a lot of the emotion you can experience by bidding in person. Many dealers are afraid to be discovered in an audience bid as an absentee. Because my time is at such a premium these days, I prefer to submit a silent bid. I do recommend, however, that if you are a first-time buyer you *attend at least one auction* so you can get a feel for this crazy environment.

If you are interested in bidding on an item but don't wish to attend the auction in person, *try telephone bidding*. The bidder makes arrangements before the auction to have someone call him just moments before the lot number will be called by the auctioneer. The bidder calls the auction house and tells them which lot number he is interested in and that he wants to place a phone bid. The bidder is given a time he will be called to place his verbal bid. The time of the call is determined by the lot number. If 100 lots are called each hour and you are bidding on lot #50, you will be called one-half hour into the auction. What I like about phone bidding is that I am told how audience members are bidding and what the atmosphere is like at the auction.

The latest craze today is *online auction shopping*. Large houses like Sotheby's and Christie's have online auctions where thousands of lots are offered. Many of these online auctions don't occur on a specific date—the bidding takes place over a range of a few days. At the end of the period, no more bidding is allowed.

What Are the Buyers' Fees?

Buyers pay fees called *buyers' premiums*, often calculated as a percentage of the sale price. Historically, a higher-percentage commission is paid the lower sale price, and vice versa. If not located nearby, buyers need to arrange shipping for the goods. The auction house will make shipping arrangements for a fee.

Selling at Auction

If you decide to sell at auction, you will be putting your faith in the auction house to do a good job of marketing your piece. You will hope to get top dollar for an accurately described item. I have found that some sellers are treated better than others; for example, a seller who has a strong relationship with an auction house may be treated better than someone walking in off the street.

We would expect that famous clients or celebrities ask for and get a higher auction estimate than the average seller. Think Jacqueline Onassis. Everyone wants to own a piece of a celebrity.

How you look, ironically, can affect the sale estimate. Here is a true story: A man who looked like a street person entered a prominent auction house. He said he had found an emerald ring in his mother's jewelry box after she died. He was going to throw it out but decided first to find out how much it was worth. The jewelry appraiser quickly brushed off this man, telling him the ring looked like something out of a bubble gum machine, not worth keeping.

The man decided to go to another auction house where a jewelry appraiser told him that he owned a very rare emerald worth over $40,000. This odd-looking man ended up selling the ring at auction for over $40,000! The lesson: *get a second opinion* if you are interested in selling anything of value.

What Do You Need to Do to Sell at Auction?

First, you should photograph the item you wish to auction. On the photo, include the following information: where the piece was purchased, the dimensions, any relevant information about the piece, like the manufacturer or where it is from, if the piece is signed or dated, or if there is original-looking fabric. This information will allow the auction house to more accurately appraise the item. The auction house will then review the information and respond with a "Yes, we're interested" or "No." If not interested, they will call the piece an *NSV, or no sale value*. If they are interested, they will send a contract to the seller.

What Are the Seller's Costs?

Sellers, like buyers, have to pay the auction house a *seller's premium*. This is usually based on a percentage of the sale price. Sellers also have to pay insurance costs for holding the goods at the auction house, along with shipping expenses. Sometimes sellers also have to pay for professional photographs that will go into the catalog. Color pictures are more expensive than black and white.

Once I Sign a Contract to Sell, Do I Have to Sell at Any Price?

No, you don't. You can set a *reserve*, in which the sale price can't fall below a certain predetermined price that you set with the auction house. The reserve is important because it is your only protection that you won't be forced to give away the item. If your item doesn't sell, you can try to sell it again at the next auction or take it home.

The Thrill of Shopping at Auction

One of the great features of the auction business is that you, the buyer and seller, have some control over the process. You don't have to worry that the decorator will charge some fuzzy commission off the top. In fact, I rarely hear of anyone saying that their decorator *recommended* shopping at auction. Many designers sway their clients into shopping at design centers where the client often doesn't know the true price because the tags are "missing," confusing, or hidden away.

I have come a long way since my first auction experience, and I can truly tell you that the auction industry is one of the most interesting businesses I know. You should try it!

CHAPTER 2

Shopping at Flea Markets and Antiques Shows

How to Shop at Flea Markets

We have all shopped at flea markets of one kind or another sometime in our lives. Spending a lazy day in my favorite floppy hat and jeans, leisurely cherry-picking through endless mounds of wares at a flea market, always makes me feel as though I want to move to the country. We all expect to find treasures awaiting us. Some approach flea market shopping a little like playing the slot machines in Vegas, certain they will hit the jackpot with the very next coin. Others of us just enjoy the relaxing scenic drive to these out-of-town emporiums, stopping along the way for a bite at some quaint country inn.

In Europe, and especially in Paris, the flea markets are absolutely spectacular. Paris, which is often referred to as the "nation of markets," takes its flea markets seriously, with over 80 markets spread across the city playing a vital role in the local business community. The one I love is the popular Marche aux Puces, located just north of Paris. Not only is the flea market filled with some of the most extraordinary antiques I have ever seen, it is a place to go for superb French café food.

In the U.S., flea markets are more hit-or-miss. Dealers come to U.S. flea markets from all around the country and many dealers don't even have a "home address." They simply go from flea market to flea market with their trucks and bring their wares. Some flea markets feel more like garage sales than like flea markets. This is because the flea markets are not ongoing; they are seasonal and usually occur only on the weekends. Just a temporary stand is installed; unlike in Europe where flea markets are more like stores and dealers have the same stalls each day. Clients of mine have told me that they are nervous about shopping at flea markets in the U.S. because they don't know which ones are good and which ones are not so good. They are also worried that if they buy something and it falls apart, they don't know how to reach the dealer. I have some tips to help you shop at flea markets.

Tips for Buying at Flea Markets

I have some words of wisdom about flea market shopping. Don't go in with great expectations of finding the exact thing you want. You will be disappointed if you come home empty-handed. I think flea markets are a great place to find accessories for your house because there are so many dealers and a large selection. Flea markets are a wonderful alternative to fancy antiques stores for someone who loves antiques but can't afford the high prices. They are also more fun to browse because you never know when you will find that perfect treasure. Over the years, people have shown me their unbelievable finds that came from flea markets. They are always so proud of their purchases. My sense is that they are more proud of their flea market finds than of their retail purchases.

1. Be prepared to never see or be able to find the dealer again. Many of these vendors travel throughout the country to sell their stuff and often live right in their trucks.

2. If you are worried about the price to pay, hire an appraiser or knowledgeable friend to join you. You wouldn't want to make an expensive mistake.

3. As you would with dealers selling expensive furniture, ask for a seller's certificate. You may need it later if you discover the piece is a fake.

4. Don't feel compelled to buy everything at your first flea market. Most people make the mistake of buying a lot of junk they will never use.

5. When buying furniture, bring a truck or car big enough to transport

the piece. Many people make the mistake of buying furniture with no thought of the logistics of getting it home. Sometimes a dealer who lives near you will agree to deliver your goods. At European flea markets, there is usually a shipping service on site to wrap and ship your goods for you. At U.S. flea markets, such services are usually not available.

How to Shop at Antiques Shows

Antiques shows come in many varieties. There are the shows in big commercial buildings selling more "collectibles" than anything else—virtually a flea market, only indoors. In the big cities, many antiques shows serve as fundraising tools for a charity, usually with a party thrown along with the show. Often there is a black-tie gala event the night before the auction in which people willing to pay a lot of money for a ticket are entitled to come. This can be a high-society event in a local community.

Booths are set up in several aisles just like a grocery store. Booth prices for a dealer can cost anywhere from $3,000 to $10,000.

Tips for Buying at Antiques Shows

1. Get a list of the dealers who will be at the show (unlike most flea markets, antiques shows usually have a glossy book that lists the dealers who will have booths at the show), and do a little research about any dealers who have the kind of products you may want. Try to locate their Web site.

2. If you buy something, get the dealer's business card and make sure you can contact him if there is a problem.

3. Negotiate—usually a dealer will go down 10% to 20% because he doesn't want to have to transport the piece all the way across the country. Also, the dealer wants to be able to cover his booth costs.

4. Check the Web site to see if the goods the dealer is selling at the show seem more expensive than the furniture online. This will help you negotiate the best deal.

5. Ask if the dealer can arrange for and take care of the shipping expenses. Some will pay for shipping as a courtesy or as part of the negotiating process.

CHAPTER 3

Shopping at Furniture Stores and Showrooms

Shopping at Retail Antiques Shops and Malls

The most popular kinds of antiques sold are English and French. Although English antiques from the 17th and 18th century are classics that will never go out of style, the demand for traditional English furniture is on the decline. Fancy gilded French furniture from the 18th century is also not as popular as it was a few years ago. Today, style and function are equally important to most people and periods in furniture design like Art Deco and other 20th-century furniture satisfies both of these needs. Across the country stores everywhere are selling either the real thing or contemporary interpretations of Mid-Century furniture. Art Deco refers to French furniture from 1925–1940 and signified a time in France when high style, both in fashion and furnishings was a major part of everyday life. Art Nouveau, a short period which began at the end of the 19th century in France, featured asymmetrical lines and nature elements in its carved wood pieces, but never became as popular as Art Deco. Art Deco is popular today because it transcends antiques with modern furniture. Most Deco pieces are made from unusual, exotic and beautiful woods, like ebony, palisander and emboyna. Retro furniture refers to furniture designed in the middle of the 20th century. This furniture was made from plastics, steel, bentwood and other innovative materials to create a chic, yet functional design. Early American furniture resembles English and French furniture from the 18th and 19th centuries and is difficult to find today, even in places like Boston, New York and Philadelphia. Much of the Early American furniture made has been donated to American museums. Its high prices (many of the pieces available cost in the tens of thousands), make Early American furniture cost prohibitive. Mission-style furniture is still popular in the U.S., but I think people will begin to move towards simple, more refined styles to match the more popular styles offered today.

Now that you know that many antiques dealers, themselves, buy their inventory at auction, let's talk about shopping at antiques stores. Shopping in antiques stores can be intimidating, especially if you don't know what you are looking at and don't know its value. In some cities, like Los Angeles and New York, it is common to find price tags that say a famous person designed a piece. Even the experts will not necessarily know if a famous furniture designer designed a piece. Of course dealers hope that by saying a piece was designed by a famous designer they can get a higher price for their furniture. Beware of this kind of activity—it is common for dealers to want to make a big markup. If you are unsure whether the piece is authentic, ask the dealer to provide you a certificate of authenticity. If he refuses to give you a certificate, I would not buy the piece.

You can also inspect the piece to see if it was signed or dated. Pre-20th-century furniture was often signed and dated if someone famous designed it. If it was not signed or dated, you should question the dealer who tells you that someone famous designed it. I love when a dealer tells me he has no idea who designed the piece and he isn't sure where the piece was made. I like the honest approach best.

As I have done in my reviews, ask the dealer what kind of discount he would be willing to give you. Again, more than 85% of the stores I reviewed who give designer discounts said they would also give the same discounts to the public. Don't hesitate to try to get a better price. Dealers expect to sell their inventory for less than it is marked.

I don't expect the same level of service or knowledge when shopping at an antiques mall. For the novice antiques shopper, I recommend going to a few different antiques malls to get acquainted with the antiques world. Malls are usually relaxed and bargaining is easier because the dealer is not often present.

Do not confuse antiques with vintage furniture. Vintage furniture refers to furniture designed in the early-to-mid-20th century. Vintage furniture has become extremely popular in the 21st century as we bridge the gap between traditional and contemporary styles. Antiques refer to furniture designed over 100 years ago. Today, the trend is eclectic. Pre-Victorian antiques are still in demand, but vintage furniture is also popular because of the fact that it is old furniture that reflects modern-day features and materials, and generally costs less than antiques, although vintage furniture is getting more expensive as the demand for these classics rises. Still there are those who are interested in buying reproductions, either because the prices of reproductions are less than the prices of original pieces of furniture or they like the modern features that reproductions offer. Either way, gone are the days when reproductions look obviously new. Today, designers are taking great steps to update antiques while giving furniture a contemporary look and feel.

There are a few simple steps you can follow to ensure you make an educated purchase while buying antiques. First, make sure the wood on the piece matches the kind of wood that would have been used during that period. Second, if a piece has been repaired or had a part replaced, show the piece to an appraiser to make sure that the value will not be affected by this event. Wear and tear are good and even expected with antiques—legs and feet are often repaired or replaced without affecting the piece's value.

Shopping at Retail Stores

Retail stores are offering a wider variety of styles, fabric choices, and materials than in previous years. I am truly amazed at how many new styles and materials are popping up in the furniture world. While an eclectic mix of new and old is popular today, furniture is becoming increasingly more functional and simple in its design. This trend in furniture design comes from the way we live now. The world is getting thinner, less bulky designs in our home technology, from flat-screen televisions to smaller, less bulky stereo equipment. Our needs are different than they were ten years ago, when armoires were the most popular method of storing televisions. Today, I am told that stores can't give away armoires. Reproductions now offer contemporary designs and functional elements that make living in our spaces better organized.

Knowing what to buy can be confusing. Salespeople and designers can really help you figure out what exactly you want or need. When shopping at contemporary furniture stores, don't be afraid to ask the dealer to explain the construction of a piece. I recently selected the best futons for *Consumers Digest* magazine. I visited several futon stores to compare different brands. At many of the stores, the salespeople I spoke with had no idea how to compare the different futons they had in their own shops. They couldn't explain why one futon cost more than another futon. They couldn't explain the construction of the futons. Make sure that you feel comfortable with the explanation a dealer gives you before embarking on a big purchase.

In this day and age, when consumers have so many options for choosing where to buy furniture, service is becoming increasingly important. I like visiting stores where the dealers and their staff greet me, offer to answer any questions and seem knowledgeable when I ask questions. I also like to know that the dealer will offer fair delivery and assembly charges. Too many large chain outlets charge too much for shipping and assembly these days. Many of the smaller stores will offer to deliver free-of-charge or for a small fee. You need to ask what these charges will be upfront. I also like to see a return policy that gives the shopper a chance to return the piece within a few weeks. A good dealer, antiques or contemporary, will allow the customer to return the inventory if it is not satisfactory. When buying at a chain store, make sure a written warranty is provided. This warranty is your only true protection when you are trying to return a piece one year later when your salesperson no longer works at that store. Some dealers will even offer payment options, which are not usually posted. If you do not ask dealers these questions you will not make an educated purchase.

Shopping at Design Centers and Working with Designers

Design centers are usually closed to the public and only open to the trade, or interior designers. When going to a design center without a designer, you will usually not be allowed to buy directly from the showroom. You will need a designer to make your purchases for you. Showrooms in design centers usually offer higher quality than that of retail stores and the ability to customize. One downside of ordering furniture from a design center is that you will have to wait an average of 12–16 weeks to get the furniture. You will also pay a high price that will include a 35%+ markup for the designer. One benefit of shopping in design centers, though, is that they offer a large variety of showrooms all under one roof. Many showrooms today are also selling through retail stores though they claim that the quality of the inventory in the design centers exceeds that of the retail stores.

Whether or not you shop in design centers, interior designers can help you save time, avoid hassles and guide you in the process of decorating your house. Designers offer a range of services, like creating floor plans, color schemes, and selecting fabrics and furniture. Historically, designers have charged an hourly fee plus a commission. I believe, and hope, that the industry will change its fee structure. I do not like the fact that a designer can get paid more for a more expensive furniture purchase. In this kind of fee arrangement, the designer is not rewarded financially when finding furniture that is the best value for the client. I recommend clients asking for either a flat design fee for actual design time and/or a flat fee for all furniture purchases.

Shopping Online and Through Catalogs

Consumers are busy shopping online for everything these days. Furniture Web sales, in particular, are increasing exponentially. In 2004 furniture Web sales reached $650 million, according to *Jupiter Research*. Furniture Web sales are expected to reach $1.2 billion by 2008. I feel that it is important to review all of the mom-and-pop Web sites that few people ever shop because they don't know they exist. Many of the stores I reviewed have tremendous Web sites which make shopping for furniture easier. Either you can browse the inventory before shopping at these stores or you can buy directly from these stores online. What makes shopping for furniture from these Web sites so great is that you avoid the fear factor. You can also save time and communicate directly with the dealer online. Many of these stores offer excellent online images of their furniture, so you can really see what you are buying.

Catalog sales are also rising in popularity. Catalogs are popular because they are a book that you can peruse at your leisure. Many catalogs offer fast shipping programs, even for upholstered furniture. As Americans become better acquainted with popular manufacturers of furniture they will be more comfortable buying through catalogs. A word of caution is to find out exactly what the shipping costs will be and make sure the business has a fair return policy. Some catalogs offer a written warranty. I recommend finding these things out so you won't be disappointed when you get your furniture.

CHAPTER 4

Chain Stores

Shopping Retail Chain Stores

Chain furniture stores represent a large percentage of the furniture purchased today. In fact, according to a recent study by *InFurniture* magazine, 95% of all Web furniture sales are to Crate & Barrel, Pottery Barn and Williams-Sonoma. These chain stores have visibility in the furniture industry and Americans recognize their names and logos. You should note that many stores reviewed in this book have multiple locations but are not considered "chain stores."

Chain stores offer the benefit of generally quick shipping because they stock more inventory than small boutique stores. Chain stores not only offer their own name brand recognition, but they also carry lines that are well-known by consumers. One word of caution is that every large furniture manufacturer has a few different lines. Just because a couch was designed by a manufacturer with a good reputation doesn't mean that a particular chain store carries the same level of quality from that manufacturer.

While chain stores generally have a lenient return policy, I have found some fairly big chains that don't offer a written warranty to their customers. I feel a written warranty is important for consumers because of the large turnover rate at these kinds of stores. If something should break, you need to feel that the store will give you your money back. Only a written warranty guarantees against defects.

Shipping expenses can be high for chain stores. Many stores charge $60 for a local delivery plus an assembly charge. These charges are not as high as they are if you purchase furniture from a design center showroom. In that case, you may pay a double shipping charge—one for national transit and the other from a local warehouse to your home. These charges can be more than 10% of the entire purchase price.

While it is difficult to negotiate at a chain store, it is possible to wait for sales and try to include without charge one of the store's own designers to help you as part of your purchasing arrangement.

In the appendix, I list the chains that I have studied for this book, and reviews each store along with its location, terms, pricing, shipping, etc.

PART II

GUIDE TO FURNITURE HOT SPOTS BY CITY

CHAPTER 5

Atlanta

Atlanta is definitely a furniture hot spot heavyweight! As many times as I have been to Atlanta, I am always amazed by the way this city has grown, expanded, and greatly diversified its furniture selection. Atlanta is not only the hub of the South, but is also known for its large melting pot of corporate transfers, a result of the city's surge in business development. Atlanta offers a bounty of furniture styles as diverse as its population. The Atlanta area consists of nearly 30 counties. I have reviewed stores not far from the downtown area in Buckhead, Midtown, Virginia-Highland, Decatur, and East Atlanta Village. Clearly you could spend weeks furniture shopping in Atlanta and not even cover many counties. I highly recommend that you rent a car or hire a cab, as public transportation is a difficult way to shop for furniture here.

ATLANTA RETAIL STORES

Virginia-Highland

Just five to ten minutes outside of downtown Atlanta, Virginia-Highland is a small neighborhood that has become one of Atlanta's favorite furniture destinations. Developed in the early 1900s, it is a mix of the old historical South and the new. Populated by mostly young people, it is filled with cute outdoor cafés, trendy restaurants, and charming homes. This neighborhood is basically where Virginia and Highland avenues intersect.

20TH CENTURY ANTIQUES

20th-Century Furniture, 1925–1970
1044 North Highland Avenue; 404-874-7042;
20thcenturyhome@bellsouth.net; Hours: Daily 10–6;
www.20thcenturyantiques.net; Credit Cards: MC, Visa, AmEx;
Owner is Vic Matich

Price: Personnel:

Ambiance: Quality:

20th Century Antiques has one of the best collections of 20th-century furniture I have seen anywhere in the country. This owner knows his stuff, as he has been in business for 25 years selling the same kind of inventory year after year. If you like French furniture from the 1920s through 1970s, this place is for you. I love the way Vic displays vintage furniture with a contemporary flair. He carries props (like big oars, paintings, and sconces) and the most unusual occasional tables. You'll even find dishes and light fixtures of this period of design. I flipped over some wonderful Lucite chairs and ottomans that were priced under $400. Most of the furniture comes from France, and the inventory turns over frequently. What truly impresses me is the fact that there is something appealing here for anyone with a sense of style, from a college student to a sophisticated homeowner. Prices are great, and 90% of the inventory sells for less than $1,000 with much under $500. Everyone gets a discount (I don't know what it is), and Vic is negotiable. The Web site does not have great pictures and lacks descriptions, but you should know that 20th Century participates in eBay auctions. The store self-delivers around the East Coast. Shipping is reasonable at $100 per item or, if you live locally, $20 per item. Lots of celebrities shop here.

BACK TO SQUARE ONE

Primitive Antiques and Garden Furniture
1054 North Highland Avenue; 404-815-9970;
Hours: Daily 10–6; Credit Cards: MC, Visa, AmEx;
Owner is Vic Matich

Price: Personnel: Ambiance: Quality:

Just next door to 20th Century Antiques and with the same owner, Back to Square One has a terrific selection of rustic furniture, garden furniture, and folk art. There are a number of enchanting painted pieces and delightful decorative items. Be prepared to spend the afternoon, as this store is lots of fun to explore and the prices are very reasonable. Just as with 20th Century, all customers get discounts, and there are frequent sales. The delivery charges are the same as for 20th Century. A great find.

DELAWARE RIVER TRADING CO

Contemporary Furniture and Housewares
1198 North Highland Avenue; 404-874-5583;
customerservice@delawarerivertrading.com;
Hours: Mon–Sat 9–8, Sun 12–6; www.delawarerivertrading.com;
Credit Cards: MC, Visa, AmEx; No checks; Owner is Willis Watts

Price: Personnel: Ambiance: Quality:

Delaware River Trading Co. is up the street from 20th Century Antiques and is recognizable by its bright blue awning. Willis Watts is an interior designer, as I might have guessed by his fabulously designed store. If this store were in Chicago, my hometown, I would be shopping here regularly for furniture, gifts, and art. Besides furniture, if you're after housewares (bowls, linens, and flatware), you're in for a treat, as they have an outstanding assortment. Check out the selection of chests and chairs made of leather and wood. They remind me of Hermès, but with substantially lower price tags. Designers receive a 10% discount if they spend more than $1,000. The Web site is excellent, with pictures and prices, though no dimensions are included, and you can even buy online.

East Atlanta Village

East Atlanta Village is about 20 minutes outside downtown Atlanta. Affectionately tagged "the small town in the big city," it is home to funky shops, a rich ethnic mix, and some restaurants to die for. I ate at Australian Bakery Café on Flat Shoals Avenue and found the food awesome, particularly the Aussie pies!

TRADERS NEIGHBORHOOD STORE

Contemporary Furniture and Accessories
485B Flat Shoals Avenue; 404-522-3006; Hours: Mon–Sat 11–9,
Sun 12–6; www.tradersatlanta.com; Credit Cards: MC, Visa, AmEx;
Owners are Shawn Ergle and Michael Knight

Price: Personnel: Ambiance: Quality:

Traders is a fun, intimate little store in East Atlanta Village loaded with lots of accessories (I will forever remember the exotic scents permeating from their army of candles), comfortable, overstuffed couches (most by Rowe Furniture), rich wooden beds and tables, and Indonesian rosewood cabinets. The façade is painted a light blue and on the day I came here, I saw some great painted red tables and chairs out in front. I don't think the furniture is unique, but it is a pleasant neighborhood shop. If you like chimes, Traders is the place for you. Discounts are available to designers only after the third purchase. The pictures on their Web site carry no descriptions or prices. There is a mix of traditional and contemporary but nothing that particularly stands out as unique. Prices are fair, and most big furniture items cost less than $1,000.

EAST ATLANTA ARTS & ANTIQUES BAZAAR

470 Flat Shoals Avenue S.E.; 404-581-0105; Hours: Mon–Fri 11–9, Sat 11–10, Sun 12–6; www.eaaab.com; Credit Cards: MC, Visa, AmEx

Price: Personnel:

Ambiance:  Quality:

East Atlanta Arts & Antiques Bazaar is located in a Colonial-style building painted red with white columns. You're in luck if you've come here hunting down wonderful dining sets and kitchenettes that are affordable and stylish. With over 50 vendors to choose from in this 10,000-square-foot building, there is a vast selection, and I like the low prices. The place is a virtual treasure chest filled with retro pieces that many young people like to collect.

Dawson Boulevard (Access Road)

About 25 minutes from downtown Atlanta is Dawson Boulevard, an ugly duckling that has evolved into a furniture hot spot in Atlanta. Most of the shops, which parallel 85 North, are nothing special, but there are a few gems worth mentioning. Though I am not reviewing baby furniture stores, Georgia Baby & Kids has a great collection of furniture for children of all ages.

ARTE FORMA

Large General Furniture Store
6248 Dawson Boulevard (AKA Access Road); 770-263-0818
sales@arteformaatlanta.com; Hours: Mon–Sat 10–7, Sun 12–6;
www.arteformaatlanta.com; Credit Cards: MC, Visa, AmEx;
Owner is Michael Gill

Price: Personnel:

Ambiance: Quality:

Arte Forma is a great store with a wide variety of inventory from all around the world. Located on the popular Access (Dawson Boulevard), with another location at 1544 Piedmont Road, Atlanta, this store is one that you might quickly drive by . . . the façade, a blond brick warehouse building, is unappealingly ordinary. Once inside, though, you'll find nothing ordinary about the inventory. Strikingly diverse and casual, it includes a good selection of traditional, contemporary, and ethnic furniture. Much of the furniture is from India, Brazil, China, and Peru. I particularly like the selection of chairs and cabinets. Discounts happen only when there are sales. Most items are priced under $500. There are a variety of fabric choices for the upholstered products, and you'll even find some nice antique pieces. The Web site includes some pictures but no prices or descriptions.

MANORISM

Asian Furniture Antiques and Contemporary
6410 Dawson Boulevard; 770-416-1947; Hours: Mon–Sat 10–7;
www.manorism.com; Credit Cards: MC, Visa, AmEx;
Owner is Warren Goodstone

Price: 🪑🪑🪑 Personnel: 🪑🪑🪑🪑🪑

Ambiance: 🪑🪑🪑🪑 Quality: 🪑🪑🪑

Manorism has recently opened at this location. They are also located at 1494 Ellsworth Industrial Boulevard in Atlanta (404-603-8300). Much of the furniture comes from Indonesia and China. They have some interesting antique Chinese pieces, such as chests and cabinets, as well as fun contemporary Indonesian pieces. Some of the furniture is painted in vibrant colors. Most of their inventory is priced under $700 for big-ticket items. The quality is fair, but I didn't care for the way the furniture is finished. There is an odd coating on top of most pieces that feels abrasive to the touch, not the finish that is usually representative of furniture from these countries. Designers receive a 20% discount. The Web site has some pictures but no prices. They also have a big warehouse.

Decatur

Four to five miles east of Atlanta is Decatur. I was referred to one special place here and decided to check it out since I enjoy finding any unusual store that is off the beaten path.

KUDZU ANTIQUES

Antiques Mall

2874 East Ponce de Leon Avenue; 404-373-6498;

Hours: Mon, Thu, Fri, Sat 10:30–6, Sun 12:30–6;

Credit Cards: MC, Visa; Owners are Kate and George Lawes

Price: Personnel:

Ambiance: Quality:

Kudzu Antiques, named after the climbing vine that is engulfing the South, is well worth a trip if you like good-quality antiques, flea markets, vintage fashion, and a really top-notch antiques mall. Lose yourself in its exceptional selection of antiques, retro furniture, vintage clothing, and jewelry. But don't expect plush surroundings or much of a comfort zone in the hot summer months. Truth be told, the building looks like a barn and there is no air conditioning. But Atlanta shoppers have been shopping here for 25 years and love coming back time and time again. A brand-new coffee shop serves as an oasis for you to relax and unwind after an exhausting shopping experience. There are 30 dealers here, but the Laweses own about 25% of the inventory themselves. Overall, a fabulous antiques mall—the selection is excellent and the prices are fair. Discounts are made on an individual basis.

Buckhead

Catch the wave of action in Atlanta's trendy Buckhead. Located just a few minutes outside of the downtown, Buckhead is a shining star that offers something exciting for everyone. On the one hand there is a sizzling night life, including lots of "in" clubs, a sizable selection of terrific restaurants, and a large single population. Yet the same area has its share of upscale homes and married people with children. This upbeat, diverse neighborhood has marvelous shops of all kinds and in particular, furniture shops. Warning: During rush hour, traffic can be abominable.

ANTIQUES & BEYOND

Antiques Mall

1853 Cheshire Bridge Road NE; 404-872-4342; Hours: Daily 11–7;
Credit Cards: MC, Visa, AmEx; Owner is Darrell Pierce

Price: 🪑🪑🪑   Personnel: 🪑🪑🪑🪑

Ambiance: 🪑🪑🪑🪑🪑   Quality: 🪑🪑🪑🪑

Antiques & Beyond has been in business for 12 years, and has just moved back into its spacious digs since a fire damaged the building last year. Over 80 dealers call this massive complex home, each offering many good-quality antiques in a wide range of prices, so bring your roller blades because you'll want to check out as much as you can in the time you have. There is also a good selection of 20th-century furniture. This is a popular spot for designers, and well worth a trip. Discounts are made on an individual basis.

Midtown

Right in the downtown area, Midtown has a number of furniture stores that have opened in the past few years. These are the "happening furniture hot spots" of Atlanta, catering to a young professional, upscale clientele that is also very hip. There is a Kartell, a trendy furniture store in the neighborhood on Peachtree Street, and during my visit, several new stores were opening in the area.

RETRO MODERN

1950s–'70s-Style Furniture

805 Peachtree Street NE; 404-724-0093; mail@retromodern.com;
Hours: Tue–Sat 11–6; www.retromodern.com; Credit Cards: MC,
Visa, AmEx; Owner is Scott Reilly

Price: 🪑🪑🪑🪑🪑   Personnel: 🪑🪑🪑🪑🪑

Ambiance: 🪑🪑🪑🪑   Quality: 🪑🪑🪑🪑🪑

Few furniture stores have begun as a Web site, but that's how Retro Modern got its start. The store is stark white and black with lots of brightly colored fabrics and finishes on the furniture. The furniture pieces are reproductions of pieces made between 1950 and 1970, and the prices are varied. Nice selection here and the service is great. The only thing that bothered me was the really loud rock music. I left the store with my ears ringing. There are monthly specials, and discounts are on an individual basis. The Web site is one of the best I have seen for any furniture store. It is easy to shop and buy online. Most goods ship free of charge and it is possible to shop by designer (they carry reproductions of furniture designed by well-known Mid-Century Modern designers), by price, furniture category, or room. Descriptions, measurements, and pricing are included on the Web site.

SPACE

Contemporary Furniture
800 Peachtree Street NE; 404-228-4600; info@spacemodern.com;
Hours: Mon–Fri 10–7, Sat 10–6; www.spacemodern.com;
Credit Cards: MC, Visa, AmEx; Owner is Tim Hobby

Price: 🪑🪑🪑🪑🪑 Personnel: 🪑🪑🪑

Ambiance: 🪑🪑🪑🪑🪑 Quality: 🪑🪑🪑🪑🪑

An "out-of-this-world" furniture store where you'll feel right at home if you're a diehard fan of Star Wars. Despite its sci-fi futuristic look, Space does have many interesting pieces of ultra-contemporary furniture from Europe. Space represents 35 lines of furniture, much of which looks as though it belongs in a contemporary art museum. Well-known designers represented here include Cassina, Minotti, Matteo, and Angela Adams. I like the elegant, clean lines of many of the pieces and the sumptuous fabrics. Lots of yuppies shop here for the "latest," but I think the atmosphere and service could seem cold and intimidating for the regular person. That said, I think the store has some really fun and intriguing pieces—lights, chaise lounges, and tables. I also like the interesting colors surrounding the showroom and fabrics on the furniture. Prices are high, and discounts are given to the trade only, according to the individual manufacturer. The Web site is colorful and creative, with pictures and descriptions of inventory but no prices.

ATLANTA DECORATIVE ARTS CENTER
Design Center; sells to the trade only
351 Peachtree Hills Avenue NE; 404-231-1720; Mon–Fri 9–5;
www.adacdesigncenter.com

The Atlanta Decorative Arts Center (ADAC) is one of the finest design centers in America. This is a trade-only building. There are no special privileges to the public, although you are welcome to shop in any of these showrooms with your designer. Most prices shown are the list price from which the designer gets a discount. The main building is large, containing several floors filled with exquisite furniture. There is also a separate building next door with more showrooms worth exploring. Many of the antiques stores are located in the lower level, by the street. Some of my favorite Atlanta-based showrooms include Ainsworth-Noah, Jerry Pair, and Regalo Antiques. Other well-known showrooms include Baker, Patina, Donghia, and of course, all of the fabric showrooms that are present at other design centers around the country. Regalo Antiques, with its unusual European painted wood and glass pieces, is my personal favorite antiques showroom in the building, but Jerry Pair also has some wonderfully unique items. Prices for antiques are high here, so be prepared when you shop with your designer.

Next door to the ADAC, another concentrated building of show-rooms will soon be opening, catering to the general public. **The Galleries of Peachtree Hills** will house numerous antiques stores, galleries, and designer offices. Many dealers are talking about this new building with a lot of excitement, and some stores are relocating to The Galleries.

OBJECTS
Rustic Antique Furniture
345 Peachtree Hills Avenue; Suite 200; 404-262-0423;
rsmith@objects-decorations.com; Hours: Mon–Fri 9–5;
www.objects-decorations.com; Credit Cards: MC, Visa, AmEx;
Owners are Hal Ainsworth and Winton Noah

Price: Personnel:

Ambiance: Quality:

Objects wowed me! Featuring antique country furniture, the store also has a great assortment of decorative objects and wall hangings. There is a fabulous selection of farm tables and painted furniture. I experienced great service, too. I did think the prices were high, especially because only designers get a discount, which is 20%. The shop is open to the public, though, and is owned by the same people who own Ainsworth-Noah in the Design Center, which is only open to designers. The store receives four to five shipments each year from Europe, and the inventory moves. Furniture here comes from all over Europe and Canada. The Web site has pictures, small descriptions, and prices. I especially like the large vintage signs in French.

SOUTH OF MARKET

Antiques and Contemporary Furniture
345 Peachtree Hills Avenue; Suite 100; 404-995-9399;
somarket@bellsouth.net; Hours: Mon–Fri 9–5, Sat 10–4;
www.southofmarket.biz; Credit Cards: MC, Visa, AmEx, Discover;
Owner is Kay Douglass

Price: Personnel:

Ambiance: Quality:

South of Market, positioned right next door to Objects, is a large showroom with great inventory. The furniture, lighting, and some antiques are real head-turners. Mitchell Gold sofas are upholstered in monochromatic colors, and the couches are surrounded by very unusual decorative objects. Much of the inventory is from France and one-of-a-kind. I especially like the selection of vintage metal cabinets and the signage on the walls. There is a sister store in Charleston, South Carolina. While the inventory in this store is something to write home about, unfortunately the service is not. Sales help was difficult to find, and when I finally did track a salesperson down, he acted rather annoyed at having to answer any questions and would not disclose the store's discounts to designers. The Web site includes pictures, small descriptions, and prices.

JEFF LITTRELL

Mostly Italian Antiques (Some French) and Custom Lampshades
178 Peachtree Hills Avenue NE; 404-231-8662; Hours: Mon–Fri 10–5;
Credit Cards: N/A; Owner is Jeff Littrell

Price: Personnel:

Ambiance: Quality:

A small shop located near the Design Center, Jeff Littrell has been in business here for 10 years. He carries unique, mostly Italian, antiques. Jeff is an extremely personable, upbeat guy with a good sense of humor who makes shopping here an enjoyable experience. Designers get a 20% discount. There is no Web site, but Jeff is willing to be helpful in explaining his inventory.

LAURA WALKER, LTD.

17th- to 20th-Century Italian Furniture and Accessories
176 Peachtree Hills Avenue NE; 678-488-6895;
Hours: Tue–Fri 12–4; Owner is Laura Walker

Price: Personnel:

Ambiance: Quality:

Although Laura Walker has a small shop, she fills it well with treasures she has dug up while scouring Italy for the best. After living in Italy for many years and shopping for antiques dealers in the U.S., she has decided to come to Atlanta and start her own shop. Her passion is selling Italian mirrors and lighting, although some of her inventory is originally from France. She loves her work, and it shows. Designers receive a 20% discount if they spend more than $1,000 and 10% discount for any purchases under $1,000. Laura has no Web site yet.

BEAMAN ANTIQUES

English and French Antiques/Reproductions
25 Bennett Street; 404-352-9388;
info@beamanantiques.com; Hours: 10–5 Mon–Sat;
www.beamanantiques.com; Credit Cards: MC, Visa, AmEx;
Owner is Lynford Beaman

Price: Personnel:

Ambiance: Quality:

Housed in an all-white building with a contrasting black awning, Beaman Antiques is located in the Bennett Street area just off Peachtree Hills Avenue. The block looks like a row of warehouses, but most of the businesses in the area are antiques stores. Beaman Antiques, owned by an Englishman who has been here for about 15 years, sells traditional brown wood furniture, English and French. Aside from selling antiques, Beaman also uses a lot of old woods to make new, reproduction furniture. This furniture also comes from England. The furniture, a mixture of formal and rustic pieces, is sturdy, practical, and presentable. The finishes are done well. What I will remember most about the place is its wild walls, which were painted such a bright red they almost seemed to pulsate (I had the feeling that at any moment they were going to swallow up all the furniture and me!). Designers receive a 20% discount. The Web site gives descriptions and prices as well as pictures. I believe the merchandise is fairly priced.

INTERIORS MARKET

Antiques Mall
55 Bennett Street, NW #20; 404-352-0055 or
800-375-9963; info@interiorsmarket.com; Hours: Mon–Sat 10–5;
www.interiorsmarket.com; Credit Cards: MC, Visa;
Owner is Kathy Guyton

Price: Personnel:

Ambiance: Quality:

Interiors Market has been in Atlanta selling high-end antiques with their 50 dealers for 10 years. The inventory consists of mostly European antiques, though there are a few dealers of modern furniture. On the day I reviewed the business, I noticed some great painted antique Swedish furniture from the 1700s and 1800s. As a whole, this is an interesting place worth scouting out. I usually don't like shopping in malls, as I find them commercial and generic, but Interior Markets never really made me feel like I was in a mall, thanks to a marvelous warm little café nestled in their space and a cozy, upscale atmosphere. Designers receive a 10–20% discount. The owner has one other location on this block and one each in Birmingham, Alabama, and Jackson, Mississippi.

ROBUCK & COMPANY ANTIQUES, LTD.

Continental Antiques
65 Bennett Street; 404-351-7173; Hours: Mon–Fri 10–5;
www.robuckandcompany.com; Credit Cards: MC, Visa, AmEx;
Owner is Shane Robuck

Price: Personnel:

Ambiance: Quality:

Robuck & Company has a most unusual selection of Continental antiques. Shane Robuck travels about 12 times a year to Spain and France to seek out pieces. Much of the inventory comes from Spain and Italy. On the day I visited, they were moving many pieces into the shop. In shopping here, I found it hard to get as up close and personal with the inventory as I wished, as the store's several display rooms are dimly lit. I did, though, particularly like the beautiful light fixtures and interesting chairs, many of which are from the 17th and 18th centuries. Discounts vary. The owner, a very busy, hands-on young entrepreneur, was too absorbed in the daily chores of running his store to spend much time talking with me. The Web site has pictures with limited descriptions and no prices. I personally feel the prices are too high, even though some negotiating is possible.

JACQUELINE ADAMS

Mostly French Provincial Antiques

2300 Peachtree Road, Suite B110; 404-355-8123;

jadamsantiques@bellsouth.net; Hours: Mon–Fri 10–5, Sat 11–4;

www.jacquelineadamsantiques.com; Credit Cards: MC, Visa,

AmEx; Owners are Jacqueline and James Adams

Price: 🪑🪑🪑🪑🪑🪑 Personnel: 🪑🪑🪑🪑🪑

Ambiance: 🪑🪑🪑🪑🪑🪑 Quality: 🪑🪑🪑🪑🪑🪑

Jacqueline Adams sells mostly French Provincial in the store's two locations (the other one is at 425 Peachtree Hills Avenue). Francophiles will love this store's larger-than-life French atmosphere. Each time I visit the place, I feel as though I have jetted off to the South of France. The inventory is extensive, with a large selection of charming armoires, sofas, chairs (most of which are covered in white canvas cloth), clocks, and tables. My service experience was excellent, and well it should be for the high prices Jacqueline Adams charges. Discounts are available to designers (20–25%) and the public, however. The Web site shows pictures, dimensions, and prices. Worth a visit.

CITY ISSUE

Mid-Century Modern

2825 Peachtree Street NE; 404-262-3500;

Hours: Mon 12–5, Tue–Thu 11–7:30, Fri 11–5,

Sat 11–7:30, Sun 12–5; www.cityissue.com; Credit Cards: MC, Visa,

AmEx; Owner is Jennifer Sams

Price: 🪑🪑🪑 Personnel: 🪑🪑🪑🪑🪑

Ambiance: 🪑🪑🪑🪑🪑 Quality: 🪑🪑🪑🪑🪑

City Issue is located in a strip shopping center on busy Peachtree Street in Bucktown. If you blink, as I did, you may pass by the shop because the façade is bare. City Issue sells furniture from the 1950s–'70s, most of which is Danish Modern. Jennifer Sams has an eye for selecting pieces with a lot of personality . . . I was crazy about some Hermès-like chairs that were extraordinarily unique and fairly inexpensive for the pair (less than $1,000). Knock yourself out with all the vintage lunch boxes, doorknobs, and contemporary, colorful paintings that cover the walls. Most pieces cost less than $400, and there are flexible payment options. Local delivery is $35. Designers receive a 10% discount. The Web site shows pictures of the inventory, and gives dimensions and prices.

Miami Circle

Miami Circle is a well-established spot to go antiques shopping in Atlanta. The strip looks industrial, but there are some well-known dealers on this street worth visiting. Keep in mind that while designers get good discounts, prices here are high to the public. Miami Circle gets a lot of tourists shopping for antiques sent by concierges, and prices tend to reflect that.

ACQUISITIONS

Country Furniture/Antiques and Reproductions
631 Miami Circle NE; 404-261-2478; Hours: Mon–Fri 9:30–5:30,
Sat 10–5; Credit Cards: MC, Visa; Owner is in Charleston, SC

Price: Personnel:

Ambiance: Quality:

Acquisitions is a great store to visit if you are in the market for a rustic look with a flair. There are many reproductions here, but the store has a high energy and a youngish beat that is far removed from being stodgy. Prices range widely, but for furniture items they can be high. The inventory includes painted pieces in fun pastels and primary colors. The main store is in Charleston, South Carolina, with another location in Charlotte, North Carolina.

BOBBY DODD ANTIQUES, INC

English and Continental Antiques

695 Miami Circle; 404-231-0580; Hours: Mon–Fri 10–5,
Sat 11–4; Credit Cards: N/A; Owners are Margie and Bobby Dodd

Price: Personnel:

Ambiance: Quality:

Bobby Dodd is equally famous throughout Atlanta both as a furniture store and as a family name. The Bobby Dodd football stadium in Atlanta is named after the store owner's father who was the beloved football coach at Georgia Tech for many years. Although Bobby Dodd the son began his career as a lawyer, he is well known for a long-standing career selling excellent examples of English, French, and other European period furniture. I like coming to this store because of the service and the reliable information presented to customers. While much of the furniture is what we have seen before, the furniture is classic with honest descriptions. The shop has been here since 1988. You'll really enjoy rummaging through all the furniture items, many of which are piled on top of each other, adding a lot of character to the large and otherwise plain showroom.

WILLIAM WORD ANTIQUES

European Antiques

707 Miami Circle, NE; 404-233-6890;
wmwordantiques@mindspring.com; Hours: Mon–Fri 10–5,
Sat 11–5; www.williamwordantiques.com; Credit Cards: N/A;
Owner is William Word

Price: Personnel:

Ambiance: Quality:

William Word Antiques is a long-standing favorite in Atlanta. The store has been here for 14 years. The owner and namesake of the store, William Word, began in the antiques business by restoring old furniture. His passion for restoring finely crafted wood pieces is as strong today as it was back when he first began. He is an enthusiastic dealer, proudly giving tours of his shop and explaining his inventory. Designers receive a 20% discount. The Web site shows inventory and prices.

HENSON & HENSON HOME

Eclectic Furniture and Accessories
741 Miami Circle; 404-949-9191; Hours: Tue–Fri 10–4, Sat 11–4;
Credit Cards: MC, Visa; Owner is Kimberly V. Henson

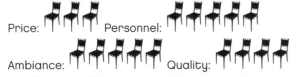

Price: Personnel:

Ambiance: Quality:

Henson & Henson, one of the newer additions to Miami Circle, is a breath of fresh air worth experiencing. I was so intrigued by the big, colorful beach balls that decorate its front window, I just had to stop in and check the place out. I had no idea as to what kind of store it was. Then I was greeted by the owner, who has a personality as cheerful and colorful as her decorative window. Indeed she has created a store she can be proud of. There are some great pieces, like wonderful club chairs from the early 20th century and some Gothic-style chairs. The store is eclectic and fun, a refreshing switch from some of the more serious shops on the row. Designers receive a 20% discount. There are also some great gift items, too, like candlesticks and picture frames.

PIECES

Eclectic Antiques and Contemporary Furniture
3234A Roswell Road; 404-869-2476;
leeboren@piecesinc.com; Hours: Tue–Fri 10–6, Sat 11–5;
Credit Cards: MC, Visa, AmEx, Discover; Owner is Lee Boren

Price: Personnel:

Ambiance: Quality:

Pieces is an amazing new store that is a must-see if you like traditional Swedish furniture, and/or contemporary furniture that is fun with an electric energy. I particularly liked some vintage club chairs upholstered in a hot pink wool fabric. Other colorful furnishings I saw included some bright (hot) green wicker chairs and some very shapely, colorful lamps. This is also a good store to visit if you are looking for an unusual gift for someone's home. Designers receive a 15% discount.

NO MÁS! PRODUCTIONS

Handcrafted Rustic Mexican Furniture

790 Huff Road at Foster Street; 404-350-0907;

Hours: Mon–Sat 10–6, Sun 12–5; www.nomasproductions.com;

Credit Cards: MC, Visa, AmEx, Discover; Owners are

Walt Bilinsky and Steve MacNeil

Price: Personnel:

Ambiance: Quality:

No Más! Productions, a 10-year business, is in a festive-looking terracotta-colored building. The inventory comes from over 100 artisans, and its look is influenced by Mexican and Spanish designs. The furniture looks old and weathered, which adds to the charm of the store. Knock yourself out with an appealing bevy of collectible chests, statues, chairs, and lighting. There is also a lively selection of garden art worth seeing. I highly recommend stopping here. The space can even be rented out for parties. Designers receive a 15% discount. It is possible to shop online, and the Web site is easy to browse.

SWITCH

Contemporary Furniture

1193 Howell Mill Road NW; 404-605-0835;

doug@switchatlanta.com; Hours: Tue–Fri 11–6, Sat 11–3;

www.switchatlanta.com; Credit Cards: MC, Visa, AmEx;

Owners are Doug Henderson and Roy Otwell

Price: Personnel:

Ambiance: Quality:

Although the façade is a cold metal structure, Switch is an inviting store for those with bon vivant taste and an interest in unique contemporary furniture that doesn't necessarily belong in a museum. Switch, also a rep of Poliform cabinetry, carries some spectacular pieces that transcend between early 20th century and contemporary. Many of the elegant fabrics, most of which are monochromatic and plush, are of commercial grade so they are made to last. The service is noteworthy and the staff is proud of their inventory, much of which comes from Europe. Ask and ye shall receive—a 40% discount is available off the floor sometimes.

BUNGALOW CLASSIC

Contemporary Furniture

1197 Howell Mill Road; 404-351-9120; bungalowatl@aol.com;

Hours: Tue–Sat 10–6; Credit Cards: MC, Visa, AmEx, Discover;

Owners are Courtney and Randy Tilinski

Price: 🪑🪑🪑 Personnel: 🪑🪑🪑🪑

Ambiance: 🪑🪑🪑🪑🪑 Quality: 🪑🪑🪑🪑

Bungalow Classic is a busy store with more contemporary inventory than its sister store across the street called "Bungalow," which has a slightly more traditional bent than Bungalow Classic. Most big-ticket furniture pieces in Bungalow Classic cost less than $1,000, yet the furniture has true class and sophistication. There are many young people who like to shop here for furniture and accessories.

ATLANTA AUCTION HOUSES

Jim Depew Galleries

1860 Piedmont Avenue

404-876-2405

Four Seasons Auction Gallery

2075 Liddell Drive NE

404-876-1048

ATLANTA FLEA MARKETS

Lakewood Antiques Market

2nd weekend of every month
2000 Lakewood Avenue SE Bldg. 4
404-622-4488

North Atlanta Antiques Show

November
1700 Jeurgens Court
Norcross
770-279-9899

Scott Antiques Markets

2nd weekend of every month
Atlanta Expo Centers
3650 Jonesboro Road
404-361-2000

CHAPTER 6

Boston

I found Boston, our nation's oldest major city, to be one of the most fascinating and surprisingly diverse furniture hot spot cities I have reviewed. After tooling all about its cobblestone streets by foot, I realized why Oliver Wendell Holmes dubbed Boston "the hub of the Universe." Aside from its beautiful, old architecture and rich historical background (being famous for Paul Revere's midnight ride and "the shot heard around the world" that marked the beginning of the American Revolution), this city has much to offer in the way of education, the arts, cuisine, and of course, furniture.

One great advantage of shopping for furniture in Boston is that unlike most of the other big cities, which have spread-out furniture districts, Boston's furniture stores are centrally located in the downtown area and are easy to get to by cab, public transportation, or car—the latter only if you are familiar with the city. (I don't recommend driving around Boston if you haven't done so before. Traffic is a killer, and the phrase "you can't get there from here" was actually coined just for Boston's many narrow one-way winding streets.) Another advantage is the food: while shopping for furniture in Boston, you'll happen upon any number of great restaurants around just about every corner.

You may be surprised to learn that this historical old-furniture mecca offers far more than just antiques. Many stores in this city specialize in contemporary furniture. The areas I reviewed in Boston include Back Bay, the South End, Beacon Hill, and Cambridge.

BOSTON RETAIL STORES

Beacon Hill

Beacon Hill, considered to be one of the most affluent neighborhoods in the country, is a well-preserved 19th-century neighborhood known for its cobblestone streets, quaint gas lamp street lighting, and charming Federal-style red brick row houses that are typical old-Boston architecture. Aside from being famous for its many fabulous antiques shops (there are no contemporary furniture stores here), Beacon Hill is equally famous for its reputation of being snobby. The majority of antiques stores in Beacon Hill are located in a concentrated four-to-five-block radius on Charles Street, where a wellspring of neat cafés, clothing stores, and bakeries also await your discovery.

A ROOM WITH A VIEUX

Mostly French Antiques
20 Charles Street; 617-973-6600;
Hours: Mon–Sat 10–6; Credit cards: MC, Visa, AmEx, Discover;
Owner is Jeff Diamond

Price: Personnel: Ambiance: Quality:

With one other location a few miles away in Brookline, A Room With a Vieux is a popular Boston antiques store, and rightfully so. The ambiance is not special, but the inventory is. There are lots of worthy collectibles to see, but what I like about shopping here is the large variety of mostly French antique furniture. Holding true to Beacon Hill's well-earned snobbish reputation, some of the tags on the furniture in this shop can be intimidating, like "firm," referring to pricing, or "do not touch." While the tags were a bit of a turn-off, I must say the interesting Art Deco furniture and room suites were awesome. I also enjoyed viewing the great selection of mirrored tables and club chairs. Discounts to designers and the public are possible but vary depending on each individual piece.

GALLAGHER-CHRISTOPHER ANTIQUES

18th–20th-Century European and American Antiques
84 Chestnut Street; 617-523-1992; Hours: Mon–Sat 10:30–6;
Credit Cards: MC, Visa, AmEx, Discover; Owner is Chris Mazewski

Price: | Personnel:

Ambiance: | Quality:

Gallagher-Christopher Antiques is a cute, smaller antiques store just off Charles Street. Keep your eyes peeled for the "Antiques" flag in the front of the store, as this is its only marker. A presence here for the past 14 years, Gallagher-Christopher has positioned itself as a well-known and respected part of the local community. I liked some of the pieces and especially their impressive mix of both old and new. Don't be shy about trying to negotiate a price here, as members of the trade and the general public may be able to receive a discount depending on the item. I must say, though, I wasn't thrilled with the indifferent treatment that I received from the sales help. Should I attribute the poor service to the fact that I had come in from a rainstorm with a dripping umbrella and soaking-wet clothes, or did the sales help come down with a sudden case of good old Beacon Hill snobbishness? Perhaps it was a good measure of both.

CHARLES RIVER ANTIQUES

European Antiques
45 River Street; 617-367-3244; Hours: Tue–Sat 11–5;
Credit Cards: MC, Visa, AmEx, Discover; Owner is Madeleine Gens

Price: | Personnel:

Ambiance: | Quality:

Charles River Antiques is an adorable, cozy shop just behind Charles Street on narrow little River Street. Madeleine Gens is one of the friendliest shop owners I have ever come across in my travels. She is as delightful as the marvelous collection of little "prop" and garden pieces that I discovered in the shop. Shop inventory is as interesting as it is varied. In what is a fancy neighborhood with not always the friendliest service, Charles River Antiques is a refreshing change. Designers are able to receive a 15% discount.

EURO EXPORTS

Biedermeier and Neoclassical Furniture
70 Charles Street; 617-720-7886; Hours: Mon–Sat 10–6;
www.euroexportsantiques.com; Credit Cards: MC, Visa;
Owners are Annette and Victor Bashensky

Price: Personnel:

Ambiance: Quality:

    I highly recommend Euro Exports if you, like me, are an ardent fan of Biedermeier furniture. I have rarely seen such an unusual selection of furniture from this period (1815–30). Surprisingly, the quality of service in this store is actually on par with the outstanding selection. Many shop owners with merchandise of this caliber make shoppers feel nervous upon entering their showrooms, but Victor Bashensky couldn't have been a warmer or more gracious host. He did a fine job of explaining his inventory, going out of his way to share details. The Web site has nice pictures and descriptions of the inventory, but no prices. Designers and sometimes the public can receive a 15% discount. I think prices are reasonable given the quality of the merchandise. After your shopping adventure here, stop at Café Vanille next door for some out-of-sight pastries!

DANISH COUNTRY ANTIQUE FURNITURE

European and Asian Antiques
138 Charles Street; 617-227-1804; Hours: Tue, Wed,
Thu 10–6, Fri, Sat 10–5, Sunday 12–5; Credit Cards: MC, Visa;
Owner is Jim Kilroy

Price: Personnel:

Ambiance: Quality:

If you have a yen for a great selection of uniquely styled, high-quality rustic, then you must visit Danish Country ASAP. This store has a truly remarkable and distinctive line of rustics that are so unlike the everyday generic ones you find today which appear to have been made out of low-grade plank wood yanked off a barn floor. All the rustics here, and especially the pine, are constructed with the most exquisitely refined high-quality wood. The wood, though, isn't the only thing that makes them stand out. One piece after the next seems to be blessed with a uniquely beautiful and individual style of its own. Many of the pieces here are from Sweden and Denmark. Even the Chinese furniture selection at Danish Country reflects a special style that is out of the loop. The atmosphere here is very laid back—so laid back I had to wait some time before I could get the salesperson's attention. That said, I still highly recommend shopping here if you at all fancy the unique and hard-to-find. Be forewarned: prices aren't cheap when it comes to this unusually unorthodox selection. Designers receive a 15% discount.

Back Bay

"You've come a long way, baby" might best describe this growing furniture hot spot. Indeed, Back Bay, once a boggy Boston marsh filled with stagnant water, has come into its own, offering everything from high fashion to hip shopping. Situated in the heart of Boston's thriving commercial downtown district, it is dotted with many fancy designer chain stores and some specialty boutiques. Back Bay serves as home to a three-block strip filled with an unusually large collection of mostly contemporary furniture stores. Many of these stores have opened here in the past few years, making this neighborhood a destination for furniture/home accessory shopping. I found its furniture shopping along with the choice eateries and other shops so irresistible that I spent one whole day in Back Bay.

SHOOMINÉ
Contemporary Furniture
8 Park Plaza; 617-227-2021; contact@shoomine.com; Hours:
Mon–Thu 10–6, Fri 10–7, Sat 10–6, Sun 12–5; www.shoomine.com
Credit Cards: MC, Visa, AmEx, Discover; Owner is Fabby Abbasi

Price: Personnel:

Ambiance: Quality:

If you're mad about very modern furniture that is highly artistic in form, this store will make you think you have died and gone to heaven. I liked the fact that many of the pieces are multipurpose—like a couch that turns into a love seat and then can be resized by simply pushing out a section and reconfiguring it. I also favored the dining tables that have easy storage for leaves. Their leather chairs were both elegant and comfortable. I appreciate the craftsmanship, creativity and artistry. Prices are high here; it is possible to achieve a similar look for less at other stores. Designers receive a discount of approximately 10%. The Web site has some pictures of the inventory but no prices.

ADESSO

Contemporary Furniture
200 Boylston Street; 617-451-2212;
info@adessoboston.com; Hours: Mon–Sat 10–6, Sun 12–5;
www.adessoboston.com; Credit Cards: MC, Visa, AmEx;
Owner is Francoise Theise

Price: Personnel:

Ambiance: Quality:

Next to the Four Seasons Hotel in Boston and just across the street from Shoominé, Adesso is a wonderful store with the most soothing atmosphere—truly the "Nirvana" of furniture hot spots. With no loud music or pushy salespeople hovering over, I thoroughly enjoyed lounging on the comfortable sofas and chairs. I also fancied the interesting lamp selection. Adesso has a great inventory of European contemporary furniture, including well-known manufacturers like Ligne Roset, Montis, Kartell, Pallucco, and MDF Italia. No one receives discounts here, which helps to make the shopping experience more pleasant than in other stores where you are constantly focused on getting the best price. The Web site includes pictures but no prices.

THE MORSON COLLECTION

Contemporary Furniture

31 St. James Avenue; 617-482-2335; Hours: Mon–Fri 10–6, Sat 11–6, Sun 12–5; www.themorsoncollection.com; Credit Cards: MC, Visa; Owner is Caroline Morson

Price: Personnel:

Ambiance: Quality:

The Morson Collection has been in operation in the Boston area for the past eight years. At one time they did have a second store in Chicago, but that closed long ago. The store is located in a generous space inside a building that reminds me of a large commercial downtown bank. Perhaps it's only fitting that the place resembles a bank, because you can expect to pay some hefty prices at Morson. Much of the furniture is by well-known, sought-after designers and is imported. Most of the pieces are contemporary, squared in form, often combining a variety of woods and generally upholstered in muted colors. I was particularly impressed with the Fornasetti screens and the simply designed wardrobe closets. On the afternoon I visited Morson, service was weak. The sales help didn't go out of their way to answer questions, leaving me pretty much on my own. Furniture takes 14 to 16 weeks to arrive. Designers receive a discount of 20%. For you fans of 21st-century designers, Morson has two sales each year for the public. Check out their awesome Web site. There's a variety of terrific online pictures and even a fancy sound system. Alas, there are no prices listed in cyberspace.

IN HOME FURNISHINGS

Full-Service Traditional Furniture Store

364 Boylston Street; 617-266-2255; info@inhome.com; Hours: Mon–Wed 10–6, Thu 10–7, Fri, Sat 10–6, Sun 12–5; www.inhome.com; Credit Cards: MC, Visa, AmEx, Discover; Owner is Bob Darvin

Price: Personnel:

Ambiance:  Quality:

In Home has four other locations in Massachusetts. Before coming to the store, I previewed their Web site which had quite a large variety of furniture, including some nice-looking antiques. When I entered the store, though, and saw the slim pickings in antiques inventory, I did a double-take. I thought I must have had the wrong address. NOT! Even though I had seen many antique pieces online, there were few to be found in this store location. In addition to the sparse antiques inventory, the majority of the pieces in the store seemed to be nothing more than ordinary traditional furniture with very high prices. Also disappointing was the too-dark showroom and the service which left much to be desired. Absolutely no one was around to help me the entire time I was shopping until right as I was leaving. Designers receive a 15% discount or a sale price, whichever is lower. A big turn-off for me was seeing big sale signs that made me feel even more strongly that these prices are too high. The Web site has some pictures of the inventory but no prices or descriptions. Note that I only reviewed the Boylston location; the other locations may have better inventory than the Boylston shop, based on the selection shown on the Web site.

CARL TODISCO

European Antique Furniture
141A Arlington Street; 617-357-5050; Hours: "by chance or by appointment"; Credit Cards: MC, Visa, AmEx, Discover; Owner is Carl Todisco

Price:  Personnel:

Ambiance: Quality:

Carl Todisco is an endearing little mom-and-pop-type store located in a small red brick vintage building. Its sleepy small-town ambiance doesn't quite jive with the rest of the bustling downtown area. The store's owner, Carl, is quite a personality and very engaging. He claims he is able to run his little business as a one-man show because most of his customers are designers "who only want him to help them." The selection here is modest, but there are some impressive 19th-century Italian and French antiques and reproductions. I would not give the selection, uniqueness, or quality of the pieces the highest mark, but it is a cute shop worth visiting when you are furniture shopping in this neighborhood. One negative is that there are no price tags. This may have something to do with the designers who frequent the store. Many of these designers may wish for Carl to have no prices on his inventory so they can "create" their own prices based on some mutually agreed upon decision.

MONTAGE
Contemporary European Furniture
75 Arlington Street; 617-451-9400; sales@montageweb.com;
Hours: Mon–Sat 10–6, Sun 12–5; www.info@montage.com;
Credit Cards: MC, Visa, AmEx, Discover; Owners are
Liz and Chris Bates

Price:　　　　　Personnel:

Ambiance:　　　　Quality:

Montage, a well-known Boston favorite, is a large store taking up two full floors. Selling popular lines like B&B Italia, Cassina, Maxalto, and Walter Knoll, Montage is not a store for the budget shopper. To give you an idea of the pricing, a sofa can start at $6,000. The look here is Italian Contemporary, and there are many leather sofas, squared in form, as well as rectangular and square tables. Most of the fabrics are monochromatic. This store is a little sleek, with lots of showy displays, and is affected with a slight case of Boston snobbery. Personally, I feel Montage to be a little intimidating in its presentation and I find the prices high relative to the quality. But don't get me wrong, other stores that sell these brands also charge the same high prices. There are, however, other stores in Boston that sell this same look for much less. While I like the simplicity of the inventory, I feel that you can get similar simple, rectilinear furniture at other stores without giving much up in terms of quality. The Web site shows pictures of some inventory, though no prices. Only designers receive discounts, and their discounts depend on each manufacturer.

KARTELL

Fun, Multicolored Plastic Furniture
10 St. James Avenue; 617-728-4442;
dloffredo_kbo@kartellus.com; Hours: Mon–Sat 10–6, Thu 10–7;
www.kartellus.com; Credit Cards: MC, Visa, AmEx, Discover;
Owner is Kartell (KBO, LLC)

Price: Personnel:

Ambiance: Quality:

Kartell is a blast. Much of the furniture (lots of clear and bright-colored pieces) is something I would never consider if I were filling an entire room, but I do think just about everyone can find one really outstanding piece to accessorize their other furniture. Most of the furniture here is so creatively designed, usable and practical. I like much of the Philippe Starke–designed furniture because it is so imaginative and isn't meant to be taken seriously, yet at the same time it is quite functional. I saw a fabulous chair with Lucite legs and a tufted box cushion on top— a brilliantly designed chair, mixing traditional style with modern-day chic. I also liked a liquor cart that looked like it had a lacquered top but is actually plastic and can be quickly cleaned, folded up, and stored away. The good news is that most of the fun furniture and accessories here are less than $500. The Web site has pictures of inventory with descriptions but no prices. Both the public and designers can receive a discount based on a quantity purchased.

AUTREFOIS ANTIQUES

Italian and French Antiques
125 Newbury Street; 617-424-8823; Hours: Mon–Sat 10–5:30;
www.autrefoisantiques.com; Credit Cards: MC, Visa, AmEx;
Owner is Francesca Rowe

Price: Personnel:

Ambiance: Quality:

Autrefois is a boutique on the popular Newbury Street. With another location in Brookline, Autrefois has been in the business of selling Italian and French antiques for 20 years. The owner travels abroad to handpick her merchandise, and it shows. The inventory is of an excellent quality. I do feel, though, that the shop could be a little more service-oriented, considering the high prices. On the afternoon I entered incognito, no one expressed the least bit of interest in even acknowledging me, much less in coming over and asking if I needed help. Despite the apathy, the store is a pleasant place to shop. The merchandise on the detailed tags is well-described, and there is a worthwhile selection to choose from. The Web site shows inventory and prices, but it is not possible to buy online. Designers receive a 20% discount.

FURNITURE BY DOVETAIL
Handmade Wood Furniture
216 Clarendon Street; 617-236-1067 or 800-773-2513;
info@furniturebydovetail.com; Hours: Mon–Sat 10–6, Sun 12–6;
www.furniturebydovetail.com; Credit Cards: MC, Visa, Discover;
Owners are Annette and Robert Loring

Price: Personnel: Ambiance: Quality:

Furniture By Dovetail has been in business for 16 years, with its main location in Holden (70 Industrial Drive, Holden, MA). Much of the handmade furniture is in the Arts & Crafts style, with oak and cherry being the primary woods used. The furniture is made locally. There are some contemporary styles, though, and you can special-order your furniture with woods other than oak and cherry for a 20% upcharge. There are also a few vintage pieces here which enhance the flavor of the inventory. There is usually no discount for the public, but designers receive a 15% discount. The Web site has good pictures and descriptions. Prices are included, but you cannot buy online.

Fort Point Channel District
(South Boston)

MACHINE AGE

Mid-Century Modern and Contemporary Furniture
354 Congress Street; 617-482-0048; info@machine-age.com;
Hours: Tue–Sat 12–5; www.machine-age.com; Credit Cards: MC,
Visa, AmEx; Owner is Normand Mainville

Price: | Personnel: |

Ambiance: | Quality: |

As the demand for Mid-Century Modern furniture has grown, so has the popularity of Machine Age. For the past 13 years this store has gained quite a loyal following in Boston and continues to do so. The store, located in an enormous space inside a cold-looking industrial building, takes up two huge floors. Most of the furniture is from the 1950s–'70s. I have to say that much of the prize collectibles on the lower level looked more like "bargain basement" resale items to me. Prices are high for pieces that in my opinion appear to be more like flea market finds than treasures. Mid-Century Modern fanatics, knock yourselves out . . . the owner of the store, a native of Montreal, with a charming personality and a flair for design, always sees to it that both floors are spilling over with an abundance of "stuff" to choose from. There is also a wonderful selection of light fixtures to match the inventory. There are no discounts. The Web site shows some of the inventory but gives no descriptions or pricing information.

South End

South End, a funky-flavored neighborhood made up of an unusual blend of young urban professionals, college kids, and the elderly, is fast becoming one of the more popular furniture hot spots in Boston to live. The area boasts some great furniture stores and cafés. You will definitely need a car or cab to check out this neighborhood because the stores are not always close to one another.

LEKKER

Unique Home Furnishings Store
1317 Washington Street; 617-542-6464;
info@lekkerhome.com; Hours: Tue–Sat 10–7, Sun 12–6;
www.lekkerhome.com; Credit Cards: MC, Visa, AmEx, Discover;
Owner is Natalie van Dijk Carpenter

Price: Personnel:

Ambiance: Quality:

Lekker is a good store to cruise because there is something interesting here for everybody and in all price ranges. Although the store sells mostly simply designed housewares from Europe, you'll also find a select number of beautiful, rustic, yet modern pieces of furniture from Belgium and the Netherlands which are well-priced considering the quality of the teak and oak the furniture is made from. There is also a good selection of some interesting Chinese furniture and antiques. The Web site offers pictures and prices, but to purchase you need to contact the store directly. Designers receive a 15% discount.

RED RIVER TRADING COMPANY

Asian Antiques and Decorative Objects
1313 Washington Street; 617-542-2223; Hours: Tue–Sat 11–7,
Sun 12–5; www.redrivertradingco.com; Credit Cards: MC, Visa,
AmEx, Discover; Owner is Jonathan Gulnick

Price: Personnel:

Ambiance: Quality:

Red River Trading Company is a great South End neighborhood shop specializing in Asian Antiques, mostly from the late 19th century. The furniture is nice, but most notable for me is the great selection of decorative arts, both antiques and reproductions, and contemporary pieces. I love many of the benches, figurines, and pottery. Prices are reasonable relative to other stores around the country selling a similar inventory. The

Web site is excellent, offering pictures of the inventory, measurements, prices, and even shipping charges. Designers receive a 15% discount, but sometimes there are storewide sales.

SEDIA

Contemporary European Furniture/Modern Classics
535 Albany Street; 617-451-2474 or 800-BAUHAUS;
colby.andrus@sedia.com; Hours: Mon–Fri 10–6; open 1st Sat of
the month; www.sedia.com; Credit Cards: MC, Visa, AmEx;
Owner is Colby Andrus

Price: 🪑🪑🪑🪑 Personnel: 🪑🪑🪑🪑🪑

Ambiance: 🪑🪑🪑 Quality: 🪑🪑🪑🪑🪑

I was referred to Sedia by several people living in the Boston area. Sedia is a no-frills store in the South End selling Modern classics. The store, located in an old, nondescript red brick industrial-looking warehouse, is easy to miss if you drive by too quickly. Like its austere front façade, the inside of this dimly lit store also lacks in atmosphere. But don't be deceived by Sedia's plain-Jane looks as this store, which has been in business for 25 years and has a large national following, offers a very impressive and sizable selection of Modern classics and Italian contemporary furniture. Sedia is a good store to visit if you're in the mood for quality Modern and a relaxed, no-stress shopping experience. Designers receive a discount that is 55% off the list price. The public also receives discounts (40% off list). The Web site has very good descriptions, including the name of the designer, the dimensions, and price. You cannot purchase online.

Cambridge

This fascinating and fun area has an amazing electric vitality generated by its diverse population of blue-collar workers, immigrants, Harvard intellectual highbrows, and young blood (over one-fourth of the population being college students). The furniture shops, restaurants, and other stores in Cambridge also reflect the high energy of this town. Be prepared for driving in traffic here.

ANTIQUES ON CAMBRIDGE STREET

Antiques Mall
1076 Cambridge Street; 617-234-0001; Hours: Tue–Sat 11–6;
Credit Cards: MC, Visa; Owners are Frank Giglio,
Bert Rosengarten, and Rob Werner

Price: Personnel:

Ambiance: Quality:

    Antiques on Cambridge is a popular spot for Bostonians who want to shop for a little of everything. With 100 dealers and 12,000 square feet, Antiques on Cambridge is a destination hot spot for antiques lovers, regardless of whether you're on a shoestring budget or the sky is the limit. If Mid-Century Modern is your cup of tea, you're out of luck, as you won't find very much of it. Most of the furniture you will find is from the 19th century. This sprawling complex, marked by two antiques flags in front, has a very unattractive façade but boasts a big testimonial from the *Boston Globe* in the window. Having been in business for eight years, the owners seem to have a large following here. The mall offers free appraisals and gives everyone at least a 10% discount. This is a great place to shop if you are a young couple who just bought a home and now need everything and want very good service. Supposedly there is a waiting list of dealers trying to get booths here.

MOHR & McPHERSON

Asian Antique and Contemporary Furniture
75 Moulton Street; 617-520-2000;
info@mohr-mcpherson.com; Hours: Tue–Sat 10–6, Sun 12–6;
www.mohr-mcpherson.com; Credit Cards: MC, Visa, AmEx;
Owner is Kevin McPherson

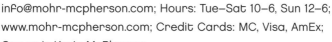

Price: Personnel:

Ambiance: Quality:

    Mohr & McPherson (with another location at 290 Concord Avenue,

Cambridge) offers a fabulous selection of very unusual Asian furniture, new and old. They also have what I consider a top-gun staff: well-trained, friendly, and knowledgeable. Much of the inventory comes from Japan, China, Korea, and Indonesia, but some is from Morocco as well. Prices are reasonable, as many of the pieces cost less than $1,000. There is also a great selection of accessories, like rugs and fabrics. The Web site is fantastic, with pictures, measurements, and prices. Designers receive a discount of 15% with a purchase over $500. Buying one piece of furniture or art here will really add interest to any room in your house. Come with an empty stomach, because when you're done shopping for furniture you'll want to grab a bite just next door at one of Boston's great seafood restaurants called Summer Shack—it's kid-friendly, so bring along the brood.

CIRCLE FURNITURE
Large General Furniture Store
199 Alewife Brook Parkway; 617-876-3988;
Cambridge@circlefurniture.com; Hours: Mon, Tue, Sat 10–6,
Wed–Fri 10–8, Sun 12–5; www.circlefurniture.com;
Credit Cards: MC, Visa, AmEx, Discover;
Owners are Harold and Richard Tubman, and Peggy Burns

Price: 🪑🪑🪑🪑 Personnel: 🪑🪑🪑🪑🪑
Ambiance: 🪑🪑🪑🪑🪑 Quality: 🪑🪑🪑🪑🪑

Circle Furniture is so unlike any chain furniture store I have ever seen (hint, hint: you know the kind I'm referring to with the lousy service, generic-looking stock, and endless maze of no-mans-land to get lost in). This chain store is exceptional because it offers so many styles, manufacturers, fabrics, and inventory that whether your taste is contemporary or traditional, you're bound to find the perfect piece on either of its two floors. Fifty years ago, Circle Furniture was founded by Robert Tubman to sell unfinished furniture to Harvard students. Today, the store has five locations (I visited the Cambridge one). The store and the merchandise cater to a wide variety of shoppers who want to pull together their own individual eclectic look. Even much of the traditional furniture is uniquely designed. Maine

Cottage furniture is painted traditional-style furniture, yet the color choices are bright and playful. This line shows very well here at Circle Furniture. Other lines are designed and produced by local wood furniture manufacturers. I highly recommend this store for anyone.

Boston Design Center
Design Center; sells to the trade only
One Design Center Place; 617-338-6610; Hours: Mon-Fri 9-5;
www.bostondesign.com

The Boston Design Center is in a large building with 78 showrooms. Of all design centers in the country the Boston Design Center is one of the strictest with respect to allowing the public to browse the showrooms. In fact, the design center has a "club" that you can join for $275 which will allow you to use an on-site interior designer's services while at the design center for only $90 per hour! I am curious how many people have actually joined this club. Some of my favorite showrooms which are not in other showrooms around the country include: Brookline Village Antiques, Antiques on 5, and Sharon B. Jorgensen, all of which sell antiques.

BOSTON AUCTION HOUSES

Skinner, Inc.
63 Park Plaza
617-350-5400

Sotheby's
6 Chestnut Street
617-367-6323

BOSTON ANTIQUES SHOWS

Brimfield Antiques and Collectibles Show
May, July, September
www.brimfieldshow.com
60 miles west of Boston off Interstate 90

Ellis Antiques Show

November
The Castle at the Boston Park Plaza Hotel and Towers
64 Arlington Street
617-248-8571

CHAPTER 7

Chicago

Finally I get to review my own hometown! I must admit, though, that I felt a bit queasy about the prospect—it's a little like being asked to review your mother's cooking in writing.

Almost everyone I have ever met from the Midwest who is at all into furnishing their home comes to Chicago at some point in time to check out the furniture stores. In my travels I've often met dealers from the coasts who come here to shop for furniture because they think the prices are less than in their home cities. Aside from reasonable prices, there are plenty of other good reasons why out-of-towners will enjoy shopping for furniture in Chicago. I am extremely proud of the increasingly good furniture store selection here and find the overall service in Chicago to be above average. Chicago's furniture shops are a wonderful mixture of all periods and styles. Chicago is also an easy place to navigate because the streets are on a grid system and the addresses generally make sense.

Some great non-furniture must-do's in Chicago include out-of-sight summer festivals, the Navy Pier, world-famous Chicago deep-dish pizza (Lou Malnati's, Wells Street; Gino's East, Superior Street; Uno's & Due's on Wabash), Magnificent Mile shopping on Michigan Avenue, and trendy River North and Rush Street clubs and restaurants.

Chicago's public transportation includes the "El" (elevated train), bus, and taxi. If you call the city's trans hotline at 312-836-7000 on your cell phone and tell them your Chicago location and preferred destination, they will quickly map out an exact route that will get you to nearly anywhere you want to go. Traffic can be a problem, so plan ahead to try to avoid rush-hour traffic. Come prepared, as Chicago weather is notoriously unpredictable. Winters are especially cold.

CHICAGO RETAIL STORES
Lakeview/Wrigleyville

When traveling through this side of town, you can't help but notice its relatively young, under-40-year-old population including many college post-graduates. This area has experienced an amazing spurt in development and growth in recent years. There is much ongoing residential home construction as young professionals raze, rehab, and rebuild costly brownstone homes. In your furniture shopping experiences here, you'll discover many innovative shops, theaters, restaurants, and cafés. Since this part of town is also home to Wrigley Field where the Cubs play, you'll have to be careful to avoid game traffic.

TRAGARA

Vintage Modern Classics and Accessories
3827 North Lincoln Avenue; 773-248-3699
and 708-567-5687; billymwilcox@hotmail.com;
Hours: Wed–Fri 12–7; Sat, Sun 12–6; Credit Cards: MC, Visa, AmEx, Discover, and Diners; Owner is Billy Wilcox

Price: Personnel: Ambiance: Quality:

Color Tragara a winner! I cannot describe to you how excited I am over this new find. Like some other furniture stores on this block, Tragara has recently opened in a small space, but considering the reasonable prices of the remarkable early-mid-20th–century furnishings this store carries (I have seen stores in other cities that charge triple the prices for the same inventory!), I am certain this store is here to stay. There are marvelous must-see combinations of materials here, like metal, woods, funky lighting, glass accessories, and Lucite. I hope Billy Wilcox announces a Web site for all the chic vintage shoppers. Designers get a 20% discount. The entire inventory is priced under $500! There are also some nice vintage garden furniture pieces. The inventory is carefully displayed and shows well.

RED EYE ANTIQUES

Eclectic Antiques and Modern Furniture and Accessories
3715 North Ashland Avenue; 773-975-2020; Hours: Wed 11–6,
Thu 11–8, Fri, Sun 11–6; Credit Cards: MC, Visa, AmEx, Discover,
Diners; Owner is Robert Lutz

Price: Personnel: Ambiance: Quality:

Red Eye, situated on busy Ashland Avenue, is a big store with a very relaxed, pleasant, small-town atmosphere. But don't let its mom-and-pop sleepy ambience fool you—Red Eye is a destination. There are dealers who come from both coasts to seek out special pieces and good prices here. Although the owner told me that the pieces here are from the 1600s to the 1970s, I observed mostly furniture and accessories from the 19th and 20th centuries. There is a nice range in prices and inventory—everything from flea market finds to the more unique, impressive items. Prop rentals are available. Designer discounts depend on the individual pieces. There is no Web site.

PRAHA

Rustic Eastern European and
American Antiques and Painted Reproductions
3849 North Lincoln Avenue; 773-549-1227; designbytodd@aol.com;
Hours: Wed, Thu 12–6, Fri 12–9, Sat, Sun 12–6; Credit Cards: MC,
Visa, AmEx, Discover; Owner is Todd M. Nyenhuis

Price: Personnel: Ambiance: Quality:

From Amsterdam with love, Praha is one of the few rustic antique shops in the area that boasts furniture from Eastern Europe. A recently opened shop, it has a wonderful contemporary flair. The owner says he based Praha on a store he's crazy about in Amsterdam. There are big, old pine cabinets and dressers as well as some wonderful painted reproductions of country pieces done in great colors. Prices are extremely reasonable for the goods. Praha also sells specialty gourmet food items, and on the weekends serves some of this food to its shoppers. The jazz music makes the atmosphere feel lively here. There are no discounts.

ZIG ZAG ANTIQUES

Art Deco and Mid-Century Modern
3419 North Lincoln Avenue; 773-525-1060;
Hours: Wed–Fri 2–6, Sat 1–6, Sun 1–4; Credit Cards: MC, Visa;
Owner is Marsha Evaskus

Price: Personnel:

Ambiance: Quality:

Stop right there! Although you might be tempted to walk away when you reach the front door of this building, don't. While the façade and inside of the space may be far from glamorous, the inventory is something else! Although its physical space may be tiny, Zig Zag is gaining a big name as it has been written up in many of the well-known interior design magazines for having an unusually wide selection of Deco metal chairs. Prices are quite reasonable here and "everybody gets discounts." Marsha Evaskus has been in this business for 25 years and spends much of her time attending antiques shows around the country. There is also an impressive selection of Bakelite jewelry here.

ARCHITECTURAL ARTIFACTS, INC.

Architectural Artifacts and Antique/Vintage Furniture
4325 North Ravenswood; 773-348-0622;
stuart@architecturalartifacts.com; Hours: Daily 10–5;
www.architecturalartifacts.com; Credit Cards: MC, Visa;
Owner is Stuart Grannen

Price: Personnel:

Ambiance: Quality:

About 15 minutes north of Chicago's loop, Architectural Artifacts is one of only a handful of large architectural artifact stores left in the country. In business for 17 years, Architectural Artifacts now has expanded into an 80,000-square-foot building. The building is a red brick loft parallel to train tracks on a somewhat industrial block. It looks like nothing from the outside, but the inside is a stunning space, as these kinds of businesses go. There are four floors of furniture, lighting, doors, stained glass, fireplace mantels, wrought-iron, and garden furnishings. The inventory is original and there are no reproductions. Some of the furniture is online, but only a small portion of what is in the showroom. Service is excellent, with several people who can really help a shopper who is lost here. Prices are high, but because this kind of merchandise is in demand, they can charge these prices. Designers get a 15% discount.

Lincoln Park

Lincoln Park is about seven minutes north of Chicago's Loop. Here in this popular, congested neighborhood reside both young people in their twenties and thirties, and well-established yuppies in multimillion-dollar homes. Lincoln Park is worth a visit just for the fun of browsing its streets. Along with a good concentration of furniture stores, there are hundreds of restaurants, shops, and bars here.

CB2

Crate & Barrel's Contemporary, Chic Furniture Store
800 West North Avenue (also at 3757 North Lincoln Avenue);
312-787-8329; Hours: Sun 11–6, Mon–Fri 10–9, Sat 10–7;
www.cb2.com; Credit Cards: MC, Visa, AmEx, Discover;
Owner is Crate & Barrel

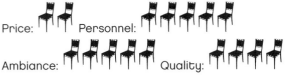

Price: 🪑🪑 Personnel: 🪑🪑🪑🪑🪑
Ambiance: 🪑🪑🪑🪑🪑🪑 Quality: 🪑🪑🪑🪑🪑

CB2 is Crate & Barrel's less expensive, contemporary, fashionable store, the first for this well-known mail-order and online furniture store. Much like IKEA, (another popular and prolific chain store), CB2 offers contemporary furniture designs with a youthful feel in a colorful, inviting atmosphere. Prices are extremely reasonable, and there is a wonderful selection of contemporary accessories, like vases, glasses, bowls, bags, etc. The furniture is an excellent value. Almost everything here costs less than a few hundred dollars. I would recommend CB2 to a person just starting out or just about anyone who wants the look of high style without the price. Worth a visit.

JAYSON HOME & GARDEN
Garden Furniture and Nursery, Asian Antiques and
Contemporary Furnishings
1885 North Clybourn Avenue; 773-248-8180;
info@jaysonhome-garden.com; Hours: Sun 11–5, Mon, Thu 9–8,
Tue, Wed, Fri 9–6; www.jaysonhomeandgarden.com; Credit Cards:
MC, Visa, AmEx; Owner is Jay Goltz

Price: Personnel:

Ambiance: Quality:

Jayson Home & Garden is a popular spot in Lincoln Park. It began as a nursery that sells plants, flowers, trees, and garden furniture, and has grown into a big home and garden business. The furniture is attractive, and I like the mix of Asian antiques and contemporary furniture. The look is rustic-chic. Jayson has a large selection of fabrics for the upholstered goods. Well-known furniture manufacturers here include Mitchell Gold and Richter, with many large-scale pieces. There is also a nice selection of housewares and bedding. Designers receive a 10% discount. The Web site is limited.

PACIFIC INTERIORS
Asian Antiques and Accessories
653 West Armitage Avenue; 312-397-1188;
pacificinteriors@sbcglobal.net; Hours: Sun 12–5, Tue–Fri 11–7, Sat
10–6; Credit Cards: MC, Visa, AmEx; Owners are Lisa and John Spears

Price: Personnel:

Ambiance:  Quality:

Pacific Interiors is a wonderful, friendly store specializing in Asian antiques and artifacts, 60% of the inventory coming from China and 40% from the rest of Asia. I like the shelving units in lacquered finishes, gorgeous cabinets that go from simple to ornate, and round serving tables, all in beautiful colors. The shop is busy, and it is sometimes difficult to find the prices on the pieces. Designer discounts depend on the individual piece. There is no Web site yet.

PINE & DESIGN IMPORTS

Antique and Reproduction Pine Furniture
511 West North Avenue; 312-640-0100; Hours: Sun 11–5, Mon, Thu
10–8, Tue, Wed, Fri, Saturday 10–6; www.pinedesignimports.com;
Credit Cards: MC, Visa; Owner is Kevin McGivern

Price:  Personnel:

Ambiance: Quality:

Pine & Design, with its green-and-white-striped awning, is a popular, well-established store on busy North Avenue. Selling rustic pine furniture, this shop has done well for many years in this spot. Even though the rest of the country isn't buying as much pine these days, there are many people here still wanting a rustic look. Many of the pieces are made from old wood, but the pieces themselves are not old. This store can get busy, and when it does service suffers. The Web site doesn't give prices or dimensions or complete descriptions, but you can contact the store for more information. I wasn't able to find out the designer discount.

ANDREW HOLLINGSWORTH

Nordic Vintage and Contemporary Furniture
and Accessories
1708 North Wells Street; 312-440-9554;
andrew@andrewhollingsworth.com; Hours: Sun 1–4, Mon–Sat 11–6;
www.andrewhollingsworth.com; Credit Cards: MC, Visa, AmEx;
Owner is Andrew Hollingsworth

Price: Personnel: Ambiance: Quality:

Unlike many stores around the country selling regular Danish Modern furniture, Andrew Hollingsworth sells mostly Danish Modern furniture with a twist. Upholstered in beautiful fabrics and colors, his furniture is chic and modern-looking. Now selling some contemporary pieces, the store seems versatile and carries some highly unusual pieces. I also love the accessories, which start at around $15 and make wonderful presents. The furniture here is expensive. Designers get a 15% discount on furniture and 10% on accessories. The Web site has great pictures and descriptions but no prices.

Bucktown/Wicker Park

Bucktown and Wicker Park sit side by side in a neighborhood that is hip, diverse, and filled with some of Chicago's best restaurants and shops. This area is only about 10 minutes from the Loop and has been rehabbed in the past several years. I recommend taking a look at some of the wonderful furniture stores in the neighborhood.

CASA LOCA
Mexican Handcrafted Furniture
1130 North Milwaukee Avenue; 773-278-2972; Hours: Sun 12–5,
Tue, Wed, Thu, Sat 11:30–6, Fri 11:30–7; www.casalocafurniture.com;
Credit Cards: MC, Visa, AmEx; Owner is Angelo Varias

Price: Personnel: Ambiance: Quality:

Casa Loca is a great find for anyone looking for rustic furniture with a twist. The store, which has been here for 10 years, really dresses up this quiet block. Casa Loca specializes in rustic Mexican furniture that comes in a variety of luscious primary colors and fun styles. Most of the furniture is between $200 and $600. Designers get a 10% discount. There are occasional sales. Accessory items are also a good value and festive in feel. I like the attractive table runners in bold colors. The Web site has pictures and some descriptions but no prices on the individual pieces.

ORANGE SKIN

Contemporary Furniture and Accessories
1429 North Milwaukee Avenue (and 223 West Erie Street main store, 312-335-1033); 773-394-4500; info@orangeskin.com;
Hours: Daily 11–7; www.orangeskin.com; Credit Cards: MC, Visa, AmEx, Discover; Owners are Giuseppe Cerasoli and Obi Nwazota

Price: 🪑🪑🪑🪑🪑 Personnel: 🪑🪑🪑

Ambiance: 🪑🪑🪑🪑🪑 Quality: 🪑🪑🪑🪑🪑🪑

Orange Skin has been making the news with their mod, contemporary furniture and home accessories store on Milwaukee Avenue. Newly opened in River North is yet another Orange Skin location that specializes in furniture made from designers from around the world. Well-known designers represented here include Phillipe Starck and Panton, Minotti and Bernhardt. There is a nice mix of materials—wood, plastic, and foam—and the furniture is colorful and comfortable. Check out the housewares department downstairs, where along with a few pieces of furniture are some nice home accessories. There are many wonderful gift possibilities here. If registered with Orange Skin, designers get a 10% discount on furniture, excluding Kartell. Kartell is a company who carries science fiction-like furniture made of materials like plastic and Lucite. Colors at Kartell are vibrant and appear fluorescent to me.

MODERN TIMES

Mid-Century Modern Furniture
1538 North Milwaukee Avenue; 773-772-8871;
Hours: Wed–Fri 1–6, Sat, Sun 12–6; www.moderntimeschicago.com;
Credit Cards: MC, Visa, AmEx, Discover; Owners are Martha Torno and Tom Clark

Price: Personnel:

Ambiance: Quality:

Modern Times has been here for many years and has perfected the art of selling Mid-Century Modern classics by well-known designers like Panton, Arne Jacobsen, Charles and Ray Eames, and George Nelson. Most of the furniture is from the 1950s and '60s. There are some wonderful lamps and light fixtures. The service is excellent, and the group seems well informed about the furniture from the period. Designer discounts depend on the individual piece. The Web site is excellent, showing pictures, descriptions, and prices. Worth a trip.

PAVILION ANTIQUES

Early–Mid-20th-Century Furniture and Accessories
2055 North Damen Avenue; 773-645-0924;
pavilionantiques@ameritech.net; Hours: Tue–Sun 12–6;
www.pavilionantiques.com; Credit Cards: MC, Visa, AmEx;
Owners are Deborah Colman and Neil Kraus

Price: Personnel:

Ambiance: Quality:

Pavilion Antiques is one of the best shops in the country for early-to mid-20th-century European designer pieces. Specializing in French 1940s, Pavilion has an excellent selection of sconces, light fixtures, and furniture. The store's owners have a real flair for style, though the shop could be intimidating to the layperson. Designer discounts vary, but on furniture the discounts range from 10% to 20%. The Web site shows pictures of the furniture and gives some descriptions but no prices.

STITCH

Home Accessories and Some Contemporary Furniture
1723 North Damen Avenue; 773-782-1570; Hours: Sun 12–5, Mon–Fri
12–7, Sat 11–7; www.stitchchicago.com; Credit Cards: MC, Visa,
AmEx; Owner is Pamela Hewett

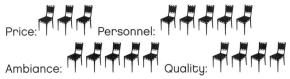

Price: Personnel:

Ambiance: Quality:

With parking in back (a huge plus in this neighborhood), Stitch has been a favorite spot in Bucktown for six years. Stitch has a wonderful array of home accessories like pillows, rugs, and chairs, also interesting purses, bags, lamps, and vases. Most of the pieces are reasonably priced and well selected. Designers receive a 10% discount. The Web site shows pictures and gives prices of the inventory, and it is possible to buy online.

PAGODA RED

Asian Antiques and Accessories
1714 North Damen Avenue; 773-235-1188; bnathan@pagodared.com;
Hours: Mon–Sat 10–6; www.pagodared.com; Credit Cards: MC,
Visa, AmEx; Owner is Betsy Nathan

Price: Personnel:

Ambiance: Quality:

Pagoda Red is located in an attractive walk-up that looks like an Asian garden. Once up the flight of stairs, you'll find the store's inventory laid out on two large floors. The furnishings are primarily from northern China, with some items from Tibet, and the inventory includes some special pieces and interesting and colorful chairs. I also like the assortment of unusual accessories. Designers receive a 20% discount. The Web site doesn't have pictures of the entire inventory or the prices yet.

ABODE

Contemporary Handmade Furniture
1904 West North Avenue; 773-227-6400; jason@abodechicago.com;
Hours: Sun 12–5, Tue–Fri 11–7, Sat 11–6; www.abodechicago.com;
Credit Cards: MC, Visa, AmEx; Owners are Jason Ballew
and Darrick Draper

Price: Personnel:

Ambiance: Quality:

Abode is a new contemporary, LA-style furniture store carrying designer pieces from all over the world. Much of the inventory is not out but can be seen in the artists' own catalogs. The service is excellent here and the atmosphere is relaxed, not stuffy. Designer discounts depend on the individual pieces. The Web site doesn't show the entire inventory, nor does it give prices or descriptions.

LILLE

Home Accessories and Custom Tables and Desks
1923 West North Avenue; contact@lilleashop.com;
Hours: Sun, Mon 12–5, Tue–Fri 11–7, Sat 11–6; www.lilleashop.com;
Credit Cards: MC, Visa, AmEx, Discover, Diners;
Owner is Lydia Lando

Price: Personnel:

Ambiance: Quality:

Lille has a beautiful assortment of home accessories from France like dishes, bowls, and flatware. They also have wonderful desks and tables that look very Deco and are made with sharkskin and parchment. All the furniture comes from France. The lighting is also very unusual. I highly recommend visiting Lille if you're in the market for something really different and special. There are no designer discounts. Most of the inventory is online, with the exception of the furniture pieces. It is possible to buy online.

River North

About two blocks north of the downtown Loop area is Chicago's Art and Furniture District. River North reminds me a little of Western Avenue in Seattle because of the kinds of stores in this neighborhood—very artsy with many loft buildings. River North has recently become a more residential neighborhood, with new loft apartment buildings, many new and trendy restaurants, art galleries, and shops. If you could only go furniture shopping in one neighborhood in this big city, River North would be the place. By the way, my favorite accessories shop in the city is a small boutique called Fly-By-Night Gallery, located at 714 North Wells Street, surrounded by many other galleries. The collection here includes European decorative arts, Art Nouveau and Art Deco, from 1890–1930. Not to be missed interesting vintage jewelry, ceramics and art glass. There is not much in the way of furniture here.

MANIFESTO
Contemporary Furniture
755 North Wells Street; 312-664-0733;
bmb@manifestofurniture.com; Hours: Mon–Fri 10–3, Sat 11–4;
Credit Cards: MC, Visa, AmEx, Discover; Diners;
Owners are Barbara and Richard Gorman

Price: Personnel:

Ambiance: Quality:

Manifesto is a well-known River North shop that is owned by a husband-and-wife architect/design team. The store carries popular European lines like Cassina, Armani Casa, and Pomemoria, and their prices are high. There is no Web site yet, but the store is easy to shop. The look here is simple, straight-lined modern furniture. Designers receive a 15% discount for most lines, except for Cassina, which charges a net price and gives no discounts. Designers receive a 10% discount for accessories.

DOUGLAS ROSIN

Mostly 20th-Century Furniture and Accessories
730 North Wells Street; 312-337-6556;
douglasrosin@aol.com; Hours: Tue–Sat 11–5:30;
www.douglasrosin.com; Credit Cards: MC, Visa, AmEx, Discover;
Owners are Gene Douglas and Barbara Rosin

Price: [chairs] Personnel: [chairs]

Ambiance: [chairs] Quality: [chairs]

Douglas Rosin is one of my favorite shops in Chicago, and one of the best in the country. Claiming to not stick to furniture or accessories of only one or two periods, Douglas Rosin really specializes in decorative arts, jewelry, and furniture from the early 20th century. Most of the pieces are European, and everything in the place is extremely unusual. I love the sconces and some of the more unusual furniture, and the nice selection of rugs. The owners are friendly, and the store atmosphere is relaxed. There are no price tags, but there is a book listing all the prices. Designers receive a 10% discount. The Web site is well done, with good pictures and clear descriptions and prices. You won't be disappointed. You can not buy online yet.

MIG AND TIG FURNITURE

Rustic and Contemporary Furniture
549 North Wells Street; 312-644-8277; Hours: Mon–Sat 10–6;
www.migandtig.com; Credit Cards: MC, Visa, AmEx;
Owner is Vicki Sempke

Price: [chairs] Personnel: [chairs]

Ambiance: [chairs] Quality: [chairs]

Mig and Tig, also located on Green Bay Road in Winnetka (20 miles north of Chicago), has become a big Chicago hit for their nice selection of both rustic and clean-lined contemporary furniture at fair prices, with good service as a bonus. There is a little of everything here, from large upholstered pieces such as sofas to bar stools, tables, etc. Custom finishes and measurements are available, and there are many fabrics from which to choose. The store doesn't share its list of manufacturers, but the furniture is an excellent value for the money. There are no sales and no designer discounts. The Web site shows pictures and gives descriptions and some pricing information. This is an easy store to shop.

SVENSKA MOBLER

Swedish Furniture From 1840 to 1940

516 North Wells Street; 312-595-9320;

Hours: Tue–Fri 11–6, Sat 11–5; www.svenskamobler.com;

Credit Cards: MC, Visa; Owner is Andrew Wilder

Price: 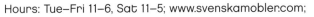 Personnel:

Ambiance: Quality:

Svenska Mobler, also in Los Angeles, is one of the only dealers in America specializing in Swedish furniture from 1840 to 1940. Much of this style resembles furniture from the Biedermeier period but has a more modern edge. There is a lot of handsome Swedish Deco furniture (very expensive), which is a nice transition between pre-1900 and contemporary furniture. Designers receive a 20% discount. The Web site shows pictures of the inventory and gives descriptions but no prices. This is a chic place.

RITA BUCHEIT

Biedermeier, Vienna Secession, and

Art Deco Furniture and Accessories

449 North Wells Street; 312-527-3316; info@ritabucheit.com;

Hours: Tue–Sat 10–6; www.ritabucheit.com; Credit Cards: MC, Visa; Owner is Rita Bucheit

Price:  Personnel:

Ambiance:  Quality:

Rita Bucheit is one of the most well-known Biedermeier dealers in the country. Well-respected and worthy of her reputation, Rita Bucheit, with her husband Floyd and daughter, Michelle, have created a store that feels like a museum. The furniture is glossy, and the atmosphere may be intimidating because of the high prices, but the inventory is beautiful. They have a wonderful selection of Biedermeier pieces, along with furniture and accessories from the Vienna Secession and Deco periods. Don't forget to ask if you can visit the rest of the inventory next door in a newly remodeled space. Designers get a 20% discount. The Web site is nice, showing pictures and giving excellent descriptions but no prices. Worth a trip.

MICHAEL FITZSIMMONS

Arts & Crafts Furniture, Accessories, and Reproductions
311 West Superior Street; 312-787-0496; mfda311@ameritech.net;
Hours: Tue–Fri 10–6, Sat 11–5; www.fitzdecarts.com;
Credit Cards: MC, Visa, AmEx; Owner is Michael Fitzsimmons

Price: / Personnel:

Ambiance: / Quality:

Michael Fitzsimmons has been in the River North area for many years. He has developed a reputation as being one of the nation's most well-respected Arts & Crafts dealers. Now with a line of reproductions (not inexpensive), he offers a nice selection of furniture in the Arts & Crafts style. My personal favorites here are the Arts & Crafts rugs, which are beautiful, and the pottery. Designer discounts vary. The Web site is easy to use, showing pictures, descriptions, and prices. It is easy to buy online here, too.

LUMINAIRE

Contemporary Furniture
301 West Superior; 312-664-9582; info@luminaire.com;
Hours: Mon–Sat 10–6; www.luminaire.com; Credit Cards: MC, Visa, AmEx; Owner is Nasir Kassamali

Price: / Personnel:

Ambiance: / Quality:

Luminaire has a 30-year reputation for being a furniture hot spot in Chicago, with shops also in Miami and Coral Gables, Florida. Selling high-end contemporary furniture like Eames, Panton, and Nelson, the store is spread out over two floors and has a museum-like feel. There are also many cutting-edge European designers whose designs are shown here. Service can be cold and impersonal. On my visit, when asking for some help, I was asked, "Have you bought from us before?" Designers do not receive a discount here. The Web site gives minimal description and no pricing.

COSULICH
European Antiques and Accessories
120 West Hubbard Street; 312-832-0757;
info@cosulichinteriors.com; Hours: Tue–Sat 10:30–6:30;
www.cosulichinteriors.com; Credit Cards: MC, Visa, AmEx,
Discover; Owners are Fabienne and Franco Cosulich

Price: 🪑🪑🪑🪑🪑 Personnel: 🪑🪑🪑🪑🪑

Ambiance: 🪑🪑🪑🪑🪑 Quality: 🪑🪑🪑🪑🪑

Cosulich has recently opened a charming shop in River North. The owners are originally from Italy, though they have come recently from England to set up this shop. The inventory is European antiques. I especially love the Murano light fixtures from Italy and the beautiful glass bowls and vases. Also the vintage picture frames are really unusual. Designers receive a 10–20% discount. The Web site is not up and running yet.

MATERIAL CULTURE

Asian Antiques and Accessories
401 North LaSalle Street; 312-467-1490;
Hours: Mon, Wed, Fri 10–6 Tue, Thu 10–7, Sat 10–5;
www.materialculture.com; Credit Cards: MC, Visa, AmEx, Discover;
Owner is an East Coast rug company

Price: 🪑🪑🪑 Personnel: 🪑🪑🪑🪑🪑

Ambiance: 🪑🪑🪑🪑🪑 Quality: 🪑🪑🪑🪑🪑

Material Culture is a cozy store with really nice Asian antiques. I especially like the cabinets and the hammered copper tables from Turkey; also the Asian jewelry, which is not very expensive. Rugs, displayed in a large room, are the shop's specialty. There is another store in Philadelphia. Designer discounts vary, and there is not much inventory online. The atmosphere is what I love most about Material Culture, not to mention its friendly staff and interesting inventory. Worth a visit.

GOLDEN TRIANGLE

Asian Antiques
72 West Hubbard; 312-755-1266;
info@thegoldentriangle.biz; Hours: Mon, Tue, Wed, Fri 10–6, Thu 10–7, Sat 10–5; www.goldentriangle.biz; Credit Cards: MC, Visa, AmEx; Owners are Chauwarin Tuntisak and Douglas Van Tress

Price: | Personnel: | Ambiance: | Quality:

Golden Triangle is a sophisticated shop specializing in Asian antiques. Most of the inventory is Chinese, and there is a large selection of furniture on two floors. The atmosphere is relaxed and the service is excellent. I like the selection of wood chests and decorative arts. There is also a new warehouse just two blocks away (very California), and I recommend seeing the inventory there. The showroom is large (though it doesn't feel large) with over 11,000 square feet. Designer discounts vary depending on the item. The Web site doesn't show individual pieces of furniture or prices.

MODERNICA

Mid-Century Modern Style Furniture
555 North Franklin Street; 312-222-1808; chshowroom@modernica.net; Hours: Tue–Sat 10–6; www.modernica.net; Credit Cards: MC, Visa; Owner is Modernica Corporation in Los Angeles

Price: | Personnel: | Ambiance: | Quality:

Modernica, located also in New York and Los Angeles, is the place to find Mid-Century Modern–style furniture. Modernica manufactures its own line of chic, simply designed furniture, much of which can be found at Design Within Reach, a chain store with several locations around the country, (see appendix in the back of the book). There are no price tags on the inventory, however, which makes shopping more time-intensive. Prices are also high. There are no designer discounts, but there is an annual floor-sample sale. The Web site is excellent, showing pictures, descriptions, and prices. It is even possible to buy online.

WHITE ON WHITE

(see description of their New York location in Chapter 11)
Copies of Mid-Century Modern Furniture
226 West Kinzie Street

ORANGE SKIN

(see also in Bucktown/Wicker Park)
Contemporary Furniture
223 West Erie Street; 312-335-1033; info@orangeskin.com; Hours: Mon–Fri 10–6; www.orangeskin.com; Credit Cards: MC, Visa, AmEx, Discover; Owners are Giuseppe Cerasoli and Obi Nwazota

Price: Personnel:

Ambiance: Quality:

Orange Skin has had so much press that I was dying to see their two stores, both here and in Bucktown/Wicker Park (not my favorite). This location features more in the way of furniture, whereas the other store has more accessories. I love the pulse here at this River North hot spot, and recommend this store if you are striving for a chic, urban look. There are some wonderful pieces by famous designers like Minotti, Panton, and Phillippe Starck. The furniture is beautifully displayed. Prices are high, but the quality and style make up for it. Designers get a 10% discount.

Merchandise Mart

Design Center; sells to the trade only,
except for Luxe Home, in which public can buy
222 West Merchandise Mart Plaza; 312-527-7600;
Hours: Mon–Fri 9–5; Luxe Home is also open on Saturdays 10–3;
www.merchandisemartproperties.com

Chicago's Merchandise Mart is the largest and perhaps most well-known of all design centers in the country. Formerly owned by the famous Kennedy family, (yes, as in John F. Kennedy's family) the Mart is a traditional design center with list prices (only the trade really understands them), and showrooms that sell to the trade only (designers). The public is welcome to browse but may feel uncomfortable entering showrooms here without a designer. If you have a passion for antiques, visit Mike Bell and Richard Norton. The Mart is becoming more public-friendly these days, though, with more shows open to the public and the recent opening of Luxe Home, a gallery filled with boutiques of medium to high-end kitchen and bath designers. The products here are showcased beautifully in this first-floor space. Well-known boutiques here include Waterworks, Christopher Peacock, Clive Christian, Paris Ceramics, and Poggen Pohl, to name a few. There are many events in this space. For more information, check out www.luxehome.com.

Gold Coast

The Gold Coast is Chicago's ritzy neighborhood with all the great shops, department stores, and restaurants. Stores like Bloomingdale's, Marshall Field's, Barney's, and Prada anchor the area whose key markers are Lake Shore Drive and Michigan Avenue. Until recently, the Gold Coast did not have many furniture shops (rent too high), but lately more stores are popping up. For home furnishings, besides what is listed, check out the excitement at Urban Outfitters for some remakes of Mid-Century Modern classics and vintage pieces. Up the street on Rush, find Urban Outfitters' sister store, Anthropologie, with its unexpectedly wonderful selection of home accessories.

MALCOLM FRANKLIN

English Antiques
34 East Oak Street, 2nd Floor; 312-337-0202; malfrank@aol.com;
Hours: Mon–Fri 10–4:30, Sat 10–3; www.malcolmfranklin.com;
Owners are Paul Franklin, Susan Gancer, and Dan Sullivan

Price: Personnel:

Ambiance: Quality:

Malcolm Franklin, on the fashionable Oak Street, next to Prada and across from the well-loved Barney's, is for the English antiques aficionado; there is no furniture from any other country here. I still prefer a mix, but Malcolm Franklin does have beautiful furniture and it is all finished well and authentic. Named as one of the best in its class in the National Antique and Art Dealers Association of America, Malcolm Franklin has been around for several generations. The atmosphere here is a little cold—maybe because of the high price tags. But everyone who buys here receives a certificate of authenticity (I like that), and at any time Malcolm Franklin will take back their furniture as a trade for anything else in the store. Another perk: the store will repair and polish furniture free of charge for one year after purchase. Designers get a 15% discount. The Web site shows pictures and descriptions but no prices.

THOS. MOSER CABINETMAKERS
Handmade Arts & Crafts–Style Furniture
58 East Walton Street; 800-708-9032 or 312-751-9684;
pamm@thosmoser.com; Hours: Mon–Fri 10–6, Sat 10–7, Sun 10–3;
www.thosmoser.com; Credit Cards: MC, Visa, AmEx;
Owner is Thos. Moser

Price: Personnel:

Ambiance: Quality:

Thos. Moser has been a Chicago favorite for over 20 years. Handmade furniture from Maine, the look is Arts & Crafts and the wood is generally cherry. The Midwest is still passionate about Arts & Crafts–style furniture, and this is the place to come. Thos. Moser's pieces are all well-designed and handcrafted, and prices are high, but I was reassured that every item is finessed to perfection. Some updated looks are going to be shown here soon in response to interest in a more updated look. If you are in a rush, this isn't the place to buy furniture—it takes about three months to finish a piece. Shipping is generally 10–12% of the cost of the item. The Web site offers pictures and prices. You can easily order even custom pieces online.

HOME ELEMENT

Contemporary Furniture, Art, Asian Antiques
700 North Michigan Avenue, 5th Floor; 312-587-8752;
homeelement@earthlink.net; Hours: Mon–Fri 10–6, Sat 10–7,
Sun 12–5; Credit Cards: MC, Visa, AmEx, Discover;
Owners are Xin Yang and Mike Cao

Price: 🪑🪑🪑🪑 Personnel: 🪑🪑

Ambiance: 🪑🪑🪑🪑 Quality: 🪑🪑🪑

Home Element has replaced Room & Board in the 700 North Michigan Avenue building, which also houses Talbot's and Saks. The furniture comes from mostly the U.S., China, and Italy. The quality isn't great on the contemporary furniture, but the Chinese antiques are very interesting, authentic and well priced. The art is not expensive here, and there is a big variety. Return policy is four weeks for store credit only. There are no designer discounts. I have a little difficulty understanding the store's concept, and it took what seemed like forever to find someone to help me. There is no Web site yet.

The Loop

Named for the route of the "El," or elevated train, The Loop is the destination for Chicago's business district. Not only is The Loop a worthwhile visit to see some of the country's best architecture, it is also home to the original Marshall Field's, an old-time Chicago department-store favorite that is now part of Target.

MARSHALL FIELD'S

Department Store
111 North State Street; 312-781-1000;

Hours: Mon–Sat 9–8, Sun 11–6; www.fields.com; Credit Cards: MC, Visa, AmEx, Novus, Marshall Field's; Owner is Target

Price:  Personnel:

Ambiance: Quality:

Marshall Field's has one of the largest collections of furniture in the city. The furniture department, on the eighth floor, seems to always be changing and rearranging. Selling popular lines like Ralph Lauren, Baker, Bernhardt, and Thomas O'Brien, Field's is known to have sales all the time, and its long-standing customers await the big Field Days events and other weekend sales. The store honors manufacturers' warranties, but attempts to repair damaged goods rather than replace them. Service could be improved, as I waited what seemed like an eternity for a salesperson to help me. It is not possible to order furniture online.

South Loop

South Loop is just five minutes south of The Loop and is home to McCormick Place Convention Center and Chinatown. The neighborhood has been re-gentrified in the last 10 years or so to accommodate new homes and businesses. This is a quickly expanding community that has many industrial pockets.

REVIVAL
Architectural Artifacts, Furniture, Art
19 East 21st Street; 312-842-4002; Hours: Mon–Sat 11–5, Sun 12–4;
Credit Cards: MC, Visa, AmEx, Discover; Owners are
Schemek Drabio and Mark Steinke

Price:  Personnel:

Ambiance: Quality:

Revival just opened in one of ComEd's oldest former power plants. But you'd never guess it was a power plant at one time, because this two-story brick building located right on the train tracks has been entirely gutted and metamorphosed into an art gallery. A famous Chicago restaurateur (who owns Red Light and Marche, among other famous restaurants) owns the building, which also has a large party room that he will be renting out for events. Yes, you hear the trains flying by, but you're so mesmerized with the neo-outer-space environment that you don't really notice them. Far surpassing any space in this city, you feel as though you're on the movie set of some science fiction flick. The shop is on two floors and has a variety of art, objects, furniture, and architectural artifacts. I think the store will do well in this fabulous space, and I am hoping it will expand its inventory. There isn't much of a theme at Revival, but that may change in the months ahead. Designer discounts vary.

West Loop

West Loop is just a few minutes west of The Loop. Until five to seven years ago, there were only industrial buildings, meat packers, and a few trendy restaurants on Randolph Street. Today, the West Loop has opened some nice new furniture stores and even more trendy restaurants. As more and more people move to the loft buildings that surround this neighborhood, furniture stores are popping up to accommodate these mostly young urbanites. While in the neighborhood, eat in any of the restaurants on Randolph Street (my favorite is Red Light for Asian-inspired food), and stop in at Morlen Sinoway Atelier, a little shop open to the trade only with some very chic custom-made furniture and accessories from around the world. There is almost no furniture to view because most of the furniture is custom and not sold retail.

DOUGLAS DAWSON
Asian Art and Furniture
400 North Morgan Street; 312-226-7975;
info@douglasdawson.com; Hours: Mon–Fri 10–5:30, Sat 10–5;
www.douglasdawson.com; Credit Cards: MC, Visa, AmEx;
Owner is Douglas Dawson

Price: Personnel:

Ambiance: Quality:

Douglas Dawson just moved from River North to this building, which feels more like a museum than a store. It will be beautifully landscaped and the garden filled with Asian garden antiques to complete the experience. There is some furniture, spectacular and pricey, but mostly what you will find here are Asian artifacts and sculptures. Not all merchandise has price tags, so you will need to grab a salesperson if one is available. Designers receive a 20% discount. The Web site is not up yet.

EL PASO IMPORT COMPANY

Mostly Painted, Rustic Furniture
1820 West Hubbard Street; 312-226-7209;
Hours: Mon–Sat 9:30–5; www.elpasoimportco.com;
Credit Cards: MC, Visa, AmEx; Owner is Jack Dunlley

Price: Personnel:

Ambiance: Quality:

El Paso Import Company, next to Salvage One, is one of my favorite stores for rustic furniture. You will absolutely flip when you see the low prices (around $300 for a large cabinet) for this very chic country look, which I have seen priced five times as much in many other chain stores around the country. With over 15 store locations nationwide (Los Angeles, Dallas, Phoenix, Berkeley, Austin, etc.), El Paso imports its furniture from India, China, Romania, and Mexico. The furniture is a great value, and the quality is decent. This showroom has 14,000 square feet of warehouse space, and the shopping environment is truly relaxing. Local shipping ranges from 10% to 20% of the purchase price. Designer discounts vary.

CASATI

Italian Mid-Century Modern Furniture
949 West Fulton Street; 312-421-9905;
ualfano@casatigallery.com; Hours: Wed–Sat 1–6;
www.casatigallery.com; Credit Cards: MC, Visa;
Owner is Ugo Alfano Casati

Price: Personnel:

Ambiance: Quality:

Casati is a real treasure chest filled with hard-to-find Italian Mid-Century Modern furniture by famous designers like Gio Ponti and Bugatti. Prices may throw you, but many of the pieces are documented as designer pieces and the prices reflect that. Service is extremely personal (what a refreshing change), and the help is knowledgeable. In particular, there are some amazing chaise lounges and chairs. Lamps are another specialty here. It is possible to pay $35,000 or more for a table, but there are also some fabulous original leather-covered chairs and accessories for less than $2,000. The owners have been collectors for years and began the shop as a way to pursue their passion in this niche business. Designer discounts vary. The Web site shows pictures and descriptions but no prices.

CHICAGO AUCTION HOUSES

Christie's
John Hancock Building, Suite 3810
312-787-2765

Leslie Hindman
122 North Aberdeen
312-280-1212

Sotheby's
188 East Walton Street
312-475-7900

Susanin's
900 South Clinton
312-832-9800

Wright, Inc. (20th-century furnishings)
1140 West Fulton Market
312-563-0020

CHICAGO ANTIQUES SHOWS

Botanic Garden Show
April
Glencoe, IL
212-255-0020 or 847-835-6952

Chicago Antiques Fair
April
The Merchandise Mart
2nd Floor Market Suites
800-677-6278

Hinsdale Antiques Show
September
Hinsdale Community House
Hinsdale, IL

Modernism Show
November

Winnetka Community House
620 Lincoln Avenue
Winnetka, IL

Winnetka Antiques Show
March
Winnetka Community House
620 Lincoln Avenue
Winnetka, IL
847-446-0537

CHICAGO FLEA MARKETS

Kane County
1st Sunday and preceding Saturday of every month
520 Randall Road
St. Charles, IL
630-377-2252

Morgan Productions
375 North Morgan Street
312-455-8900

Sandwich Fairgrounds
Sandwich, IL
815-786-2389

CHAPTER 8

Dallas

The movies have traditionally portrayed Dallas as being grand: big country breakfasts, sprawling cattle ranches, towering oil wells, elegantly appointed homes with beautiful furniture, and billionaires in their cowboy hats wheeling and dealing, (like, J. R. Ewing from the old "Dallas" TV series). In real life, Dallas is better known for its trendy restaurants, great football team, and ideal year-round climate. There's one holdover about Dallas from the movies that is true: Dallas is big when it comes to its hospitality and its terrific furniture shopping. It would be hard to see all the great mix of new and old, expensive, and just plain fun furniture that Dallas has to offer in just a few days. If you are planning a short visit here, I would recommend hitting two major areas: Uptown and the Dallas Design District. Other noteworthy neighborhoods include Highland Park, Deep Ellum, and the Bishop Arts District.

In reviewing these stores I have found that each city has a different concentration of a particular kind of furniture. I think Dallas's bend is definitely toward antiques shops, but there are also some good contemporary stores. In general, store owners couldn't have been warmer or more helpful. Many of them even offered to take me around Dallas—without even knowing I was writing this book! Because Dallas is "plenty big," you definitely need a car to get around town. Most stores I reviewed in Dallas don't have Web sites.

DALLAS RETAIL STORES

Uptown

Uptown has some wonderful shopping pockets and great restaurants. Many art galleries, restaurants, and home furnishings stores are on or just off McKinney Avenue (I ate at a terrific Mexican restaurant called Chuy's on McKinney). Uptown is just a few minutes north of downtown Dallas.

FORTY FIVE TEN, INC.

Unique Vintage and Contemporary Furniture and Home Accessories
4510 McKinney Avenue; 214-559-4510 or 888-567-4510;
Hours: Mon–Sat 10–6; www.fortyfiveten.com; Credit Cards: MC, Visa, AmEx, Discover; Owners are Brian Bolke, Bill Mackin, and Shelly Musselman

Price: 🪑🪑🪑🪑🪑 Personnel: 🪑🪑🪑🪑
Ambiance: 🪑🪑🪑🪑🪑 Quality: 🪑🪑🪑🪑🪑

The name of this store is also its address on McKinney. Located in an elegant white building next to Design Within Reach and El Paso Imports, this is a terrific place to shop for furniture and at the same time pick up really great gifts. Look for the unusual selection of colorful bowls and serving pieces, one-of-a-kind jewelry, and pretty clothing. I especially liked the iron furniture—some of the most distinctly designed pieces I've ever seen. Prices are high, but I think this store is definitely worth the trip.

JOHN ROBERT CLARK ANTIQUES

Specializing in Unusual French Empire Furniture
2723 Routh Street; 214-871-3388; jrc@jrcantiques.com;
Hours: Tue–Fri 10–5, Sat 11–4; Credit Cards: MC, Visa;
Owner is John R. Clark

Price: 🪑🪑🪑🪑🪑 Personnel: 🪑🪑🪑🪑🪑

Ambiance:  Quality:

Just off of McKinney is a great shop to browse if you are at all into 19th-century Empire furniture. This store is in a beautiful old red brick house. The elaborate storefront, with its beautifully landscaped entranceway and elegant fountain, helps sets the stage for what lies inside. Filled with a selection of mostly very formal and gilded furniture, the shop makes you feel like you're in someone's private home—someone like the Rockefellers! Needless to say, this is not a shop for the budget-conscious or those with a squeamish stomach when it comes to price. Although the prices are high here, even perhaps inflated, the goods are real and John Clark knows his stuff. He takes excellent care of his inventory, and it shows. He is also very helpful to his customers. Designers receive a 20% discount.

UNCOMMON MARKET

Unusual Decorative Arts and Architectural Ornaments
2701 Fairmount; 214-871-2775;
uncommonmktinc@mindspring.com; Hours: Mon–Sat 10–5:30;
Credit Cards: MC, Visa, AmEx; Owners are Don, Scott,
and Ward Mayborn

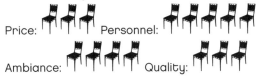

Price: Personnel:

Ambiance: Quality:

Lights, camera, action! One block from John Robert Clark and also just off McKinney, this is another of my favorite furniture stores—or should I say, favorite stores to shop movie props! Set designers for motion pictures have shopped here for unusual props, like vintage pictures, draconian iron gates, and sports equipment. The accessories here come from all over the world. You'll want to check out the shop's backyard garden where you'll find a great supply of beautifully displayed antique garden furniture. The store's three buildings and property out back make you feel like you're on a beautiful old farm. The service I received was Texas-style warm and friendly. Designers receive a 15% discount. Well worth a trip. You will fall in love with this place. Don't miss it.

THE WHIMSEY SHOPPE
French Provincial Furniture
2923 North Henderson; 214-824-6300; Hours: Mon–Sat; 10–5:30;
Credit Cards: MC, Visa, AmEx; Owners are Suzie and
Wendell Patterson

Price: Personnel:

Ambiance: Quality:

    The Whimsey Shoppe is located in a charming, vintage-looking strip shopping center in the Knox-Henderson area of Dallas located just off Freeway 75 and a few blocks from McKinney. This is a large showroom made up of many smaller rooms all filled with French Provincial pieces, a considerable number of which are quite lovely. I loved the many antique dining chairs with the original brown leather and large nailheads. If you are interested in buying a great farm table for your family, this is the place for you. The owners even put out a newsletter. Service is very good, even though prices are high. Designers receive a 25% discount here.

NICK BROCK ANTIQUES
18th- and 19th-Century European Antiques
2909 North Henderson; 214-828-0624; Hours: Mon-Fri 10-5
Sat 10–5:30; Credit Cards: MC, Visa, AmEx, Discover;
Owner is Nick Brock

Price: Personnel:

Ambiance: Quality:

    This store is Texas on the outside, but has a heart of old Europe. Although the beautiful, rustic-looking exterior with its large, Texas-size wooden front door might give you an appetite for steak and eggs, once you're inside the shop you'll probably crave some truffles. The store, which has mostly all 19th-century European, has an Old World charm, especially with the French music playing in the background. From the way the customers seemed so well acquainted with the gentleman who was helping them, I'd say this is a popular place to shop in Dallas. Prices are high but they don't deter customers. Designers receive a 20% discount, and some discounts are available to the public.

BRANT LAIRD ANTIQUES

18th- and 19th-Century European Furniture
2901 North Henderson Avenue; 214-823-4100; Hours: Tue–Sat 10–5;
Credit Cards: MC, Visa, AmEx; Owner is Brant Laird

Price: Personnel:

Ambiance: Quality:

Brant Laird is a man who wears many hats. Next door to his fine antiques shop, but treated as one business, is Laird's busy Dallas consignment shop. He owns what he describes as the best consignment store in all of Dallas. His clientele is largely designers here at the antiques store and many of the designers actually also shop at the consignment store. His selection is diverse and complete. He is also an accredited appraiser and a gemologist, and often runs high-end estate sales in town. I liked both shops, but I particularly liked the consignment shop. This is a busy showroom, so be prepared to wait behind other customers as I did. Designers receive a 20% discount on all antiques.

MILTON KENT ANTIQUES

European Antiques and Interior Design
2819 North Henderson; 214-826-7553;
miltonkent@sbcglobal.net; Hours: Mon–Sat 10–6; Credit Cards:
MC, Visa, Discover, Diners, AmEx; Owner: Milton Kent

Price: Personnel:

Ambiance: Quality:

If you are in the Knox-Henderson area just off McKinney, this is a store you won't want to miss. The storefront looks like an old-fashioned ice cream parlor, with everything painted in yellow and white stripes—even the furniture outside. Inside, however, is another story . . .. Milton Kent has a fabulous showroom with a diverse mix of furniture from everywhere and many rooms to peruse. I especially enjoyed talking with Milton, a friendly man who is clearly proud of his shop. He has a great eye for the expensive and the inexpensive. He has been here for 15 years. I definitely like the great English leather library couches. Designers receive a 20% discount.

Dallas Design District

The Dallas Design District is located in the downtown and covers several blocks of stores and showrooms, most of which are open to the public. This is not an attractive area—it looks industrial and is not a place where you can just walk up and down the streets. You definitely need a car to shop here. This is also a place where you need to plan on spending a full day to fully appreciate all there is to offer. I especially enjoyed antiques shopping on Slocum Street. There are not many restaurants in the district, but the surrounding areas have plenty of chain restaurants.

THE GATHERING
Art and Antiques Mall
1515 Turtle Creek Boulevard; 214-741-4888;
caffey@thegatheringantiques.com; Hours: Mon–Fri 9:30–5:30,
Sat 10–5; www.thegatheringantiques.com; Credit Cards: MC, Visa,
Discover, AmEx; Owner is Jack Caffey

Price: [4 chairs] Personnel: [5 chairs]
Ambiance: [5 chairs] Quality: [4 chairs]

The Gathering is a large antiques mall, but it has such an intimate feel and excellent service, I felt like I was shopping in an antiques store. The building is a newer red brick building with ample parking. There are a considerable number of French antiques available. Designers receive a 20% discount. I love the Web site, which can even calculate shipping costs per item, but it is not yet possible to buy online.

SCOTT + COONER, INC.

Contemporary Furniture
1617 Hi-Line Drive; Suite 100; 214-748-9838;
josy@scottcooner.com; Hours: Mon–Fri 9:30–5:30, Sat 10–4;
www.scottcooner.com; Credit Cards: MC, Visa, AmEx;
Owners are Lloyd Scott and Josy Cooner

Price: | Personnel: | Ambiance: | Quality:

This is definitely the place to come if you love contemporary, sleek European (mostly Italian) furniture. Forty-seven lines are represented, including Cassina and Poliform, with an unusual selection of woods, leathers, and fabrics. Initially, I found the place a little quiet and intimidating, but after meeting owner Josy Cooner I had a wonderful shopping experience. There are no price tags (a pet peeve of mine), so you need to ask someone to help you if you are interested in learning what something costs. Discounts to designers and the general public vary depending on the individual lines. You can shop and place an order online. Great Web site.

JAN SHOWERS & ASSOCIATES, INC.

20th-Century Furniture and Accessories; Design Services
1308 Slocum Street; 214-747-5252;
Hours: Mon–Thu 9–5 Fri 9–4, other days by appointment;
www.janshowers.com; Credit Cards: MC, Visa, AmEx, Discover;
Owner is Jan Showers

Price: | Personnel: | Ambiance: | Quality:

This is a great shop with unusual furniture and accessories from the 1930s and '40s. Much of the inventory is French and Italian. The furniture is special in part because of the rare materials used, like goatskin, parchment, and ivory. I love the great vintage mirrors and light fixtures, also the pretty glass accessories. Jan Showers is also a well-known designer who has created her own furniture line that is represented in a few showrooms around the country. Her own furniture designs are reproductions of the kinds of furniture she has in her shop. The Web site does not list prices or the inventory in the store, but displays her manufactured line of furniture. Designers receive a 20% discount.

JOHN GREGORY STUDIO

18th-, 19th-, and 20th-Century Modern Furniture
1201 Slocum Street; 214-741-9858; Hours: Mon–Fri 9–5;
www.johngregorystudios.com; Credit Cards: MC, Visa;
Owner is John Gregory

Price: Personnel:

Ambiance: Quality:

I highly recommend seeing this store, one of my favorite furniture stores ever. The inventory is diverse, spanning more than 200 years in furniture design. I found John Gregory to be a personable man who has a great eye. Also an interior designer, he knows how to put it all together and decorates some wonderful homes. He has an incredible selection of vintage Venetian light fixtures and sconces. I also loved some of the great tables and game tables. The Web site is not yet up and running but will be soon. Designers receive a 20% discount.

DEBRIS

Antiques/Art/Design, Antiques Mall
1205 Slocum Street; 214-752-8855;
debrisantiques@msn.com; Hours: Mon–Fri 9–5, Sat 10–4;
Credit Cards: MC, Visa, AmEx; Owner is Josef Edwards

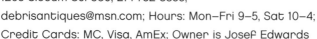

Price: Personnel:

Ambiance: Quality:

This is my pick for the nicest antiques mall in Dallas. It is a large, high-end antiques mall—I am actually embarrassed to use the word "mall" to describe the place, because the building has much nicer things than one would normally expect to see in an antiques mall. That being said, the service is excellent. Josef Edwards also owns Found, another fabulous mall located on Industrial Boulevard, featuring more 20th-century furniture; prices there are generally a little less than here at Debris (see review below). Designers at both malls receive a 20% discount. Some discounts are available to the public, too.

PITTET CO.

19th-Century, Mostly French Furniture
1215 Slocum Street; 214-748-8999; info@pittet.com;
Hours: Mon–Fri 9–5; www.pittet.com; Credit Cards: MC, Visa,
AmEx, Discover; Owner is Raymond Pittet

Price: Personnel:

Ambiance: Quality:

This is a store with a lot of brown wood furniture. If you are looking for armoires, commodes, and large tables, make sure you come here. Located in a big warehouse building, they also carry a big selection of architectural elements. Some of the inventory is shown online. Designers receive a 25% discount.

JOEL COONER GALLERY

Tribal, Pre-Columbian, African Art and Furniture
1605 Dragon Street; 214-747-3603;
joel.coonergallery@airmail.net; Hours: Mon–Fri 10–5
Closed August; www.joelcooner.com; Credit Cards: MC, Visa, AmEx;
Owner is Joel Cooner

Price: Personnel:

Ambiance: Quality:

I felt a little like walking into a museum here. Joel Cooner, in business for 25 years, is nationally recognized as a foremost authority in tribal, pre-Columbian, African and Japanese art and furniture, with clients scattered all over the globe. His inventory is museum quality. Even if this is out of your budget or differs from your décor, I recommend coming here and taking a look around. The inventory is very interesting, and there is a great deal that can be learned. Discounts depend on the particular piece. The Web site has pictures of most of the inventory but no prices.

THE MEWS

Antiques Mall

1333 Oak Lawn Avenue; 214-748-8353;

Hours: Mon–Fri 9–5, Sat 10–4; Credit Cards: MC, Visa, AmEx;

Owner is Doris Hart

Price: / Personnel:

Ambiance: / Quality:

This is a great antiques mall that is located in two different buildings back to back. The inventory is extensive and there is a wide variety of antique furniture. I could have easily spent hours and a lot of money here. Designers receive a 20% discount.

EAST & ORIENT COMPANY

European Antiques

1123 Slocum Street; 214-741-1191;

bettygertz@eastandorient.com; Hours: Mon–Fri 9:30–5;

www.eastandorient.com; Credit Cards: N/A;

Owner: Elizabeth (Betty) B. Gertz

Price: / Personnel:

Ambiance: / Quality:

In a building with a green-and-white-striped awning covered with vines and a most spectacular courtyard, East & Orient is a wonderful shopping experience. The shop is owned by a woman who has been in this business for more than 20 years, and 9 years at this location. Mrs. Gertz has traveled all around the world finding the most wonderful classical European antique furniture. She has true Southern charm, and not only did I get a personal tour of this magical shop, but I was also given what the shop has become known for—the most delicious homemade iced tea and Swedish cookies. Sotheby's often uses her back room to entertain clients and give lectures. Come here for the experience! Discounts depend on the individual piece. There are some pictures of the inventory but no prices.

DALLAS DESIGN CENTER
Design Center with many showrooms; sells to the trade only
1025 North Stemmons Freeway; 214-747-2411; Hours: 10–5 Mon–Fri

The Dallas Design Center on Slocum is a trade-only outdoor shopping center. Some of the showrooms located inside this little plaza include J. Robert Scott, Holly Hunt, Dessin Fournir, Stark, and Donghia. Don't even think about trying to shop here without a designer. The layout feels more like an outdoor mall than like a design center. You can browse here but not buy without a designer.

JOSEPH MINTON ANTIQUES
European Antiques and Design Services
1410 Slocum Street; 214-744-3111;
mintonantiques@sbcglobal.net; Hours: Mon–Fri 10–5;
www.mintonantiques.com; Credit Cards: N/A; Owner is Joseph Minton

Price: Personnel: Ambiance: Quality:

Joseph Minton has an unusual selection of European antique furniture. A former lawyer who later went on to win the ASID (American Society of Interior Designers) Designer of the Year award, Joe Minton has decorated some great homes and worked with many celebrities. Much of his business is to the trade, and designers receive a 25% discount. The Web site shows only some of the inventory and no prices. The Web site pictures are a little hard to read. Service is excellent here.

FOUND

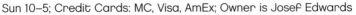

1225 North Industrial Boulevard; 214-741-5533;
debrisantiques@msn.com; Hours: Mon–Sat 10–5
Sun 10–5; Credit Cards: MC, Visa, AmEx; Owner is Josef Edwards

Price:  Personnel:

Ambiance: Quality:

This is yet another antiques mall by the owner of Debris (reviewed above). Located in a blond brick building on busy Industrial Boulevard (really the last block of the Design District), Found carries more 20th-century furniture and accessories than Debris, and has some really fun pieces. Designers receive a 20% discount and some discounts are offered to the public.

COLLAGE: 20TH-CENTURY CLASSICS

Mid-Century Modern Furniture
1300 North Industrial Boulevard; 214-828-9888;
txcollage@aol.com; Hours: Mon–Sat 11–5;
www.collageclassics.com; Credit Cards: MC, Visa, AmEx, Discover;
Owners are Abby and Wlodek Malowanczyk

Price:  Personnel:

Ambiance: Quality:

Many people in Dallas suggested I visit this store, said to have furniture by the most well-known designers of the 1930s to the '70s. That it has, along with some wonderful contemporary lines. Located on Industrial Boulevard in a blond brick building with a modern façade, this is a deceptively large showroom (8,000 square feet). From the street the store looks like a tiny store, but once you are inside, the space feels large. There is also a big warehouse in the back. The store has been here for 15 years. Designer discounts vary, and some discounts are available to the public. The inventory is well selected and the owners have taken great pride in seeking out the best in 20th-century design. They are also now carrying a line of 20th-century reproductions. The Web site shows pictures but no prices. It is not possible to buy online, but I like the ease in which you can browse the selection and the graphics are great.

CEYLON ET CIE

Eclectic Antiques and Contemporary European and Asian Furniture

1319 Dragon Street; 214-742-7632; ceylon@airmail.net;

Hours: Mon–Fri 9:30–4:30; www.ceylonetcie.com;

Credit Cards: MC, Visa; Owner is Michelle Nussbaumer

Price:  Personnel:

Ambiance:  Quality:

I happened upon this shop by chance driving down an industrial street in Dallas. The façade looked intriguing so I stopped in—and was bowled over by the shop's unusual inventory from all over the world, including Switzerland, Italy, China, France, India, and Sweden. Furniture ranges from the 18th century to present. The owner, a well-known designer in Dallas, has just opened her shop in this location after being in the other location (the one I saw) for three years. The gallery loft-like space has 10,000 square feet. I especially liked Michelle's selection of rock crystal sculptures. Much of her business is to the trade. There is a wide range of prices. The Web site includes some pictures but no prices.

Bishop Arts District and Surrounding Area

Bishop Arts District is an artsy up-and-coming neighborhood that is becoming increasingly well-known for its cute little restaurants and shops. There are a variety of vintage stores worth visiting. This neighborhood is filled with young people in their 20s and 30s.

PATINA BLEU

Eclectic Flea Market Finds

835 West 7th Street; 214-941-1131; patinableu@aol.com;

Hours: Thu–Sun 10–6; Credit Cards: MC, Visa;

Owner is Gregory Barker

Price: 🪑 Personnel: 🪑🪑🪑🪑🪑

Ambiance: 🪑🪑🪑🪑🪑 Quality: 🪑🪑🪑🪑

For anyone interested in a store that feels like a great flea market, this is the place for you. Patina Bleu was recommended to me by a well-known dealer in Dallas, and I got a little lost trying to find it. Few people in Dallas know about this little diamond of a shop, but I liked it, especially the warehouse in the back where I found some wonderful light fixtures and cute furniture. Most of the stuff here is vintage and looks like something out of a garage sale, but there is a little bit of everything. Owner Gregory Barker, originally from Baton Rouge, also works at American Airlines in the baggage department. He has a passion for his little shop and personally fixes up everything you see. He is very artistic. Don't be fooled by the façade, which looks like a car repair place. There is a big purple flag outside as a marker. This is in the Oak Cliff neighborhood. Gregory offers a 15% discount to designers and others for all goods over $100. There is no Web site as yet.

B. GOVER LIMITED

Eclectic Vintage Furniture

Bishop Arts District; 410 Bishop; 214-941-4070;

bgoverltd@sbcglobal.net; Hours: Mon–Sat 10–4; Credit Cards: MC, Visa, AmEx, Discover; Owners are Barb Gover and Randy Smith

Price: 🪑🪑🪑🪑🪑🪑 Personnel: 🪑🪑🪑🪑🪑

Ambiance: 🪑🪑🪑🪑🪑 Quality: 🪑🪑🪑

Located in the up-and-coming Bishop Arts District on Bishop and 7th (not far from Patina Bleu), B. Gover Limited sits in the middle of the block next to a cute vintage clothing shop called Zola's Everyday Vintage and some casual restaurants. The merchandise is nicely displayed, and I think designers would like coming here because of all the charming vintage accessories that can be easily mixed with more expensive and modern pieces. This place is large and looks a little like an elegant flea market. Although there is a big range of prices, I feel that many of the items are overpriced. However, designers get discounts of at least 20%, and there are some discounts possible to the public. Many people were shopping here on the day I came, and I got the impression that this is a popular neighborhood spot.

Deep Ellum

Deep Ellum is just a few minutes from downtown Dallas. It is a young, funky, but small neighborhood, mostly made up of post-college graduates. There are art galleries and some hip restaurants here.

CENTURY MODERN
Classic Modern Furnishings
2928 Main Street; 214-651-9200; Hours: Tue–Fri 11–5,
Sat 11–5, Sun 12–5; www.centurymodern.com; Credit Cards: MC,
Visa, AmEx, Discover; Owner is Joe Jones

Price: ░░░░░ Personnel: ░░░░░░

Ambiance: ░░░░░░ Quality: ░░░░░

Century Modern is located in the Deep Ellum area within downtown Dallas, in the middle of Main Street, a hip little block with some appealing restaurants and stores. I really loved this store and recommend it highly for anyone interested in 20th-Century Modern furniture. The store is fun to browse, and the help is friendly and laid-back. There is a big variety of furniture, some expensive and some inexpensive, but in general pricing is very fair here. Century Modern has a wonderful Web site that allows buyers to purchase online. They ship regularly. I liked the bold fabric colors and the way the furniture is displayed. Designers and the public receive a discount of between 10% and 15%. There is another location in New York City on Lexington and 79th.

Highland Park

Highland Park is an upscale, well-established suburb of Dallas. The homes here are beautiful and I recommend spending a little time going for a leisurely drive so you can see the interesting old homes and community.

GERALD TOMLIN ANTIQUES
Mostly English and French Antiques
Highland Park Village; Suite 54; 214-526-3702; gtantique@aol.com;
Hours: Mon–Sat 10–5; www.tomlinantiques.com;
Credit Cards: MC, Visa, Discover; Owner is Gerald Tomlin

Price: Personnel:

Ambiance: Quality:

Located in Highland Park Village, one of the prettiest and oldest shopping centers in Dallas, Gerald Tomlin gets a lot of foot traffic being next to Williams-Sonoma and a great movie theater. Gerald Tomlin is a very elegant shop with some unusual, mostly French and English antiques. Prices are high and in my opinion inflated, but discounts are possible. Designers receive at least 20% and there is some discounting available to the public. The Web site includes pictures, descriptions, and prices but it is not possible to buy online.

DALLAS AUCTION HOUSES

Dallas Auction Gallery
1518 Slocum Street
214-653-3900
866-653-3900 toll-free
info@dallasauctiongallery.com
www.dallasauctiongallery.com

DALLAS ANTIQUES SHOWS

Buchanan's Fair Park Antique Show
June
Food & Fiber Pavilion at Fair Park
1010 First Avenue
www.buchananmarkets.com

Dallas Antique Show
May
Market Hall
888-682-7420

Dallas International Art and Antiques Fair
November
The Dallas International Pavillion
Field Street and Woodall Rogers Freeway

Ralph Willard's Tower Antiques Show
December
3809 Grand Avenue
214-337-7134

DALLAS FLEA MARKETS

The Canton Flea Market
1st Monday of every month
1 hour east of Dallas
Canton

CHAPTER 9

Los Angeles

Up to now you may have thought that Los Angeles, home to Hollywood and our movie industry, is famous mostly for its celebrities, palm trees, great restaurants, and long, romantic, balmy walks on the beach. Think again, because Los Angeles is the "extreme" furniture hot spot! Los Angeles takes its furniture seriously. There is an incredibly talented new breed of furniture designers in LA coming out from the nearby Pasadena School of Design, one of the top product design schools in the world. These young designers have raised the furniture industry in Los Angeles to an art form, creating a selection of furniture as diverse as this city's eclectic population. Unlike anywhere else in the United States, LA nurtures and promotes its native furniture designers, and some of the best stores in the city feature designs by these artists. Many up-and-coming designers here have developed a following in the Los Angeles furniture industry, just like the film business that has its share of rising star "celebrity designers." Commissioning furniture in Los Angeles, a popular alternative to mass-produced designs, has become a big business here, generating big bucks. Many shoppers from all over the U.S. and the world come to Los Angeles not just to shop the stores but also to have their favorite designer whip up some furniture. These pieces are usually out of reach for most of us, running as high as five or six figures for one piece.

My only negative impression of this city is the high percentage of dealers who claim to have furniture designed by famous designers but can't show any documentation that proves the famous designer did, indeed, design the piece. In fact, because of these so-called "designer" pieces, dealers feel perfectly comfortable inflating prices. This is particularly true in places like Beverly Hills and West Hollywood. Could it be that because this is

Hollywood, furniture dealers here feel they, like the movie stars, are entitled to take a little creative license now and then? Apart from the dealers who enjoy embellishing a bit, reviewing LA was an exciting adventure and a joy.

While there are some great furniture pockets outside of Los Angeles, I stuck to LA for my reviews. I think the city is filled with enough great stores to entice and satisfy any interested buyer.

LOS ANGELES RETAIL STORES

La Cienega

La Cienega is a busy boulevard, not particularly pretty, but well known for its high-end furniture stores, most of which specialize in antiques or vintage furniture. I personally found the inventory at many of these stores overpriced, given the high percentage of "designer" pieces. Most of these shops cater to the design trade and depend on designer business, and discount accordingly. I did, however, find some stores noteworthy and worth a look for the non-professional buyer.

After a busy afternoon cruising furniture on La Cienega, stop in for some gourmet Mexican cuisine and a margarita at The Spanish Kitchen at 826 North La Cienega. Or if you're a sushi nut who enjoys Zen retreat–like eateries, try Koi at 730 North La Cienega in West Hollywood. Both restaurants are a stone's throw from some of my furniture shop picks!

PEGASO INTERNATIONAL

Vintage Furniture and Accessories, Mostly Italian
812 North La Cienega Boulevard; 310-659-8159;
pegasoi@sbcglobal.net; Hours: Mon–Fri 10–5;
Credit Cards: MC, Visa, AmEx, Discover;
Owners are Eugenio Manzoni and Brian Pinto

Price: | Personnel:
Ambiance: | Quality:

Pegaso moved here one year ago from Melrose Street. Color this store orange, from the wild frenzy of orange circles covering its outside façade to the lively orange interior walls. The inventory here is just as fresh as the bright orange décor, constantly renewed as the owners of this shop, which began in Milan, Italy, whisk off to Italy on four to five buying trips a year. The owners are knowledgeable about most of their inventory. You'll go crazy over all the unusual 20th-century Italian furniture and lighting. Wait till you see the Murano chandeliers and the selection of light fixtures! There are quite a few pieces by Gio Ponti, an Italian designer of furniture popular in the mid-20th century. Prices are very high here, but designers receive a 20% discount. There appears to be a lot of important designers represented. There is no Web site yet.

BLACKMAN CRUZ

Mostly 20th-Century Furniture and Accessories
800 North La Cienega Boulevard; 310-657-9228;
info@blackmancruz.com; Hours: Mon–Fri 10–6, Sat 12–5;
www.blackmancruz.com; Credit Cards: MC, Visa, AmEx,
Discover; Owners are Adam Blackman and David Cruz

Price: Personnel:

Ambiance: Quality:

    Blackman Cruz, a very well known furniture shop in LA with a brown façade and Tiffany blue windows, is a must-see. Having heard a lot of buzz about the store from locals here, I made this one of my first stops in LA. I can almost guarantee that you have never experienced as unique a collection of merchandise as you will in this shop. You'll find all kinds of cool, offbeat "stuff," including original New York street signs from the 1940s. The furniture comes from all over the world, and many of the pieces are so different and distinctive that I had never seen anything like them before. They had some Asian pieces from the 18th to mid-20th century that were out of sight. The majority of the inventory hails from Europe, and dates from the 1930s and '40s, but there is plenty of inventory from the 19th century. I did flip-flops over all the chairs with their original leathers, which have a very weathered look. Service warning: If you think long waits for service are a headache, bring along some aspirin. As I entered the store, I waited for what seemed an eternity for someone to greet me. In general I found the service, as at many other shops on La Cienega, to be below par (thankfully the wonderful things I saw in this store soothed the beast in me!). Designers receive a 20% discount. Blackman Cruz is pricey but well worth a visit—if for no other reason, just to get ideas.

PAT McGANN COURTYARD GALLERY
Vintage Furniture and Accessories from the 1920s–'60s
748 North La Cienega Boulevard; 310-657-8708;
Hours: Mon–Fri 10–6, Sat 12–5; Credit Cards: MC, Visa, AmEx;
Owner is Pat McGann

Price: Personnel:

Ambiance: Quality:

Stepping into Pat McGann, a small courtyard shop off this busy street, is a bit like walking into Floyd's barber shop on the old TV show "Mayberry RFD" because it has none of the showy glitz like so many of the other shops on La Cienega. I like the unusual, though small, collection of American, European, Asian, and Indian furniture and accessories. There are some beautiful textiles here and some lovely vintage garden furniture worth investigating. The shop also offers an interesting selection of art. Designers receive a 20% discount. Again, the atmosphere is relaxed here, and there is no hype.

LUCCA ANTIQUES
French Provincial, Spanish, and Italian Antiques
744 North La Cienega Boulevard; 310-657-7800;
Hours: Mon–Fri 10–5; www.luccaantiques.com; Credit Cards: MC, Visa, AmEx; Owners are Susan and Stephen Keeney

Price: Personnel:

Ambiance: Quality:

Lucca Antiques relocated here recently from Santa Monica, and from the looks of it, I think they will do well here. Even though much of the furniture is French Provincial, the majority has a distinctive twist from the usual farm tables that French Provincial brings to mind. I particularly like the grand antique beds and club chairs, most of which have their original leathers and were imported directly from France. The owner, a delightful and engaging man, seems dedicated to great service, and spent time explaining to me the story behind his very whimsical business cards. Prices are elevated. Designers receive a 20% discount. Though the Web site shows some pictures of inventory, not much inventory is on the Web site .

DOWNTOWN

Vintage Modern Furniture
719 North La Cienega Boulevard; 310-652-7461; Hours: Mon–Fri 10–6, Sat 12–5; www.1stdibs.com (a communal Web site); Credit Cards: MC, Visa, AmEx, Discover; Owners are David Serrano and Robert Wilson

Price: Personnel: Ambiance: Quality:

For those of you who love filling your home with something a little different, this is a great shop to hit. In business for eight years, Downtown is a colorful store with a wide range of inventory spanning from 1930 to 1970, including some amusing, wild, and over-the-top pieces. I had a hard time getting anyone to help me here, maybe because the store was busy or possibly even because the owners did not want to make contact with me. Hopefully you'll fare better than I did. Designers receive a 15% discount. Downtown posts its inventory on 1stdibs.com, a communal Web site that other dealers in LA and from around the country often use. It is a great Web site for people shopping for furniture because it allows you to compare inventory and prices in a multitude of shops without having to surf the Web. The people at 1stdibs run it very much like an auction business, negotiating your transaction with a dealer for you.

LEE STANTON

18th–20th-Century Continental Antiques

796 La Cienega Boulevard; 310-855-9800;

Hours: Mon–Fri 10–5; www.leestantonantiques.com;

Credit Cards: MC, Visa, AmEx, Discover; Owner is Lee Stanton

Price: Personnel:

Ambiance: Quality:

Lee Stanton was high on my list to visit. Though I arrived just after the store closed, I knocked on the door (the store was completely dark) and Lee Stanton let me in anyway. He is a tall and attractive man with the right personality for the antiques business. Extremely friendly and relaxed, he does a fine job of explaining his inventory. Every piece in his shop has a story and an unusual element that Lee goes out of his way to share with you. His look is straighter-lined wooden European furniture. The Stanton name is well regarded in the business. Many of his clients have followed him from his San Juan Capistrano shop, which he had for 12 years. Additionally, many of his clients come from New York. Lee's space is well laid–out, and he has a real flair for style. Prices are high here, but designers get a 20% discount. His Web site has pictures and descriptions but no prices.

MECOX GARDENS

Antiques and Contemporary Furniture and Accessories

919 North La Cienega Boulevard; 310-358-9272;

info@mecoxgardens.com; Hours: Mon–Sat 10–6;

www.mecoxgardens.com; Credit Cards: MC, Visa, AmEx, Discover;

Owner is Mac Hoak

Price: Personnel:

Ambiance: Quality:

Mecox Gardens has three locations on the East Coast (one in New York City and two in the Hamptons) and one in Palm Beach, Florida. The owner recently opened this LA shop. All of the stores have similar inventory, with a mix of antiques and contemporary furnishings. This is a large store with everything for your home, from housewares to furniture to accessories. I fell in love with some fun rattan dining chairs. There is also a lot of upholstered leather furniture. I like both the mix of new and old here as well as the variety of merchandise. This is also a good place to find vintage garden furniture and accessories. Mecox Gardens has developed a reputation for selling anything you could want to decorate your house. The accessories are emphasized as much as the furniture. Designers receive a 15% discount. The Web site, in my opinion, has more interesting inventory than the store. Worth a visit.

West Hollywood

Right next to Beverly Hills, West Hollywood has some fabulous, very expensive (and a few not as expensive) furniture shops that tend to attract decorators and their wealthy clients. In fact, many of these shops sell only to the trade. There are several blocks of furniture stores and many different options in this part of town. Well-known shopping streets here include Melrose Place, Beverly Boulevard, Robertson, and La Brea. Most of the merchandise here is overpriced because designers receive a discount off of the list price. National showrooms like Nancy Corzine, Kreiss, Armani Casa, Roche-Bobois, and Grange have spaces in this location.

OFF THE WALL ANTIQUES
Vintage Furniture, Collectibles, and Weird Stuff
7325 Melrose Avenue; 323-930-1185; weirdstuff@earthlink.net;
Hours: Mon–Sat 11–6; www.offthewallantiques.com;
Credit Cards: MC, Visa, AmEx; Owners are Lisa and Dennis Boses

Price: (5 chairs) Personnel: (5 chairs)
Ambiance: (4 chairs) Quality: (3 chairs)

Off the Wall Antiques is a 1950s diner-like shop that has a bunch of odd collectibles mixed with vintage classics. The business is well known in LA and has been here for 25 years. You can't miss it—look for a neon sign with an arrow outside. Many of the pieces here look like flea market finds. You'll probably enjoy this place if you're the type that likes to go cherry-picking through stuff in resale shops. Service is good, but prices are high. Designers receive a discount of approximately 20%.

PAUL FERRANTE INC.

European Antiques and Lighting
8464 Melrose Place; 323-653-4142; Hours: Mon–Fri 8–5;
Credit Cards: N/A; Owner is Paul Ferrante

Price: ▮▮▮▮▮ Personnel: ▮▮▮

Ambiance: ▮▮▮▮▮ Quality: ▮▮▮▮▮

In a pretty vine-colored building, Paul Ferrante is a large store with a great selection of vintage lighting fixtures. Ferrante has some really wonderful furniture pieces, many of which are French Provincial, but there is also a good selection of European and Oriental furniture. The shop now sells a line of reproduction pieces that they design. Most of the furniture here is made from dark woods. I found prices to be high relative to other dealers around the country. I think the service could be more inviting. Designers receive a one-third discount here.

LICORNE ANTIQUES

Spanish, Italian, and Portuguese Antiques
8432 Melrose Place; 323-852-4765;
licorne@licorneantiques.com; Hours: Mon–Fri 9–5;
www.licorneantiques.com; Credit Cards: AmEx;
Owners are Monique and Patrick de Warren

Price: ▮▮▮▮▮ Personnel: ▮▮▮▮▮

Ambiance: ▮▮▮▮▮ Quality: ▮▮▮▮▮

Licorne Antiques, a 20-year-old business, is a charming store with a fairly relaxed atmosphere, considering the very expensive antiques. Many of the pieces date back to the 16th century! The owners travel to Europe (they are French) every other month for their inventory. The store's walls are painted a vivid red, which shows off the Spanish, Italian, and Portuguese antiques well. Prices are high, but designers receive a one-third discount. Only a few pieces of the inventory appear online, and there are no prices.

LA MAISON FRANÇAISE ANTIQUES, INC.

Continental Antiques and Garden Furniture
8420 Melrose Place; 8435 Melrose Avenue;
323-653-6540 or 323-653-6534; info@lmfantiques.com;
Hours: Mon–Fri 9–5; www.lmfantiques.com; Credit Cards: Visa,
MC, AmEx; Owner is Pierre-Yves Bolduc

Price: Personnel: Ambiance: Quality:

La Maison Française reminds me of a scene in a novel. The shop resembles a castle (most castles don't have furniture this good), and the prices reflect that. The inventory is museum quality, and most of the pieces here are highly unusual. Brace yourself, though—most pieces cost over $75,000. The business has been around since 1972 and began as a French country shop, but the owner became more and more interested in exquisite pieces, so his inventory changed—and with it the ambiance, more like a museum than a store. There are two buildings, one behind the other, with an exquisite selection of antique garden furniture as well. I believe this is one of the best stores in the entire country. Service is exceptional. I found the Web site difficult to use. Most of us could never afford to furnish our house from La Maison Française, but we can all appreciate and learn from our viewing experiences here.

HAMBY

Custom-Designed Wood Furniture
8465 Melrose Avenue; 323-655-7003; hambyjcm@aol.com;
Hours: Mon–Fri 10–6; www.hamby-collection.com;
Owner is Julio C. Martinez

Price: ▮▮▮▮▮ Personnel: ▮▮▮▮

Ambiance: ▮▮▮▮▮ Quality: ▮▮▮▮▮

Although the selection is limited, I really like the offerings at Hamby. The look is chic painted- or stained-wood country and contemporary furniture, and the buyer is able to select the size and finish of his choice. Julio Martinez designs all kinds of furniture (his couches and chairs are also great) and is also an interior designer; many of his designs have been featured in design magazines, and he has a host of celebrity clients. Most pieces cost more than $2,000, a bit steep, but the look is simple and sophisticated. The Web site shows their inventory, but there is no pricing information. I love the designs and think Hamby is worth a visit.

CHARLES FRADIN

Reproduction Furniture
8471 Melrose Avenue; 323-951-1200; Hours: Mon–Fri 9–5;
www.charlesfradin.com; Credit Cards: N/A;
Owner is Charles Fradin

Price: ▮▮▮▮▮ Personnel: ▮▮▮▮

Ambiance: ▮▮▮▮ Quality: ▮▮▮▮▮

Because the atmosphere here seemed stuffy to me, I realized that this must be a "trade only" store and, sure enough, I was right. Knowing that, it is still worth it to make a stop to see the beautiful classic pieces and updated looks achieved in Charles Fradin's line of furniture. This is a sophisticated, large showroom with updated English and French designs. The furniture is simple and elegant. The Web site is being created.

J.F. CHEN

Continental Antiques and
and Accessories and Modern Furniture
8414 Melrose Avenue; Warehouse: 941 North Highland Avenue #200;
323-655-6310; jchen72105@aol.com; Hours: Mon–Fri 9:30–5, Sat
(warehouse) 12–5; Credit Cards: MC, Visa, AmEx, Discover;
Owner is Joel Chen

Price: Personnel:

Ambiance: Quality:

Joel Chen has had this business for 30 years. Nationally recognized as one of the best furniture dealers in the country (and I agree), this is a hot spot for dealers themselves. The olive green façade is hard to notice, but I encourage you to peek inside. The look here is eclectic and sophisticated, with furniture (mostly antiques) coming from around the world. The only negative is that you need a designer to shop. Ironically, I couldn't get anyone to help me until I recognized a dealer whose store I reviewed in another city. Within seconds, I had an excellent salesperson assisting me. Unfortunately there is no Web site yet. Designers get a one-third discount. There is also a large inventory in their warehouse. This is a must-see, but you will need to be accompanied by a designer.

JONATHAN ADLER

Contemporary Furniture and Accessories
8125 Melrose Avenue; 323-658-8390;
orders@jonathanadler.com; Hours: Mon–Sat 10–6, Sun 12–6;
www.jonathanadler.com; Credit Cards: MC, Visa, AmEx, Discover;
Owner is Jonathan Adler

Price: Personnel:

Ambiance: Quality:

I don't know why I feel this way, but Jonathan Adler's store reminds me of a Kate Spade store. Kate Spade doesn't sell furniture, but the look of her shoes, handbags and stationery is bold colors and youthful styles that are extremely popular with women of all age groups. Luscious combinations of colors personify the merchandise here, too. All of the furniture is designed in-house, and there are elements of old and new styles with a mix of materials used, like plastic, leather, and painted woods. I especially like the fun couches, jewelry, and animal-shaped lamps. The store is busy, with many youthful shoppers browsing around. I have also visited their Soho location in New York City, and that store, too, is full of energy and chic shoppers. Prices are reasonable compared with their counterparts in the neighborhood. The Web site shows pictures and prices and makes it easy to buy within in a 24-hour period. Designers receive a 10% discount after spending $500.

RICHARD SHAPIRO

Continental Antiques and Art
8905 Melrose Avenue; 310-275-6700;
richard@rshapiroantiques.com; Hours: Mon–Fri 9–5;
www.rshapiroantiques.com; Owner is Richard Shapiro

Price: Personnel:

Ambiance: Quality:

Richard Shapiro is clearly one of the finest showrooms in the country for one-of-a-kind early antiques from all over Europe, especially from Italy, but I thought the atmosphere was a bit cold. I was never able to get the help of a salesperson. I should tell you up   front that this store, housed in a beautifully landscaped stone building, deals in museum-quality pieces of furniture and works of art, with most of the inventory costing in the tens of thousands. The furniture dates from as early as the 14th century. Richard Shapiro also sells a spectacular line of reproduction and contemporary furniture. The Web site shows pictures of the inventory and has a nice video show. Designers receive a 20% discount.

INDIGO SEAS

Eclectic Furniture and Home Accessories
123 North Robertson Boulevard; 310-550-8758;
Hours: Mon–Fri 10–5:30, Sat 10–4; Credit Cards: MC, Visa;
Owner is Lynn Vonkersting

Price: ▮▮▮▮▮▮ Personnel: ▮▮▮

Ambiance: ▮▮▮▮ Quality: ▮▮▮▮

Indigo Seas is next door to The Ivy, a famous Hollywood see-and-be-seen restaurant. The store's theme is the Caribbean, with a wild décor and azure blue tiles; loud jazz is piped outside. The inventory is colorful with a lot of funky painted furniture and fanciful fabrics. Home accessories here include fabrics, linens, and Chinese lanterns. While this is a fun store, I left feeling a little dizzy because of all the colors and patterns. Designers do not receive a special discount here.

NATHAN TURNER

Continental Antiques and Interiors
636 Almont Drive; 310-275-1209; nathan@nathanturner.com;
Hours: Mon–Fri 10–5; www.nathanturner.com; Credit Cards: MC, Visa, AmEx; Owner is Nathan Turner

Price: ▮▮▮▮▮ Personnel: ▮▮▮▮▮

Ambiance: ▮▮▮▮▮ Quality: ▮▮▮▮▮

A friend of mine recommended stopping here en route to other stores in the neighborhood. What a find! Although the building is very small, the selection is most unusual and the service is friendly. The look is rustic, with pieces from all over the world, many of them dating back to the 17th century (these look like they came from a medieval castle). Ironically, there is also a clothing company in the back of the space. Nathan Turner also sells a nice selection of attractive 18th-century Swedish furniture. The Web site doesn't have many pieces and doesn't include prices. Designer discounts are 20%. Worth a trip if price isn't an object.

LIEF

Continental Antiques

646 North Almont Drive; 310-492-0033;

lief1@earthlink.net; Hours: Mon–Fri 11–5; Credit Cards: MC, Visa,

AmEx; Owner is Stefan Michaelsen

Price: Personnel:

Ambiance: Quality:

Lief is a huge, loft-like showroom with the most beautiful period antiques from all over the world. The owner is Swedish, and there is a bend toward antique (18th-century Gustavian) Swedish furniture. Although most of the business here is to the trade, I found the store easy to shop. The only negative is that price tags are off the furniture, but I was told that is because there is so much inventory here it would take forever to tag everything. That is probably true. I particularly like the painted pieces and the Biedermeier, Swedish, Asian, and vintage garden furniture. Designers receive a 20% discount.

STUDIO HEXAGON

Art Deco Furniture and Reproductions

8763 Rosewood Avenue; 310-859-7100;

studiohexagon@earthlink.net; Hours: Mon–Fri 11–6;

www.studiohexagon.com; Credit Cards: MC, Visa and AmEx;

Owner is Denis de la Mesiere

Price: Personnel:

Ambiance: Quality:

Studio Hexagon is sandwiched between other furniture stores in the heart of this furniture-shopping mecca. The store has a subdued look, but its individual pieces are quite special. The store has been here for five years and has been able to attract celebrities, including Brad Pitt and Jennifer Aniston, along with Art Deco aficionados. Denis owns another store in Venice (California) called Bazar. Designer discounts vary.

Reproductions are expensive here, but are good quality. The Web site displays pictures and descriptions but no prices.

BLUEPRINT

General Furniture Store

8366 Beverly Boulevard; 323-653-2439; blueprint1@earthlink.net; Hours: Mon–Fri 10–7, Sat 10–6, Sun 12–5; www.blueprintfurniture.com; Credit Cards: MC and Visa; Owner is a corporation

Price: Personnel: Ambiance: Quality:

Blueprint is a good all-purpose contemporary furniture shop for everyone, from young people starting out to older people looking to fill in. The inventory looks a little like what you might find at IKEA, but the furniture is a little sturdier here, with a range of prices. There is a big selection of chairs, tables, entertainment units, and bar carts. If shopping for furniture is an intimidating experience for you, this is a good place to shop because the store is not quiet or filled with salespeople who stand over you. The Web site shows some pictures and dimensions but gives no prices.

ORANGE

Mid-Century Modern Classics

8111 Beverly Boulevard; 323-782-6898; orangefurniture@aol.com; Hours: Mon–Sat 11–6, Sun 12–5; www.orangefurniture.com; Credit Cards: MC, Visa, AmEx, Discover; Owner is Angela Zupan

Price: Personnel: Ambiance: Quality:

Orange is a Vintage Modern store in the center of West Hollywood that is frequented by collectors of this style of furniture. The building is large and old, and the interior space is modest, not flashy. There are orange lamps in the window. The furniture reminds me of shopping at a flea market, or a notch better. The Web site does not show the entire inventory but does mention the fact that custom furniture can be ordered. Designers receive a 10% discount.

EMMERSON TROOP, INC.

Mid-Century Modern Classics and Contemporary
8111 Beverly Boulevard; 323-653-9763;
shannon@emmersontroop.com; Hours: Mon–Sat 11–6;
www.emmersontroop.com; Credit Cards: MC, Visa, AmEx;
Owners are William Emmerson and Shannon McMackin

Price: 🪑🪑🪑🪑🪑   Personnel: 🪑🪑🪑🪑🪑

Ambiance: 🪑🪑🪑🪑🪑   Quality: 🪑🪑🪑🪑🪑

Emmerson Troop is a great store to see if you are interested in unusual Mid-Century Modern classics. Most of the inventory is interesting, and several of the pieces were designed by famous Mid-Century designers. The store is simple and elegant in its presentation. The owners, William Emmerson and Shannon McMackin, design and manufacture their own line of furniture that resembles designs from the 1930s to 1970s. Much of the inventory comes from Europe. Designers receive a 15% discount. The Web site shows pictures of inventory and gives brief descriptions but not prices.

TWENTIETH

Contemporary and Mid-Century Vintage Classics
8057 Beverly Boulevard; 323-904-1200;
info@twentieth.net; Hours: Mon–Fri 10–6, Sat 12–5;
www.twentieth.net; Credit Cards: MC, Visa, AmEx;
Owner is Stefan Lawrence

Price: 🪑🪑🪑🪑🪑   Personnel: 🪑🪑🪑🪑🪑

Ambiance: 🪑🪑🪑🪑🪑   Quality: 🪑🪑🪑🪑🪑

If you want to see really unusual contemporary furniture mixed with wonderful vintage classics, Twentieth is the place to visit. One of the best contemporary showrooms in the country, Twentieth has a 10,000-square-foot showroom with an art-museum feel. Stefan Lawrence, a designer himself, supports emerging local furniture designers whose pieces are impressive and functional. I fell in love with a chaise made from foam. This is not a spot for budget-conscious shoppers; most pieces cost more than $1,000. Celebrities like Jennifer Aniston, Brad Pitt, and Ellen DeGeneres like to shop here for the newest and latest designs. Designers receive a 15% discount. The Web site is excellent, including pictures of inventory, names of designers, and descriptions. You can even buy online. Well worth a trip.

EMPIRIC

Contemporary and Vintage Furniture and Lighting
7918 Beverly Boulevard; 323-634-7323;
mtowey@sbcglobal.net; Hours: Mon–Sat 11–6, Sun 12–5;
www.empiricstudio.com; Credit Cards: MC, Visa, AmEx, Discover;
Owner is Michael Towey

Price: Personnel:

Ambiance: Quality:

Empiric is a small store with a lot of flair. Michael Towey, a Seattle native, opened the store seven years ago, and it has become a serious furniture hot spot in LA. There is a chic and eclectic mixture of vintage and contemporary. Most of the furniture is 1940s American. The owner describes his store as carrying "furnishings for the home or lab," and he is right—much of the furniture looks like lab furniture, and there are many metal chests. I especially like the big assortment of vintage lighting. Designers receive a 10% discount if paying by cash or check, and 7% discount if paying with credit cards. Celebrities like Diane Keaton and Kevin Spacey have shopped here. The Web site shows some of the inventory and gives descriptions but no prices. Well worth a trip.

LA BREA ANTIQUE COLLECTION

Mid-Century Modern Antiques Mall
334 North La Brea Avenue; 323-938-9444;

Hours: Mon–Sat 10:30–6, Sun 12–6; Credit Cards: MC, Visa, AmEx;
Owner is Steve Milner

Price:  Personnel:

Ambiance: Quality:

Just look for the sign "Vintage Fun," and you will be at La Brea Antique Collection. I found this place a refreshing change after reviewing some of the overpriced, snooty, Mid-Century Modern stores in the neighborhood. This mall is unique in that they sell only one kind of furniture—Mid-Century Modern—with a good selection and very reasonable prices. They have a nice array of chairs from the 1950s and '60s covered in vivid-colored washable fabrics. I also like the vintage lighting. The shop has been here for six years, but people are still getting to know about this mall. Some dealers consign furniture here. Designers get a 10% discount.

BOURGEOIS BOHÈME

French Antique, Vintage, and Contemporary Furniture
332 North La Brea Avenue; 323-936-7507;
info@bobo-antiques.com; Hours: Tue–Fri 10–5, Sat 12–5;
www.bourgeoisboheme.com; Credit Cards: MC, Visa, AmEx,
Discover; Owners are Frederic Lazare, Tim Norr, and Dale Skorcz

Price:  Personnel:

Ambiance: Quality:

Bourgeois Bohème has been here for about two years. It's a charming little shop with a nice mix of vintage, antique, and contemporary pieces, also some architectural and garden pieces. The inventory is all European antique furniture and accessories, including some unusual pieces. The store has a quiet elegance with a stylish look that I predict will make it a success in LA. Designers get a 15% discount. The Web site offers pictures but needs to describe and date its pieces. Prices are not listed. Worth a visit.

ECCOLA

Italian and French Vintage and Contemporary Furniture
330 North La Brea Avenue; 323-932-9922 or 310-567-1201;
eccolainc@aol.com; Hours: Tue–Fri 10–5, Sat 12–5;
www.eccolaimports.com; Credit Cards: MC, Visa, AmEx;
Owners are Kathleen R. White and Maurizio Almanza

Price: Personnel:

Ambiance: Quality:

Eccola recently opened. This husband-and-wife team have exceptional inventory. I love everything here. Maurizio Almanza is Italian and
regularly goes to Italy and France to get the inventory for this small but
exquisite space. Not to be missed is their fabulous selection of unusual
lighting fixtures from the Deco period. They also design some contemporary furniture that is as good as the Deco stuff. Designers get a 20%
discount. The Web site is not yet up and running.

MODERN ONE

20th-Century Furniture and Accessories
7956 Beverly Boulevard; 323-651-5082;
scott@modern1.com; Hours: Mon–Fri 12–6; www.modern1.com;
Credit Cards: MC, Visa, AmEx; Owner is Benjamin Storck

Price: Personnel:

Ambiance: Quality:

Benjamin Storck is well known for his taste and knowledge about
20th-century European designers. Celebrities like Kirsten Dunst, Tom
Ford, and Cameron Diaz come into the shop frequently to find the latest treasures. He has another shop in San Francisco, called Benjamin
Storck, which is a little more highbrow than Modern One. What I like
about this store is that everything is unique and there is a fairly wide price
range. The atmosphere is casual and welcoming. You will be wowed by
your shopping experience here. Designer discounts are approximately

20%, but they can vary. The Web site has a nice selection and offers pictures, descriptions, and prices. Worth a trip

Downtown LA

Besides being the location for big office buildings and a traditional business district, downtown Los Angeles houses one furniture gallery with an interesting concept—commissioned furniture from some of LA's hottest new furniture designers.

ORANGE 22

Contemporary, Unique Furniture Gallery
and Designer of Spaces
125 West 4th Street, Suite 102; 213-972-9922;
dantonioni@orange22.com; Hours: Mon–Fri 10–7;
www.orange22.com; Credit Cards: MC, Visa, AmEx;
Owner is Dario Antonioni

Price: ▯▯▯▯▯ Personnel: ▯▯▯▯▯
Ambiance: ▯▯▯▯▯ Quality: ▯▯▯▯▯

Dario Antonioni has recently opened Orange 22 in the downtown area. You may think this is a weird place for a furniture "gallery," and I do mean gallery. (This is not the only gallery in the neighborhood; just diagonally from Orange 22, on Main Street, is a well-regarded art gallery called Bank.) Orange 22 looks like a museum—very modern and sparse. This is a place to come if you want to commission a piece of furniture by one of LA's up-and-coming furniture designers. There are innovative designs here, and you can get a lot of ideas by looking at the offerings. Prices vary among the different designers.

PACIFIC DESIGN CENTER

Design Center with many showrooms; sells to the trade only
8687 Melrose Avenue; 310-657-0800; Hours: Mon–Fri 9–5;
www.pacificdesigncenter.com

Pacific Design Center is located in West Hollywood in a modern-looking complex of two buildings, one blue and one green. The size is overwhelming, but the layout is very logical. The buildings are open to the public, but only designers can buy here (with the exception of the kitchen and bath showrooms where the public may buy directly). Showrooms in the PDC offer "list" prices and the designers get a discount off that list price. In this building complex are the well-known national showrooms like Baker, Donghia, Bernhardt, and all of the large fabric companies. Noteworthy showrooms that are based in Los Angeles are Charles Jacobsen and Tenango for Asian antiques, and Micucci, a smaller showroom that sells beautiful glass objects imported from Italy.

Other Places to Shop in LA

Los Angeles has many suburbs and neighborhoods very close to the downtown area which have an eclectic feel. Venice (Abbot Kinney) is a good place to shop for rustic furniture and Mid-Century Modern. Some favorites in Venice include Neptina, Bountiful, Digs, and Michele Sommerlath. While browsing in the Venice neighborhood, don't miss Massimo's Gelato and café. The Italian cookies and gelato are terrific; so are the salads.

Silver Lake (Silver Lake Boulevard) has become a popular shopping spot for young people. My personal favorites are Rubbish and Yolk. Yolk has beautiful housewares.

LOS ANGELES AUCTION HOUSES

Bonham's and Butterfield's
7601 Sunset Boulevard
323-950-7500

Los Angeles Modern Auctions
666 South Brea Avenue
323-845-9456

Orill's Auction Studio
1910 West Adams
323-734-3123

LOS ANGELES ANTIQUES SHOWS

Los Angeles Antiques Show
April
The Barker Hangar
Santa Monica Air Center
Santa Monica
310-455-2886

Los Angeles Modernism Show
May
Santa Monica Civic Auditorium
1855 Main Street
Santa Monica
818-244-1126

LOS ANGELES FLEA MARKETS

Melrose Trading Post
Every Sunday
Fairfax High School
7850 Melrose Avenue
323-651-5200

CHAPTER 10

Miami

I am always fascinated by everything and everybody in this electrifying international city. Although the South American culture is a dominant influence in Miami, many other nationalities from every corner of the world come together to make the Miami scene as hot as its sizzling tropical sun. South American, German, French, and Caribbean restaurants all fill up the same square block; young skateboarders whiz past the porch of a retirement home as retirees bask in the sun on their lounge chairs; a myriad of accents and languages float through the air above a quaint outdoor café. You can see the flavor and creative style of Miami everywhere, including in its art and its furniture, and especially its passion for Art Deco.

There is so much in the way of furniture shopping here that it was difficult for me to choose which areas I should review. There are many great places within two hours of Miami that I could have reviewed, but that would have assumed that when people come to the Miami area they have a car and don't mind spending a whole day shopping for furniture (although if you are willing to give up an entire day on the beach in favor of antiquing in Palm Beach, you won't be disappointed—not with all the hidden treasures floating into the shops from those palatial Palm Beach mansions!). However, assuming that your day in the sun takes precedence over antiques, I have reviewed three principal furniture spots in the Miami area: Coral Gables, Dania Beach (Design Center of the Americas), and the Miami International Arts and Design District. I assure you, furniture shopping in this jewel by the sea is anything but ordinary. So buckle up your seat belt and get ready to experience Miami's furniture scene! The neighborhoods I have reviewed in Miami require you to have a car and are on the outskirts of town so be prepared.

MIAMI RETAIL STORES

Coral Gables

They don't call Coral Gables the "City Beautiful" for nothing. Picture shopping for furniture in a place with the finest restaurants, exquisite parks, an exotic spring-fed lagoon fashioned into an Italian grotto, and well-preserved Mediterranean—style homes built during the 1920s, and you'll have a pretty good idea of what it's like to furniture-shop in Coral Gables. Only 20 minutes south of downtown Miami by car, Coral Gables is a mellow and breathtaking place where terrific furniture awaits you. Many of the great furniture spots I hit are located in the Village of Merrick Park shopping center along Ponce de Leon Boulevard, just off Highway 1. Still other shops are farther up on Ponce de Leon, and some of the well-known chain stores are on the Miracle Mile Boulevard. As you shop, don't forget to take a little respite, as I did, at any of the following Coral Gable favorites: world-renowned chef Norman Van Aken's Mundo, 4251 Salzedo Street; and Chispa, 225 Altera Avenue.

VALERIO ANTIQUES

Art Deco Furniture and Accessories
250 Valencia Avenue; 305-448-6779;
Hours: Mon–Sat 10–5; www.valerioartdeco.com;
Credit Cards: MC, Visa, AmEx (adds a surcharge to use);
Owners: Antonio Amado and F. Roberto Bertran

Price: Personnel: Ambiance: Quality:

Furniture hot spot "red hot alert": This is one of the hottest Art Deco stores I have ever seen! On a small side street just off Ponce de Leon, in a small steel building, Valerio Antiques is a Deco lover's dream. The showroom is large, packed with exquisite Deco furniture, lighting, and decorative arts. I found the help to be not only fashionable but also friendly. Many hard-to-come-by pieces in the store were actually signed by their famous

Deco designers. Unfortunately, price tags are not on the pieces themselves. Most shoppers will receive a discount of 15–20% whether or not they are designers. Interestingly enough, much of the inventory comes from the U.S. and not from France. Don't expect to get a good deal here; the stuff is star quality and they know it. Their Web site shows the wonderful inventory but does not give prices.

ARTEFACTO

Contemporary Brazilian-Made Furniture
Village of Merrick Park Shopping Center; 4440 Ponce de Leon
Boulevard, Suite 1600; 305-774-0004; Hours: Mon–Sat 10–9,
Sun 12–6; www.artefactousa.com; Credit Cards: MC, Visa;
Owner is Paulo Bacchi

Price: Personnel:
Ambiance: Quality:

Artefacto has been written up in many magazines, and for good reason: This is a store with a passionate sense of style that has something exciting for everyone. Floridians really enjoy shopping here, this being one of two Artefacto stores in the U.S. (there are fifteen in Brazil). All of the furniture is made in Brazil using native woods (like imbuia, pommele, and ironwood) and leathers. Most of the furniture is rectilinear. I found Artefacto interesting, affordable, and simple in its concept. The furniture here is also practical and easy to care for. The outdoor furniture, made from plastic but a dead ringer for wicker, was absolutely dreamy—not just in looks, but also weather-proof and easy to clean. Fabrics are stocked here, though the fabric selection is not as impressive as the furniture. Designers get a 10% discount. Artefacto has a great-looking Web site which plays "The Girl from Ipanema." It posts inventory, but you cannot buy online.

MÖBLER

Mid-Century Modern Furniture
Village of Merrick Park Shopping Center;
358 Avenue San Lorenzo, Suite 3110; 305-445-4898,

cell 305-206-0323; mail@mobler.us; Hours: Mon–Sat 10–9, Sun 12–6;
www.mobler.us; Credit Cards: MC, Visa, AmEx, Diners Club;
Owner is Swen Schele

Price: Personnel:

Ambiance: Quality:

I almost confused Möbler with one of those Danish Modern stores we see in all the malls. The owner, Swen Schele, would be insulted to hear that, because he takes so much pride in his fabulous Swedish-designed furniture showroom. This is the place to go to find beautiful, comfortable kitchen and dining chairs. The materials used are cutting edge, like the red rubber dining chairs I loved trying. Aside from chairs, Möbler sells well-constructed contemporary sofas, dining tables, and even computer work stations. The look is interesting and well designed by prominent Swedish designers (whose large pictures are displayed on the walls), and the furniture is solid. Also be on the lookout for the exquisite vases and sculptures. Prices are extremely high, but there are sales periodically. Designers get 10% off. Parking is free with a validation. The Web site is not meant for shopping.

CLIMA

Outdoor Furniture
Village of Merrick Park Shopping Center;
358 San Lorenzo Avenue, Suite 3125; 305-446-1831,
cell 305-298-4988; john@climaoutdoor.com; Hours: Mon–Sat 10–9, Sun
12–6; www.climaoutdoor.com; Credit Cards: MC, Visa;
Owner is John DelGreco

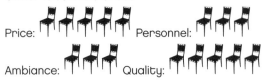

Price: Personnel:

Ambiance: Quality:

If you love entertaining outdoors, and who in Florida doesn't, you've got to visit this place. The outdoor furniture here is modern and functional but stylish enough that it looks like it could go inside the house. I had a little trouble getting service initially, but eventually the salespeople offered assistance. This shop has a collection of furniture from designers like Richard Schultz and Gandiablasco from Spain. Discounts depend on the item. The Web site has pictures of their different lines of furniture. You cannot make purchases online.

ROSARIO SALAZAR AT THE VILLAGE

Contemporary Ethnic Furniture
Village of Merrick Park; 358 Avenue San Lorenzo, Suite 3215;
305-446-6559; sales@rosariosalazar.com; Hours: Mon–Sat 10–9, Sun
12–6; www.rosariosalazar.com; Credit Cards: MC, Visa, AmEx; Owner
is Rosario Salazar

Price: Personnel: Ambiance: Quality:

I found this shop to be very busy with not a lot of help when I came to visit. Rosario Salazar, who has an interior design background, designs most of the furniture in her showroom. Salazar calls her furniture "contemporary ethnic," but much of the furniture is just of her own design and doesn't follow any traditional styles. Quality is just fair for the high prices. There is a lot of wood (much of which is very polished), woven leathers, and linen fabrics. Designers receive a 10–20% discount. The Web site shows inventory, but you cannot buy online. I found the Web site difficult to use.

HOME DESIGN STORE: FURNITURE FROM FARAWAY LANDS

Furniture from India, Indonesia, and China
Village of Merrick Park, 3rd Floor; 305-461-0330;
Hours: Mon–Sat 10–9, Sun 12–6; Credit Cards: MC, Visa, AmEx;
Owner is John Guarino

Price: Personnel: Ambiance: Quality:

This store is a joy for those wanting a tropical style for their home. Beautifully carved wood cabinets, sofas, and tables fill the showroom. I loved the gorgeous decorative pillows with Indian fabric. There is not a lot of help in the showroom, but Home Design Store is a worthwhile visit.

Dania Beach

Design Center of the Americas (DCOTA)

Design Center with many showrooms; sells only to the trade
1855 Griffin Road; 305-945-7496; Mon–Fri 9–5, 2nd Sat of each month 9–5; www.dcota.com

Located in Dania, just off Interstate 95 and only about 30 minutes north of Miami by car, the Design Center of the Americas (DCOTA) is a destination for the trade. The DCOTA is the largest design center in America, with over 775,000 square feet of showrooms. I found the DCOTA building to be the most public-friendly design center in the country. The thing that impressed me most was the fact that its showrooms show the net price (or the price a designer would have to pay) instead of the list price (the price technically the end user would have to pay). Customers are not allowed to buy goods without using a decorator, but the public can browse and even hire a designer available "on call" who will help customers who don't have a decorator make purchases. As in many design centers, all shops are housed in one large building; here there are 150 showrooms spread out over the center's four floors. Service in many of these showrooms (as in other design centers around the country) is poor or nonexistent.

Although the center has some wonderful showrooms that are in other places in the country, like Donghia, Baker, Far Eastern, and Henredon, I decided to focus just on those showrooms that are Miami-based. Showroom hours for each of the following are Monday through Friday, 9 to 5. The second Saturday of the month, the showrooms are open from 10 to 4. There are two sample sales each year, held on weekends. If you are spending the day, you'll find some restaurants at the center.

E. G. CODY

Reproduction European Furniture
1855 Griffin Road, Suite B112; 954-920-4408;
egcdania@aol.com; Credit Cards: MC, Visa, AmEx;
Manager is Mark Bernstein

Price: Personnel:

Ambiance: Quality:

Formal and fancy reproduction furniture best describes this showroom, well known in Florida. With another, smaller but more modern showroom in the Miami Design District (I liked that one better), this showroom is large and very jazzy-looking. You can find 550 lines of furniture here. Much of the furniture comes from Italy, Spain, and Argentina.

BOB SAPAN'S SHOWPLACE

Contemporary Furniture
1855 Griffin Road, Suite A123; 954-927-0333;
mary@bobsapansshowplace.com; Credit Cards: MC, Visa, AmEx;
www.bobsapansshowplace.com (not up and running yet);
Owner is Bob Sapan

Price: Personnel:

Ambiance: Quality:

This showroom reminds me of Florida 30 years ago. The owner is right at the door to greet shoppers, and he seems to know everyone in Florida. Glitzy light fixtures surround the showroom, but there are some wonderful dining chairs and Deco-style furniture and accessories. Much of what is on the floor is private-label contemporary furniture. The new lines Bob is carrying are very unusual and special.

J. BATCHELOR

Contemporary Furniture
1855 Griffin Road, Suite A428; 954-926-1881;
info@jbatchelor.com; Credit Cards: N/A; www.jbatchelor.com
(not up and running yet); Owner is Joseph Batchelor

Price: Personnel:

Ambiance:  Quality:

J. Batchelor is probably my favorite showroom in this building. The showroom is colorful, with interesting and bold modern paintings surrounded by subdued, elegant furniture and sculptures. The woods are stunning, and there is a gorgeous selection of garden furniture. The furniture is modern, and the fabrics are monochromatic and well made. I was surprised that there was no one to help me in the showroom for what seemed like an hour with no explanation. Well-known lines represented here include Pucci and Janus et Cie.

TURNER GREENBERG ASSOCIATES

Reproduction European Furniture
1855 Griffin Road, Suite B476; 954-925-8303;
turnergreenberg@aol.com; Credit Cards: N/A;
Owners are Steve Turner and Janet Greenburg

Price: Personnel:

Ambiance: Quality:

I really enjoy the inventory here, but the service needs definite improvement. I found the salespeople to be uninterested in helping me when I showed interest in or asked questions about the furniture. Famous lines sold here include Patina, Emanuel Morgz, and Mike Bell. Designers receive a 40% discount off the list prices. Furniture here is traditional.

MOBELFORM

Contemporary Furniture
1855 Griffin Road, Suite B408; 954-922-7234 or 888-662-3546 (toll-free); roie@mobelform.com; Credit Cards: MC, Visa;
www.mobelform.com; Owner is Roie Avin

Price: Personnel:

Ambiance: Quality:

Much of the furniture here comes from Italy and is very sleek modern. I was completely smitten with the awesome frosted-glass storage units. Otherwise, the oversized leather couches and chairs can be purchased elsewhere for a lot less. Well-known designers here are Eero Saarinen and Henry Bertoia. It is not possible to shop online. I found the sales staff here uninterested in helping me and wondered why I should stick around a showroom that has high prices and no service.

CAMPANIELLO IMPORTS OF FLORIDA, INC.
Contemporary Furniture
1855 Griffin Road, Suite B346; 954-925-1800;
campaniellodania@aol.com; Credit Cards: MC, Visa;
www.campaniello.com; Owner is Thomas Campaniello

Price: 🪑🪑🪑🪑🪑 Personnel: 🪑🪑🪑🪑🪑

Ambiance: 🪑🪑🪑🪑🪑 Quality: 🪑🪑🪑🪑🪑

Prices are not listed on the pieces here. If you can get someone to help you (I didn't have an easy time of it), this is a store worth exploring. My favorite things included the dining chairs made of different materials and covered in wonderful, unusual, and colorful fabrics. The showroom is ultramodern. They carry little in the way of wood. Italian lines represented here include Il Loft and Nube Reflex. There is also a showroom in New York.

RAKOVA BRECKER
Contemporary Furniture/Beds
1855 Griffin Road, Suite A309; 954-924-9878;
info@rakovabrecker.com; www.rakovabrecker.com;
Owners are Donald Brecker and Ava Rakova

Price: 🪑🪑🪑🪑🪑 Personnel: 🪑🪑🪑🪑🪑

Ambiance: 🪑🪑🪑🪑🪑 Quality: 🪑🪑🪑🪑🪑

I love this showroom. While it features beds and beautiful linens, there is also a great selection of contemporary, simple furniture. I also like the various storage systems. One thing refreshingly different about this showroom compared with the others here is the attentive, polite service. Designer discounts vary, and prices are not listed. You can see inventory on their Web site but not buy online.

Miami International Arts and Design District

If you want to spend a few hours hitting the main furniture hot spots in Miami, go to the Miami Design District. It is easy to get to—about 10 minutes from South Beach. Be careful, because the surrounding neighborhoods aren't the safest. A cab can take you there, but, as I did, make sure you tell the cabbie when and where to pick you up; otherwise you will be stranded. The best place to start is around 2nd and 39th Streets. Famous national showrooms include Holly Hunt and Ralph Lauren. If you get hungry, there are a few great restaurants in this four-square-block radius. I ate at a place called The District, a cute outdoor café and bar.

JBL INTERNATIONAL ANTIQUES

European Antiques
100 Northeast 40th Street; 305-576-1500; jbl@jblantiques.com;
Hours: Mon–Fri 10:30–5; Other times by appt.;
Credit Cards: N/A; Owners are Robert W. Parker
and J. Burton Lange

Price: (6 chairs)   Personnel: (3 chairs)

Ambiance: (5 chairs)   Quality: (5 chairs)

My experience shopping here was that like no other. I was almost refused into the shop at first because the owners suspected that I wasn't a designer; I was not dressed in my finest. Of course, things were different when they heard I was reviewing them in a book! Then I was welcomed gladly. The store has a wonderful selection of Continental antiques. Prices are high but competitive with other antiques shops. Furniture here is purchased in the U.S. and in Europe. The main owner is a character who, the day I came, was wearing a colorful top and told me great stories about his times in Chicago years ago. He has sold antiques to many celebrities, including: Bea Arthur, Katherine Hepburn, George Hamilton, Candice Bergen, Marlo Thomas, and the Gibbs brothers. Designers receive a 30% discount.

ARABESQUES ANTIQUES

Moroccan, Spanish, and British Colonial Furniture/Antiques
91 Northeast 40th Street; 305-571-8808;
arabesques@earthlink.net; Hours: Mon–Fri 10–5, Sat 11–4;
Credit Cards: MC, Visa, AmEx; Owner is Peggy Armand

Price: Personnel:

Ambiance: Quality:

This tiny store has pretty Moroccan furniture. Prices are high and discounts vary. I liked some of the chests and rugs here. Service was not great.

DÉCOR 8

Vintage and Contemporary Furniture and Accessories
35 NE 40th Street, J9; 305-573-3473; johana@decor8miami.com;
Hours: Mon–Sat 11–5; www.decor8miami.com;
Credit Cards: MC, Visa, AmEx; Owner is Johana Diaz

Price: Personnel:

Ambiance: Quality:

This is a very romantic little furniture store that recently opened. The owner is young, fashionable, and comes from Colombia. The store has the look of a fancy little lingerie store, with fluffy pillows, and soft couches and chairs, and accessories. The colors of the fabrics are red, pink, white, luscious oranges, and browns. The furniture comes from Colombia, Brazil, and Italy. Service is excellent here. Designers receive a 30% discount. The Web site is under construction.

ABITARE

Italian Modern Furniture and Kitchens
21 Northeast 39th Street; 305-573-5200; Hours: Mon–Fri 10–6, other
times by appointment; www.abitareusa.com;
Credit Cards: MC, Visa, AmEx; Owner is Nicola Belletti

Price: Personnel:

Ambiance: Quality:

Here only one year, Abitare is a large showroom filled with Italian furniture and kitchens. It is a very chic-looking store, carrying a mixture of self-manufactured furniture and other lines, like Minotti. I particularly like Abitare's highly functional storage systems. Service is personalized, and the staff is extremely knowledgeable about the inventory. Prices are not listed on the merchandise. Designers receive a 20% discount.

South Beach

While there are not many great furniture stores in the South Beach area, I would highly recommend going to Senzatempo. This one is a worthwhile trip because it is just off Lincoln Road, a wide boulevard between Washington and Alton with no cars. There are several blocks of shops, outdoor cafés, and bars. Lincoln Road is one of the hottest night-life spots in the country.

SENZATEMPO

Art Deco, Vintage French and Italian Furniture,
Accessories and Watches
1655 Meridian Avenue; 305-534-5588; matt@sanzatempo.com;
Hours: Mon–Fri 11–7, Sat 12–7; www.senzatempo.com;
Credit Cards: MC, Visa, AmEx; Owners are Matthew Bain
and Massimo Baracca

Price: Personnel:

Ambiance: Quality:

This store is fun, fun, fun! I love the retro feel here, in the casual, larger-than-life showroom. The vintage furniture is fabulous, not to mention the unusual art, accessories, vintage watches, and sculptures. You can view some of the inventory online but not make purchases. I love the Web site which even lists the prices! Much of the furniture here is purchased in Italy and the U.S. Senzatempo has been around for 12 years and has a great warehouse in the Miami River area that is open only by appointment.

North Miami

North Miami is getting to be known as an art and design district. There are many new stores and cafés opening in this location, across from the Museum of Contemporary Art (MoCA).

VERMILLION

1925–1965 Eclectic Furniture and Accessories
765 NE 125th Street; 305-893-7800;
susancutler@earthlink.net; Hours: Tue–Sat 11–6;
www.galleryvermillion.com; Credit Cards: MC, Visa, AmEx;
Owner is Susan Cutler

Price: Personnel: Ambiance: Quality:

If you love Deco, not to be missed is the recently opened Vermillion. Susan Cutler specializes in one-of-a-kind Mid-Century furniture, spanning from the 1920s to the '60s. There is a nice selection of Art Deco and more contemporary designs. The shop opened one year ago and is across from the Museum of Contemporary Art (MoCA). Designers receive a 20% discount. The Web site is under construction but will be up soon.

MIAMI AUCTION HOUSES

Christie's
550 Biltmore Way, Suite 800
Coral Gables
305-445-1487

Sotheby's
800 Douglas Road, Suite 125
305-448-7882

MIAMI ANTIQUES SHOWS

Miami National Antiques Show
January
Radisson Center
777 NW 72nd Avenue
305-261-4200 or 954-563-6747

Palm Beach Classic Antiques Show
January/February
Palm Beach Country Convention Center
West Palm Beach
561-209-1300 or log on to www.ifae.com
1 hour north of Miami

Palm Beach Winter Antiques Show
January
Marriott West Palm Beach
1001 Okeechobee Boulevard
West Palm Beach
561-833-1234
1 hour North of Miami

MIAMI FLEA MARKETS

Flagler Flea Market

Every Saturday and Sunday
401 Northwest 38th Court
305-649-3000

Lincoln Road Antiques Market

Every other Sunday all year long

CHAPTER 11

New York

Writing a review on anything to do with shopping in New York is quite a challenge. It's a little like being asked to grade the driving test for the guy who wrote the official rules-of-the-road guidebook they hand out when you go for a driver's license. Not only is this city home to the best restaurants, theater, art, and fashion in the U.S., but it's the ultimate furniture hot spot, with some of the most remarkable furniture stores in the world. There is an eclectic mix of furniture, and high price tags to go along with it. The furniture stores are spread out, but most of the good ones are on the Upper East Side, Soho, Midtown, the Village, Chelsea, and Tribeca, all in Manhattan, with a few attractive shops outside of Manhattan in Brooklyn.

NEW YORK RETAIL STORES
Upper East Side

The Upper East Side, with its posh brownstones and white-gloved doormen, is brimming over with beautiful shops and restaurants. Shoppers love to congregate in the Upper East Side and Midtown. Prices are high, but that's what you expect when you're in a place with the best of the best. This neighborhood is on a grid, and walking is the preferred method of getting around. Traffic is impossible and cab rides can be costly, especially on east–west cross streets.

DWELLINGS

Contemporary Furniture and Some Vintage Pieces
30 East 67th Street; 212-717-5753; info@dwellingshome.com;
Hours: Mon–Fri 10–6; www.dwellingshome.com;
Credit Cards: MC, Visa, AmEx, Discover;
Owners are James Huniford and Stephen Sills

Price: Personnel:

Ambiance: Quality:

Finally a shop with great upholstered furniture that fits my petite frame! This very savvy furniture store, unlike so many others, realizes that not all customers play for the NBA or live in houses with rooms as big as the Taj Mahal. The owners of this very chic store have found a great niche in unusual, not oversized upholstered furniture. The upholstered pieces are some of the best I have seen in New York. There are multiple furniture finishes available and some custom sizing options. I also like the selection of unusual lamps and vintage (mostly French) accessories. Designers receive a 10% discount. The Web site shows pictures and gives some descriptions but no prices.

BARRY FRIEDMAN, LTD.

Museum-Quality Vintage and Contemporary Furniture
32 East 67th Street; 212-794-8950;
registrar@barryfriedmanltd.com; Hours: Mon–Fri 10–6, Sat 10–5;
www.barryfriedmanltd.com; Owner is Barry Friedman

Price: Personnel:

Ambiance: Quality:

For the many years that I have been frequenting Barry Friedman, the inventory has always been antique or vintage French. However, Barry is now becoming more daring and contemporary. While he still carries his same museum-quality inventory, he is showing newer, sculptural furniture. I especially like the way Barry showcases imaginative pieces, and particularly the ones with the most unusual woods, metals, and parchments. I found the new collection to be highly creative and sophisticated, which makes for a titillating shopping experience. Selection is limited because everything is handmade. The service is usually good. There is no set designer discount, but you should know up front that most of the pieces are in the tens of thousands. The Web site shows pictures and gives some background information and descriptions but no prices. Barry Friedman is also a partner in the furniture and tribal arts shop across the street called Friedman and Vallois.

HOMER

Contemporary Furniture and Accessories
939 Madison Avenue; 212-744-7705; info@homerdesign.com;
Hours: Mon–Fri 10–6, Sat 11–5; www.homerdesign.com;
Credit Cards: MC, Visa, AmEx, Discover; Owner is Richard Mishaan

Price: Personnel:
Ambiance: Quality:

I'm a huge fan of Homer, which has been here for only five years but seems like it has been here forever. Nestled in between many chic clothing stores and restaurants, this busy Manhattan destination is worth a trip for anyone who wants the look of French '40s but with a contemporary edge. The store is on two floors and has vivid colors everywhere. There are a lot of "H" monograms on the accessories—making me feel like I am in Hermès, which by now you may know I am mad about (especially if you have read much of this book!). I particularly like the lamps, benches, and tables. Much of the furniture here is lacquered. There is also an impressive collection of paintings and housewares. The owner is an interior designer and architect. Designers receive a 20% discount. The Web site is difficult to use and does not show a lot of the inventory.

FLORIAN PAPP

English and Continental Antiques and Fine Art
962 Madison Avenue; 212-288-6770; papp@florianpapp.com;

Hours: Mon–Fri 9–5:30, Sat 10–5; www.florianpapp.com;
Owners are Melinda and William Papp

Price: Personnel: Ambiance: Quality:

Florian Papp, a family business since 1900, has long been considered one of the best antiques stores in New York. One solid bonus of shopping here is that the store guarantees quality, authenticity, and value—something that attracts a steady following of wealthy clientele who are willing and able to pay the high prices. The store is on three floors (unusual for the Upper East Side), and shoppers are free to browse at their leisure. The tags are very descriptive. I particularly like their 20th-century Deco pieces because they are a little more unusual than their classic antiques. Designers receive a 20% discount. The Web site has excellent pictures and descriptions but no prices.

CLEARLY FIRST

Vintage Furniture, Contemporary Clothing, and Accessories
980 Madison Avenue; 212-988-8242; Hours: Mon–Sat 11–6,
Sun 12–5; www.clearlyfirst.com; Credit Cards: MC, Visa, AmEx,
Discover; Owner is Helene Hellsten

Price: Personnel: Ambiance: Quality:

Take care that you don't pass this shop by! Clearly First is not an easy store to spot because of its plain-looking façade. Be assured, the inside of this store, unlike its exterior, is far from a shrinking violet. Keep your eye on this great little store, because I predict it will become a real furniture trendsetter. Clearly First is one of the few shops in the country I have seen that combine fashion with furniture and design (and then some!). On two floors, in a somewhat strange layout, the store carries some specialty, important vintage pieces as well as everything else cool under the sun: women's clothing and handbags, innovative bicycles, life-sized antique toy cars for kids, even a line of out-of-sight doggie wear. There are also some unusual housewares here that would make lovely house gifts. The owner, who is Swedish, has just announced that she will soon be selling a contemporary line of furniture at the MoMA (Museum of Modern Art) Store. I love the interactive Web site and its music. The Web site displays pictures of pieces and gives short descriptions but no prices. No discounts here.

The following four stores are located in the Interior Design Building, which sells to both designers and the public:

AMY PERLIN ANTIQUES
Unusual Continental Antiques
306 East 61st Street; 212-593-5756; info@amyperlinantiques.com;
Hours: Mon–Fri 9–6; www.amyperlinantiques.com;
Credit Cards: MC, Visa, AmEx; Owner is Amy Perlin

Price: 🪑🪑🪑🪑🪑 Personnel: 🪑🪑🪑🪑

Ambiance: 🪑🪑🪑🪑🪑 Quality: 🪑🪑🪑🪑🪑

Amy Perlin has become a well-known antiques dealer whose business has grown tremendously over the years. Most of her business is to the trade, out of her showroom here in the Interior Design Building at 306 East 61st Street; she has another location in Bridgehampton, Long Island. The showroom is open to the public but only designers receive a discount. Amy does not lack for confidence when talking about her business or her inventory. She has a 10,000-square foot space here along with a large warehouse open by appointment on 125th Street. Her inventory includes mostly larger, rustic antiques and unusual vintage pieces coming from all over Europe. The furniture is pricey, and she wouldn't tell me her designer discount. She now has a reproduction line. The Web site does not show any inventory. The atmosphere here could be a little intimidating for a novice shopper.

SENTIMENTO

Continental Antiques, Modern Furniture and Accessories
306 East 61st Street; 212-750-3111; Hours: Mon–Fri 10–6;
Owner is Toby Landey

Price: Personnel:

Ambiance: Quality:

Sentimento, a 27-year veteran in the city, is another great showroom in the Interior Design Building and one of my favorite showrooms in all of New York. The look here is completely eclectic and invigorating. The antiques are diverse and there are many unique items. I especially like the Swedish painted antique furniture, but the 20th-century furniture is equally special. Furniture here comes from around the world. Designers get a 20% discount.

ERIC APPEL

20th-Century Furniture and Lighting
306 East 61st Street; 212-605-9960;
ericappelantiques@verizon.net; Hours: Mon–Fri 10–6;
www.ericappel.com; Credit Cards: N/A; Owner is Eric Appel

Price: Personnel:

Ambiance: Quality:

Yet another incredible showroom located in the Interior Design Building. If you're anything like me, you'll fall head over heels in love with Eric Appel and all of his Deco furniture and lighting. He carries many unusual pieces; not the usual run-of-the-mill furniture from the Deco era. I think his lighting is also quite striking. A lot of furniture is crammed into this small space, but it works. Prices and designer discounts vary. There is something here for everybody. The Web site offers some pictures and descriptions but no prices. Well worth a visit.

LEE CALICCHIO, LTD.

Continental Antiques
306 East 61st Street, 2nd Floor; 212-588-0841;
leecalltd@aol.com; Hours: Mon–Fri 9:30–5:30;
www.leecalicchioltd.com; Credit Cards: N/A; Owner is Lee Calicchio

Lee Calicchio is a designer who has a very unusual showroom with inventory from all over Europe. She has been in business for more than 10 years. There is inventory from the 18th–20th centuries with an emphasis on unusual pieces, many of which cost more than $10,000. Designers receive a 20% discount here. The Web site offers some pictures and descriptions but no prices.

LIZ O'BRIEN

20th-Century French Furniture
800A Fifth Avenue at 61st Street; 212-755-3800;
doria@lizobrien.com; Hours: Mon–Fri 10–6;
Credit Cards: MC, Visa, AmEx; Owner is Liz O'Brien

Liz O'Brien is one of the few dealers that can afford such a great location on Fifth Avenue, just down the way from Bergdorf's. She sells high-end French designer pieces from mostly the 1930s and '40s. I found the classical and sophisticated inventory outstanding. One negative here, and the only one, is that there are no price tags. Many of the chairs are covered in the original leather and the tables in parchment. Designers receive a 15% discount. There is no Web site .

JAMES SANSUM, INC.

Continental Antiques, Vintage Classics,
and Contemporary Pieces
1020 Lexington Avenue, 2nd Floor; 212-288-9455;
jamessansuminc@nyc.rr.com; Hours: Mon–Fri 10–5;
Owner is James Sansum

Price: Personnel: Ambiance: Quality:

James Sansum, owned by a Harvard decorative arts graduate, is a little diamond in the rough. The listed address is confusing here, so take care not to get lost. Look for the bright red Lexington Bar and Books building, as you'll find the shop directly above them. The selection is not great but there are pictures showing much more of the store's inventory. Worth looking over here is a collection of gorgeous contemporary needlepoint rugs from India. The colors are spectacular. James Sansum has a good eye and accurately represents his goods. Designers receive a 20% discount here. There is no Web site .

MALMAISON ANTIQUES

18th–20th-Century French and American Furniture
253 East 74th Street; 212-288-7569; napo253@aol.com;
Hours: Mon–Fri 9–5; www.1stdibs.com; Owners are Yvonne and Roger Prigent

Price: Personnel: Ambiance: Quality:

Here's another store you want to be careful not to pass up because of its drab exterior. Appearing much like a boarded-up vacant building, Malmaison is perhaps one of the best 20th-century dealers in the country. The amount of inventory here is staggering. The atmosphere is a little quirky, but if you are a lover of unusual, mostly 20th-century furniture (mostly Deco and French 1940s), this is the place to hit. The business has been here for 25 years and began as a shop that sold 18th- and 19th-century furniture. Roger Prigent used to be a photographer for Vogue magazine years ago, and his artistic style shows here. Designers get a 20% discount here. The Web site is part of a collective Web site for other stores in four large cities. Worth a visit!

TREILLAGE, LTD.

Antique and Contemporary Garden Furniture
and Antiques
418 East 75th Street; 212-535-2288; info@treillageonline.com;
Hours: Mon–Fri, 10–6, Sat 10–5; www.treillageonline.com;
Credit Cards: MC, Visa, AmEx; Owners are John Rosselli
and Bunny Williams

Price: Personnel:

Ambiance: Quality:

Treillage is one of my favorite antique garden furniture stores in the country. Don't be fooled by the name, the store is much more than just a garden furniture shop. The business, which began 14 years ago, sells exquisite one-of-a-kind antiques, contemporary furnishings, and beautiful lighting. There is a wide range of prices. There aren't a lot of people around the store to help you if you are shopping, but I still highly recommend coming here to see the treasures. The inventory and customers come from all over the world. Designer discounts are 20%. The Web site shows their inventory and gives descriptions but no prices. A great find.

LEIGH KENO

Early American Antiques through 1840
127 East 69th Street; 212-734-2381; Hours: Mon–Fri 9:30–5:30;
www.leighkeno.com; Owner is Leigh Keno

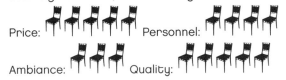

Price: Personnel:

Ambiance: Quality:

Leigh Keno and his twin brother, both noted antiques appraisers, have become TV, magazine, and book celebrities. They are best known for helping to create the "Antiques Roadshow" on PBS. Leigh Keno, in his shop, carries only American antiques, which are becoming harder to find. On the day of my visit, there were only cabinets and secretaries, but no seating options. Prices are high, with many pieces costing more than

$35,000. It seems as if the only people who shop in this second-floor showroom without signage are collectors. Designer discounts vary.

MECOX GARDENS
See review of their Los Angeles store; same review applies here
Antique, Contemporary, and Garden Furniture
962 Lexington Avenue; 212-249-5301

SKYSCRAPER
Art Deco Furniture and Accessories
237 East 60th Street; 212-588-0644; e60sky@aol.com;
Hours: Mon–Fri 10–6; www.skyscraperny.com;
Credit Cards: MC, Visa, AmEx, Discover; Owner is Sandi Berman

Price: Personnel:

Ambiance: Quality:

Skyscraper is another one of my favorite stores in the country. The atmosphere here is refreshingly casual, and there is no attitude or pressure here. There is a wide variety of pieces in a wide range of prices. The store is sophisticated and fun. My favorite pieces are the Deco tables and cabinets. Designers receive a 20% discount. Sandi Berman also owns another shop at Lexington and 74th Street, which sells art and accessories. The Web site shows some pictures of the inventory and gives descriptions but no prices. This shop is a real treat.

JOHN SALIBELLO ANTIQUES
20th-Century Furniture and Lighting
211 and 229 East 60th Street; 212-838-5767 or 212-688-7499;
Hours: Mon–Fri 10–6; www.johnsalibelloantiques.com;
Credit Cards: MC, Visa, AmEx, Discover; Owner is John Salibello

Price: Personnel:

Ambiance: Quality:

John Salibello has two locations on 60th Street, just a few doors apart. The selection in both of these stores is wonderful. The furniture comes from all over the world. The stock ranges from Deco to the 1970s. Prices are extremely high here, but even though there are other good stores where you can get the look for considerably less, I still recommend seeing the place. Though I found the service to be nonexistent, the caliber of the inventory makes this store worth a visit. Designers receive a 20% discount. The Web site shows pictures of some inventory and gives descriptions but no prices. Note that there is another location in Bridgehampton, on Long Island.

ILIAD ANTIK

Biedermeier, Neoclassical, and Empire Furniture

237 East 58th Street; 212-935-4382;

info@iliadantik.com; Hours: Mon–Fri 11–6, Sat 12–5;

www.iliadantik.com; Owners are Adam Brown and Andrea Zemel

Price: | Personnel:

Ambiance: | Quality:

Iliad Antik came from Philadelphia a few years ago, but it seems as if this shop has been here forever because of its name recognition in the industry. The inventory is Biedermeier, Neoclassical, and Empire, the furniture from this period (the first half of the 19th century) being typically made of medium to dark woods, glossy-looking and formal in its presentation. Service here is wonderful, and the sales staff is knowledgeable. Designers receive a 20% discount. The Web site is excellent, with good explanations of furniture from this period. There are pictures of inventory and descriptions but no prices.

East Harlem

Although East Harlem is not considered a furniture hot spot, there is one that is the exception. The neighborhood is not one that I would recommend walking around alone, especially at night. When there is no traffic, it will take about 20 minutes from downtown to get there by car.

ANTIQUES AT THE LAFAYETTE WAREHOUSE

Antiques Mall

401 East 110th Street at 1st Avenue; 212-722-8400;
lafayettecenter@aol.com; Hours: Sun 12–5, Mon–Sat 10–5;
Credit Cards: MC, Visa; Owner is a corporation made up of
many people

Price: Personnel:

Ambiance: Quality:

This place is truly an antiques oasis worth going out of your way for. Here only one year, this is one of the best antique malls I have seen anywhere. The inventory is both unusual and extraordinarily well selected. There are about 50 dealers in this 20,000-square-foot no-frills space. Discounts depend on each dealer and most dealers are not around, but the front desk staff is extremely pleasant and helpful. My feeling is that you could negotiate with the dealers.

Midtown

Midtown is where many of the big businesses in New York are headquartered. Also home to many wonderful restaurants and commercial stores, and hotels, this is the heart of New York City. Walking is the easiest way to get around in this part of town. Taxis are hard to get during rush hour but there are buses.

THE TERENCE CONRAN SHOP

General Furniture Store and Home Accessories

407 East 59th Street; 212-755-7249; info@conranusa.com;
Hours: Mon–Fri 11–8, Sat 10–7, Sun 12–6; www.conran.com;
Credit Cards: MC, Visa, AmEx, Diners; Owner is Terence Conran

Price: Personnel:

Ambiance: Quality:

As large general furniture stores go, the Terence Conran Shop is one of the best in the country. Conran, the famous British restaurateur, author, interior and furniture designer, has created a beautiful store that feels like a museum but warmer. He carries a variety of good-looking functional and contemporary furniture, housewares, flowers, and even wonderful children's toys. He also sells Capellini, Phillipe Starck, and Eames furniture. I like the variety of giftware, dishes, flatware, and vases in addition to the furniture. The furniture is medium-priced, and there is something here for everybody in the two-store shop located under the Queensboro Bridge and next to a Conran restaurant. Terence Conran also founded the Design Museum in London, which specializes in modern industrial design. The Web site shows some of the inventory, which can be purchased online. This is his only shop in the U.S., but Conran also has three shops in London, two in Paris, and one in Japan. Designers who first spend $5,000 get a 20% discount on subsequent purchases, excluding sale items and electronics.

NEWEL

Eclectic Antique Furniture and Accessories
425 East 53rd Street; 212-758-1970; info@newel.com;
Hours: Mon–Fri 8:30–5; www.newel.com; Owner is Lewis Baer

Price: Personnel: Ambiance: Quality:

Newel is a six-story antiques store that has one of the largest collections of antiques and 20th-century furniture in the country. As a third-generation owner, Lewis Baer takes pride in his large and eclectic inventory. The prices are unbelievably high for the merchandise, but the selection is good. The business began as a prop rental shop and evolved into a full-scale antiques store. The inventory comes from around the world. Designers receive a 20% discount. The Web site is excellent and even has specific categories to make shopping online easier. Included online are pictures, prices, and descriptions.

BLOOMINGDALE'S

Department Store
1000 Third Avenue; 212-705-2576; Hours: Sun 1–7,
Mon–Fri 10–8:30, Sat 10–7; www.bloomingdales.com
(no furniture online); Credit Cards: MC, Visa, AmEx, Discover,
and Bloomingdale's; Owner is a corporation

Price: Personnel:
Ambiance: Quality:

Bloomingdale's is a New York hallmark. One of the busiest department stores in the country, Bloomingdale's carries an extensive furniture collection. Well-known manufacturers such as Ralph Lauren, Natuzzi, and Grange are showcased here. The look ranges from traditional to contemporary. The staff is more than able to be of assistance, and I found my service experience to be excellent. There are no designer discounts, although there are regular sales. The Web site doesn't show the furniture lines.

TAKASHIMAYA

Vintage and Contemporary Home Furnishings; Clothing
693 Fifth Avenue (between 54th and 55th Streets);
212-350-0100; Hours: Sun 12–7, Mon–Sat 10–7; Credit Cards: MC,
Visa, AmEx; Owner is a corporation

Price: Personnel:
Ambiance: Quality:

Takashimaya is a New York favorite and well located near other wonderful shops in Midtown. The largest department store in Japan, Takashimaya has become a stomping ground for beautiful vintage and contemporary home furnishings. Most of the vintage pieces are early-20th-century, Deco pieces. This is also a wonderful place to find unusual flower containers, clothing, linens, books, and travel accessories. There is a nice café in the downstairs area called the Tea Box Café. Designers receive a 10% rebate here on furniture purchases only.

CASSINA

European Contemporary Furniture
155 East 56th Street; 212-245-2121; info@cassinausa.com;
Hours: Mon–Fri 9–6, Sat 11–5 (but closed Saturdays in the
summer); www.cassinausa.com; Credit Cards: MC, Visa, AmEx;
Owner is a corporation

Price:  Personnel:

Ambiance: Quality:

Cassina has been here for 10 years and is the only Cassina store in the U.S., although their line of furniture is represented within other showrooms around the country. The store has recently been remodeled and is very busy. The furniture is all kind of squarish with lots of good-quality leathers. The styles are from well-known furniture designers like Phillipe Starck, Frank Lloyd Wright, and Le Corbusier. The wall in the center of the store is bright red, just like the logo. There are good options here, even though the furniture is pricey. The Web site shows the Cassina line of furniture and gives dimensions but no pricing. I like the fact that they explain how this furniture is different from the cheap knock-offs. There is no designer discount.

TOM THOMAS

20th-Century Furniture and Accessories
318 East 59th Street; 212-688-6100; tt@tomthomasgallery.com;
Hours: Mon–Fri 10:30–6; www.tomthomasgallery.com;
Owner is Tom Thomas

Price: 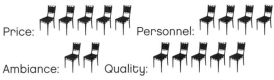 Personnel:

Ambiance: Quality:

Tom Thomas is a small shop specializing in unusual and highly collectible 20th-century furniture and decorative arts. Much of his collection is from the 1930s and '40s (there is a nice selection of furniture designed by Jacques Adnet), and the inventory is German, Swedish, and French.

There are no price tags. This is a store for serious collectors, with many of the pieces costing over $15,000. His Web site shows pictures and he also sends out his own newsletter.

Garment District

The Garment District in Manhattan isn't exactly a place where you would expect to find a plethora of furniture stores, but there are some stores worth mentioning here. The neighborhood is best known for manufacturing and distributing clothing.

VW HOME

European and Asian Antiques and Contemporary Furniture
333 West 39th Street; 212-244-5008;
vwhome.vicentewolf@verizon.net; Hours: Mon–Fri 9–5;
www.vw-home.com; Credit Cards: MC, Visa, AmEx;
Owner is Vicente Wolf

Price: ▮▮▮▮▮ Personnel: ▮▮▮▮▮

Ambiance: ▮▮▮▮▮ Quality: ▮▮▮▮▮

On the 10th floor of a shabby-looking office building (I thought I was in the wrong place) is the showroom of the famous interior designer of 28 years, Vicente Wolf, displaying a wide variety of antiques and contemporary furniture and fabric designed by Wolf. Custom pieces are also an option here. I do think prices are high for the merchandise, but designers receive a 20% discount and most of the business is to the trade. The showroom has some elegant and diverse pieces. Some of Vicente Wolf's furniture is located in high-end showrooms around the country. The Web site shows some of the interesting inventory and gives small descriptions, but many of the measurements are missing and so are the prices.

FOREMOST FURNITURE

Large General Furniture Store
8 West 30th Street; 212-889-6347 or 866-694-6678;

info@foremostfurniture.com; Hours: Mon–Fri 10–6, Thu 10–7, Sat 10–5, Sun 11–5; www.foremostfurniture.com; Credit Cards: MC, Visa, AmEx; Owner is the Broderson Family

Price: 🪑🪑🪑🪑 Personnel: 🪑🪑🪑🪑🪑🪑

Ambiance: 🪑🪑🪑🪑 Quality: 🪑🪑🪑🪑🪑

Foremost Furniture is one of the only large general furniture stores in Manhattan. Housed on five floors of an old, not-so-glamorous office building, it is one of the oldest family-run furniture businesses in New York, here for 40 years. The space is no-frills, but I encourage you to check this place out. Known for excellent service and great variety with design services available, the store offers something for everyone and in a wide range of prices. Most customers have come from word-of-mouth, and many New Yorkers still don't know about Foremost. Well-known furniture lines here include Century, Bernhardt (Martha Stewart), and Lexington. There is also a large leather gallery. The furniture styles range from traditional to contemporary. I think you can get a good value for the money here on everything from suede and leather couches to dining tables. Designer discounts depend on the individual manufacturer. There are frequent sales. The Web site doesn't show individual pieces but shows parts of different lines of furniture.

Chelsea

While Chelsea is hit-or-miss in terms of furniture stores, there are some noteworthy shops. Note that they are spread out. Chelsea is easy to get to by subway but it doesn't have the same neighborhood feel that other neighborhoods nearby offer, like Soho, Tribeca and Greenwich Village.

REMAINS
Vintage and Reproduction Lighting
130 West 28th Street; 212-675-8051; mail@remains.com; Hours: Mon–Fri 9–6, Sat (28th Street location) 11–6; www.remains.com; Owner is David Calligerows

Price: 🪑🪑🪑🪑 Personnel: 🪑🪑🪑🪑🪑

Ambiance: 🪑🪑🪑🪑🪑 Quality: 🪑🪑🪑🪑

Remains has an enormous selection of vintage and reproduction lighting. Service is excellent and needs to be for trying to view the huge lighting selection offered here! This shop is one of two locations; the other is at 213 East 59th Street. There is a new line of reproduction lights Remains is doing that is in showrooms around the country, (located in design centers). The Web site is exceptionally well laid out for easy shopping, showing the inventory with dates and pricing. I wish that all Web sites were this easy to navigate! I recommend checking out the collection online before making the trip to the stores. It is not possible to buy online yet.

PLEXI-CRAFT QUALITY PRODUCTS CORP.

Custom Lucite Anything
514 West 24th Street; 212-924-3244;
craft@plexi-craft.com; Hours: Mon–Fri 9–5;
www.plexi-craft.com; Credit Cards: MC, Visa, AmEx;
Owner is Shirley Rose

Price: 🪑🪑🪑 Personnel: 🪑🪑🪑🪑

Ambiance: 🪑🪑 Quality: 🪑🪑🪑🪑🪑

One of my favorite New York resources, Plexi-Craft will replicate or design anything in Lucite. What I like about Plexi-Craft is that they complete pieces quickly, done perfectly and at a very reasonable price. Years ago I had a wine glass rack made out of Lucite and though it was an extremely complicated project, they did it quickly and I couldn't have been happier with their work. Lots of toney shops and showrooms make similar pieces for five or ten times the price.

MANTIQUES MODERN

20th-Century Decorative Furniture and Accessories
146 West 22nd Street (between 6th and 7th Avenues);
212-206-1494; info@mantiquesmodern.com; Hours: Daily 10:30–6:30;
www.mantiquesmodern.com; Credit Cards: MC, Visa, AmEx;
Owners are Cory Margolis and Kenny Felberbaum

Price: Personnel:

Ambiance: Quality:

    Mantiques Modern has interesting and unusual 20th-century furniture and accessories. The atmosphere is casual, making it a relaxing and enjoyable shopping experience. They have recently moved to this new space from directly across the street. There are two floors of furniture. Designer discounts depend on the individual pieces. Much of the business is to the trade. The Web site is outstanding, with pictures, prices, and descriptions broken down into several categories, making shopping online easy. Worth a peek.

Q COLLECTION

Ecological Furniture
915 Broadway Suite 1001; 212-529-1400; info@qcollection.com;
Hours: Mon–Fri 9–5:30; www.qcollection.com; Credit Cards: MC,
Visa, AmEx; Owners are Anthony Cochran and Jesse Johnson

Price: Personnel:

Ambiance: Quality:

    Q Collection is unique in being one of the only contemporary ecological, or green, furniture stores in the nation. As the country goes organic with food, it is also catching on to organic furniture. The concept here is to offer attractive, transitional furniture made from certified woods from sustainably managed forests. The furniture has no formaldehydes, no polyurethanes, and no harmful dyes or carcinogens in the fabrics. The owners have a design background, and the selection, although limited, is stunning. I love the Abigail sofa, in particular. Also noteworthy are the luscious fabric choices. The only drawback, and I think a significant one, is that the store caters to the trade. This showroom has become a popular and intriguing place for celebrities and other wealthy clientele. The Web site shows pictures and gives descriptions but no prices.

ABC CARPET & HOME

Large General Furniture Store—
Antiques to Contemporary
888 Broadway (at East 19th Street); 212-473-3000;
Hours: Mon–Fri 10–8, Sat 10–7; www.abchome.com;
Credit Cards: MC, Visa, AmEx, Discover, and ABC Credit Cards

Price: 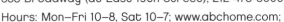 Personnel:

Ambiance: Quality:

ABC Carpet & Home is one of my favorite stores anywhere. Unlike most home furnishings department stores, ABC Carpet has the most unusual rugs, antique furniture, decorative items, jewelry, and housewares on its 10 floors. There is something for everyone here, with a wide variety of styles and prices. New Yorkers rave about the selection and love to spend hours browsing. Designers receive a 10% discount. The store has other locations in New York. I love the variety of old and new, a rare concept for such a large store. The Web site describes their lines of furniture, but there is no pricing. Worth at least a day's visit.

East Village

East Village is an artsy little neighborhood with some of the best furniture stores in Manhattan. Many of the stores are housed in old brownstones that have been converted into shops. There are also many cute restaurants in the neighborhood.

TURBULENCE

15th–19th-Century European Antiques
812 Broadway; 212-598-9030; Hours: Mon–Fri 11–6;
Owners are Antonie and Maurice Margules

Price: Personnel:

Ambiance: Quality:

Turbulence is just one of those stores I will never understand. There is graffiti on the doors and the entrance is shabby; the owner is sort of an odd character, wearing no shirt on the day I met him. But that said, the inventory is truly among the best in the country. There are many beautiful woods and a high percentage of furniture from the 15th and 16th centuries, furniture I have never before encountered. Most of the pieces are museum quality and massive, and most of the clientele are serious collectors. The building is enormous, with four floors here and an additional four floors across the street. The business has been here for 15 years. Prices are vague and so are discounts. Don't miss this place if you are a serious furniture buff.

BERND GOECKLER ANTIQUES, INC.

Antiques and Art Deco Furniture and Lighting
30 East 10th Street; 212-777-8209; bgantiques@mac.com;
Hours: Mon–Fri 9–6, Sat 10–5; www.bgoecklerantiques.com;
Owner is Bernd Goeckler

Price: Personnel:

Ambiance: Quality:

In a chic, narrow space, the well-known Bernd Goeckler shop sits amid other elegant, expensive shops, like Karl Kemp, in the neighborhood. About 90% of the business here is to the trade. The atmosphere is a little intimidating because of the high prices and the formality of the furniture. I love the look, though, and the unusual furniture selected and displayed in a modern way. I especially love the 20th-century light fixtures. Most of the furniture is from Italy, Austria, and France. Designers receive a 20% discount. The Web site shows pictures of inventory and descriptions but no prices. An intriguing shop.

KARL KEMP

Biedermeier and Art Deco Furniture and Accessories
34 East 10th Street; 212-254-1877; info@karlkemp.com;
Hours: Mon–Fri 10–6; www.karlkemp.com; Owner is Karl Kemp

Price: 🪑🪑🪑🪑🪑   Personnel: 🪑🪑🪑🪑🪑

Ambiance: 🪑🪑🪑🪑🪑   Quality: 🪑🪑🪑🪑🪑

Karl Kemp is one of my favorite stores. Ironically, I hadn't seen the shop until this past visit. Usually I see Karl Kemp's booths at antiques shows around the country. His look is Biedermeier with some modern elements of Deco and other 20th-century furnishings. His furniture and lighting selection is spectacular, and yes, the pieces come with big price tags. Designers receive a 20% discount. The Web site has pictures and descriptions but no prices.

West Village

West Village has so many wonderful furniture stores, restaurants, and clothing stores. The streets here are packed with all kinds of people, many of which are NYU students. I like all of the outdoor cafés that get crowded in the summer.

LARS BOLANDER NY

Antique (mostly Swedish) Furniture and Reproductions
72 Gansevoort Street; 212-924-1000; chris@larsbolander.com;
Hours: Mon–Sat 11–7; www.larsbolander.com; Credit Cards: MC, Visa, AmEx; Owner is Lars Bolander

Price: 🪑🪑🪑🪑🪑   Personnel: 🪑🪑🪑🪑🪑

Ambiance:  Quality:

Lars Bolander is a veteran in the design/furnishings industry. He has had this shop for 20 years, and it is a busy place, with interesting pieces everywhere you look. Most of the furniture is from the Swedish Gustavian period (18th century), but there are also antiques from other parts of the world. He now has a great reproduction line of Swedish Gustavian furniture that looks like exact replicas. The Web site has pictures of the inventory and brief descriptions but no prices. Designers receive a 15% discount.

STEVEN SCLAROFF

20th-Century Furniture
801 Greenwich Street; 212-691-7814; info@stevensclaroff.com;
Hours: Mon–Fri 11–7, Sat 12–6; www.stevensclaroff.com;
Credit Cards: MC, Visa, AmEx, Discover; Owner is Steven Sclaroff

Price: Personnel:

Ambiance: Quality:

Steven Sclaroff is a popular, casual, and down-to-earth shop. Carrying lots of mid-20th-century pieces, this is a store that designers would love. There are interesting accessories, amazing lamps, and a wide range of furniture pieces, some expensive and unusual and the rest more like a high-end flea market. Designers get a 20% discount. The Web site shows pictures, gives descriptions and prices.

BECA

Antique and Vintage Rustic Furniture
37A Bedford Street; 212-414-2684; lizashermanli@aol.com;
Hours: Mon–Fri 11–7; www.lizashermanantiques.com;
Credit Cards: MC, Visa, AmEx; Owner is Liza Sherman

Price: Personnel:

Ambiance: Quality:

Beca is a shop you can't miss with its fun, mustard-colored façade. The flagship shop is in Sag Harbor, New York. This location opened recently. Beca is the only store I have seen in this neighborhood that has antique and vintage rustic furniture and accessories—maybe that is why I like it so much. There is also a nice selection of vintage outdoor furniture and accessories. The shop is very small, and most of the inventory is in books that you can peruse. Designer discounts vary. The Web site is nice, showing pictures, dimensions, and prices.

Tribeca

Tribeca has many interesting furniture shops. An up-and-coming neighborhood that feels intimate and quiet compared with other Manhattan neighborhoods Tribeca is a charming area to roam by foot and easy to get to by the subway. I enjoy finding all of the treasures this neighborhood has to offer.

DUANE ANTIQUES AND INTERIORS

Mid-Century Modern Furniture and Accessories
176 Duane Street; 212-625-8066; duaneantiques@aol.com;
Hours: Mon–Fri 11–6, Sat 12–6; www.duaneantiques.com;
Credit Cards: MC, Visa, AmEx; Owners are Bruce Glickman
and Wilson Henley

Price: Personnel:
Ambiance: Quality:

Duane Antiques and Interiors sells some gorgeous one-of-a-kind Mid-Century Modern pieces. I like the fact that the owners have tried hard to find furniture made of unusual materials. The shop is casual, not stuffy, and not everything is perfect here. I especially like the selection of tables. Most of the inventory is priced between $2,000 and $5,000, but the selection is nice. Designers receive a 20% discount. The Web site is well done, showing pictures and descriptions but no prices.

MONDO CANE

20th-Century Furniture and Accessories
174 Duane Street; 212-219-9244; mc@mondomodern.com;
Hours: Mon–Fri 11–6, Sat 12–6; www.mondomodern.com;
Credit Cards: MC, Visa, AmEx; Owners are Patrick Parrish
and Greg Wooten

Price: Personnel:

Ambiance: Quality:

Mondo Cane has an excellent, beautiful selection of furniture from the 1930s to 1960s. The furniture comes from all around the world. The store moved here recently from Chelsea and has two spacious, elegant floors there. Designers come from all over to seek out special treasures. There are unique sculptures and works of art. Designers receive a 15% discount. I love the Web site , which has pictures, descriptions, and prices, not to mention many categories. Well worth a visit.

BURDEN & IZETT, LTD.

Eclectic Antiques
180 Duane Street; 212-941-8247; info@burdenandizett.net;
Hours: Mon–Fri 11–6, Sat 12–6; www.burdenandizett.net;
Credit Cards: MC, Visa; Owners are Jonathan Burden
and Ben Izett

Price: Personnel:

Ambiance: Quality:

Burden & Izett carries an eclectic selection of furniture from the 18th century to the present. The shop has some of the most beautiful pieces I have seen in Manhattan. I think the prices are high, though, and do not recommend this shop for anyone other than real collectors. Designers usually receive a 20% discount. The Web site is nice, and includes pictures, descriptions, and prices.

DONZELLA

Mid-Century Modern Furniture

17 White Street; 212-965-8919; donzellaltd@aol.com;

Hours: Mon–Sat 11–6; www.donzella.com; Credit Cards: MC, Visa,

AmEx; Owner is Paul Donzella

Price: [chairs] Personnel: [chairs]

Ambiance: [chairs] Quality: [chairs]

Donzella is recognizable by its yellow signage and black posts in front of the shop. This is a large gallery that has a combination of casual and more formal furniture, mostly from the 1950s to 1970s, although there are some contemporary pieces. Most of the pieces are by well-known Mid-Century designers. The salesperson referred to the look as "Hollywood-designed furniture." There are many one-of-a-kind pieces here. Designers receive a 15% discount. The Web site has pictures of inventory and descriptions but no prices. This is a collector's shop.

JOHNSON & HICKS

Art Deco Furniture and Accessories

100 Hudson Street; 212-966-4242; johnandhicks@aol.com;

Hours: Mon–Sat 11–5; www.johnsonandhicks.com;

Credit Cards: MC, Visa, AmEx; Owner is Lisa Weimer

Price: [chairs] Personnel: [chairs]

Ambiance: [chairs] Quality: [chairs]

Though Johnson & Hicks doesn't have a particularly memorable storefront, the store is as good as any Deco store I have visited around the country. The space is chic, simple, and sparse. It reflects the beautiful woods and lines of the Deco period. The owner shops all of Europe to buy her inventory. Service is excellent and very professional. There is documentation displayed to prove that some of the pieces were designed by well-known designers of the time. While in this shop, peek next door at Urban Archaeology for great lighting. Designers receive a 20% discount. The Web site is not up and running yet.

DUNE

Contemporary Furniture

88 Franklin Street; 212-925-6171; aaron@dune-ny.com;

Hours: Mon–Thu 11–7, Fri 11–5, Sat 11–6; www.dune-ny.com;

Credit Cards: MC, Visa, AmEx, Discover, Diners;

Owner is Aaron Shemtov

Price: 🪑🪑🪑🪑🪑 Personnel: 🪑🪑🪑🪑🪑

Ambiance: 🪑🪑🪑🪑 Quality: 🪑🪑🪑🪑🪑

Dune, a two-story showroom, looks like something out of a science fiction book. The furniture here is all handmade by emerging furniture designers. The look is hip, minimalist, and original. Just about anything here can be custom-made and ordered. There are even many fabric choices available. Personally, I find the atmosphere cold and the furniture expensive. I love some of the design elements and I do like the shelving units available in a variety of finishes. The owner is nice and really service-oriented. Designers (representing a big percentage of the business here) receive a 15% discount. The Web site shows pictures of the inventory.

WHITE ON WHITE

Mid-Century Modern Knockoffs

359 Broadway; 212-966-6711; Hours: Mon–Fri 10–7, Sat 11–7,

Sun 12–5; www.whiteonwhite.com; Credit Cards: MC, Visa;

Owner is Karizina Cinar

Price: 🪑🪑 Personnel: 🪑🪑🪑

Ambiance: 🪑🪑🪑🪑 Quality: 🪑🪑🪑🪑

White On White is a find, especially in New York, where everyone is into the Mid-Century thing. This is a store with knockoffs of the original Mid-Century furniture. This is one of two locations in New York, the other being at 149 Essex Street. I loved the chairs here, which are stacked up the wall. There is not a great deal of ambiance, but the staff is friendly and the prices are right. Nothing costs more than a few hundred dollars. The quality is decent and perfect for a first apartment or bachelor pad. The Web site has pictures, dimensions, prices and color options. You can order furniture online.

Soho

Soho is one of the best furniture neighborhoods in the country. There are upscale designer shops, eclectic furniture stores, and chain stores like Crate & Barrel, Pottery Barn, and Smith and Hawken. Some local favorites of shops that are in other cities include the don't-miss Jonathan Adler store (the Kate Spade of furniture) and Kartell. Unlike the Upper East Side, Soho has no grid system for its streets; you will need a map to get around here. There are wonderful restaurants. Chinatown and Little Italy are nearby. Rent and prices here have gone up considerably in the last decade, but that hasn't prevented the shoppers from making Soho their destination. While you're here, don't miss a little chocolate shop where I took a break, called Kee's Chocolates, on Thompson and Spring (80 Thompson).

GREENE STREET ANTIQUES

Swedish and Danish Biedermeier and Art Deco Furniture
65 Greene Street; 212-274-1076; gstantiques@cs.com;
Hours: Mon–Fri 10–6, Sat, Sun 12–6; www.greenestreetantiques.com;
Credit Cards: MC, Visa, AmEx; Owner is Anessa Rahman

Price: [chairs] Personnel: [chairs]
Ambiance: [chairs] Quality: [chairs]

Greene Street Antiques is one of the few shops in the country specializing in Swedish and Danish Biedermeier and Deco. There are two floors here in this crowded 8,000-square-foot shop. The owner takes great pride in her inventory, which spans from the late 19th century to the 1930s. The furniture here is all wood, much of it birch. Designers receive a 20% discount with purchases over $10,000 and a 15% discount for purchases under $10,000. Restoration services are also available. The Web site has some pictures but no descriptions or prices.

TROY

Contemporary Furniture

138 Greene Street; 646-442-2938; Anthony@troysoho.com;

Hours: Mon–Fri 10–6, Sat 11–6; www.troysoho.com; Credit Cards:

MC, Visa, AmEx, Discover; Owner is Troy Halterman

Price: Personnel:

Ambiance: Quality:

Looking more like an art gallery than a furniture store, Troy has a strong following and the shop is often busy. There are vivid colors on the furniture and red walls. Much of the furniture is reproduced from 20th-century classics from designers like Fritz Hansen. There are no price tags and the prices are high. Salespeople sit behind a wall (I don't understand that), but are available to answer any questions. There are some innovative features on the furniture, like vinyl slipcovers for sofas. I like the chairs best of all, wonderful for a kitchen or dining room. The Web site shows pictures and gives descriptions but no prices. Much of the clientele here is commercial.

MOSS

Housewares, Accessories, and Some

Contemporary Furniture

146 Green Street; 212-204-7100; info@mossonline.com;

Hours: Mon–Sat 11–7, Sun 12–6; www.mossonline.com;

Credit Cards: MC, Visa, AmEx, Discover; Owner is Murray Moss

Price: Personnel:

Ambiance: Quality:

Moss is a home store on three floors. There isn't necessarily a concentration of any one type of home essential, but all kinds of people shop here, from young to old. They have a bridal registry with a wide variety of dishes, serving pieces, and utensils, not to mention a great selection of kitchen chairs (not cheap—they can cost $500 and up apiece), pots and pans, gadgets, and art. Moss has a nice selection of jewelry and dollhouse miniatures. The atmosphere is rather cold, with much of the inventory behind plastic casing units like sculptures at a museum. There is even a sign at the door saying, "Children must be held." (That sign would eliminate many of my friends and me.) Many of these pieces are designed by artists, with their bios attached. I had to spend a lot of time finding help on my visit there, but the salespeople generally seemed good. Designer discounts vary. The Web site shows pictures and gives dimensions and pricing. You can even buy online.

GALERIE DE BEYRIE

French Designer Furniture from the 1940s and '50s
393 West Broadway; 212-219-9565; debeyrie@interport.net;
Hours: Mon–Fri 1–6; www.galeriedebeyrie.com; Credit Cards: N/A;
Owners are Catherine and Stephane De Beyrie

Price: Personnel:

Ambiance: Quality:

I was intrigued by this shop. Most of the furniture here was designed by Jean Royere, using simple, classic lines and lighter woods. The furniture of this period was meant to be functional, and it is. There are no price tags, and in fact, this doesn't feel like a store at all, being the De Beyries' apartment. When I stepped off the elevator, which opens onto the apartment, I thought I was in the wrong place at first. Most of the business is to the trade and prices are high. The Web site is not yet complete.

BDDW

Custom, Handmade Wood Furniture
5 Crosby Street; info@bddw.com; Hours: Mon–Fri 10–7,
Sat 12–6; www.bddw.com; Credit Cards: MC, Visa, AmEx;
Owner is Tyler Hays

Price: Personnel:

Ambiance: Quality:

BDDW has beautiful, many of them Asian-inspired, pieces of furniture made from all kinds of exotic woods. Many of the wood pieces are surrounded in a lacquered frame. The look is stunning! The furniture is a little rustic, a little contemporary, and features exquisite handwork and detailing. There are no price tags and the prices are extremely high, but the furniture is truly one-of-a-kind. There is a 15% designer discount. The Web site is not yet complete.

AERO, LTD.

Contemporary and Vintage Furniture and Accessories
419 Broome Street; 212-966-1500; dmiller@aerostudios.com;
Hours: Mon–Sat 11–6; www.aerostudios.com; Credit Cards: MC, Visa, AmEx; Owner is Thomas O'Brien

Price: 🪑🪑🪑🪑🪑 Personnel: 🪑🪑🪑🪑🪑

Ambiance: 🪑🪑🪑🪑🪑 Quality: 🪑🪑🪑🪑🪑

Aero has become one of New York's favorite furniture spots. Thomas O'Brien, interior designer and furniture designer, has accomplished so much with this business. Hickory is now selling O'Brien's traditionally inspired line, much of which is wood, and he has been featured in many design magazines. The two-story store has something for just about everyone and in a variety of price ranges. I love all of the vintage pieces here as well. O'Brien is featuring in his store his own collection of tabletops and bedding. Designers receive a 10% discount on accessories and lighting, 30% off on furniture and 10% off the vintage pieces. The Web site is not yet complete.

AIX INTERIORS

Mostly French Antiques, Modern Furniture, and Accessories
462 Broome Street; 212-941-7919; aix@nyc.rr.com;
Hours: Mon–Sat 11–7; www.aixnewyork.com; Credit Cards: MC, Visa, AmEx, Discover; Owner is Herve Rossano

Price: 🪑🪑🪑🪑🪑 Personnel: 🪑🪑🪑

Ambiance: Quality:

Aix Interiors has a special selection of French and Italian antiques and modern furniture. There is a variety of prices, but most of the furniture is highly unusual and expensive. I love the selection of the French tables from the 1940s and the Venetian lamps; also the original leathers and other wonderful fabrics that cover the seating. Designers get a 15% discount. The Web site shows inventory and gives descriptions and some prices.

BOCA GRANDE

Primitive and Contemporary Furniture and Accessories
54 and 66 Greene Street; 212-334-6120; Hours: Daily 11–7;
www.bocagrandefurnishings.com; Credit Cards: MC, Visa, AmEx;
Owner is Marcello Duek

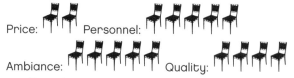

Price: Personnel:

Ambiance: Quality:

Boca Grande has been very successful in its 17 years here. There are three stores in the neighborhood, those on Greene Street selling primitive furniture and contemporary design; the third sells jewelry. Much of the furniture is Indian-inspired designs. Prices are reasonable and the atmosphere is very relaxed and inviting. There are many pieces under $500. This definitely seems like a neighborhood stop. I recommend Boca Grande for anybody who wants a fashionable pad that doesn't require a second mortgage. The Web site offers pictures and descriptions but no prices. Designers get 15% off or the sale price, whichever is lower.

ALICE'S ANTIQUES

Antique and Vintage Beds
72 Greene Street; 212-966-6867; mduek@yahoo.com;
Hours: Daily 12–7; www.alicesantiques.com; Credit Cards: MC, Visa,
AmEx, Discover; Owner is Derrick Hemingway

Price: Personnel:

Ambiance:  Quality:

Alice's Antiques has a huge selection of antique (Victorian) and vintage beds in any style, along with other odd pieces of furniture, spread out on three floors of this ornate, old cream-colored building. The business has been around for 30 years. The owner, a casual sort of guy (a character), definitely takes pride in his inventory and has been written up in many design magazines. Several TV shows and businesses have rented props from Alice's, including "Sex and the City" and Louis Vuitton. The entire inventory comes from Europe. Designer discounts vary depending on quantity purchased. They make their own chandeliers, and there is a nice selection of traditional-style lighting fixtures in all price ranges. I was not able to pull up the Web site .

WYETH

Early to Mid-20th-Century Furniture
315 Spring Street; info@wyethhome.com;
Hours: Mon–Fri 11–6 "by appointment"; Credit Cards: MC, Visa,
AmEx; Owner is John Birch

Price:  Personnel:

Ambiance: Quality:

Wyeth is a store that has special well-known designer pieces from the early to mid-20th century. The furniture comes from all over the world. You will not be allowed in without a designer or without an appointment. Prices are high, and on my visit I had an extremely unpleasant service experience. Designers get a 15% discount. I especially like the light fixtures, but even they look pretty dim in light of the attitude and hassle.

TODD HASE

Contemporary and Vintage Furniture
261 Spring Street; 212-871-9075; anthony@toddhase.com;
Hours: Mon–Fri 10–6, Sat, Sun 12–5; www.toddhase.com;
Credit Cards: MC, Visa, AmEx; Owner is Todd Hase

Price: ▮▮▮▮▮   Personnel: ▮▮▮▮▮▮
Ambiance: ▮▮▮▮▮▮   Quality: ▮▮▮▮▮▮

I recommend that you stop in and take a peek at this very recently opened and very simple, elegant-looking shop. Todd Hase has designed an entire innovative line of pieces which have won him a lot of positive press lately. There are nice sofas with clean lines that look a little like Mitchell Gold but are a little more stylish and shapely, as well as some vintage pieces worth writing home about. There are also some very simple case goods, like tables and chests. Unlike Todd Hase's other stores, this is the only one not located in a design center. Designers receive a net price, and there is no discounting on vintage items. The atmosphere is relaxed and the service is good. There is no attitude here. The Web site offers pictures and some prices.

JACQUES CARCANAGUES, INC.

Antique and Contemporary Asian Furniture and Artifacts
21 Greene Street; 212-925-8110; carcan@rcn.com;
Hours: Daily 11:30–7; www.jacquescarcanagues.com;
Credit Cards: MC, Visa, AmEx, Discover, Diners Club;
Owner is Jacques Carcanagues

Price: ▮▮▮▮▮   Personnel: ▮▮▮▮▮▮
Ambiance: ▮▮▮▮▮▮   Quality: ▮▮▮▮▮

A 35-year veteran in this neighborhood and recently with a new address, Jacques Carcanagues is a special place with people coming from all over the world just to see its unique inventory of mostly Asian furniture and artifacts. The pieces are imported from Korea, Japan, Thailand, India, and China, as well as a few other Asian countries. Check out the selection of antique chests, in particular. The inventory is very unusual and well designed, and there is a wide range of prices. The store is crowded and a popular Soho hangout. Designers receive a 20% discount if paying by cash/check and a 15% discount if paying by credit card. The Web site is being developed.

MoMA DESIGN STORE, SOHO

Contemporary Furniture, Housewares, and Books
81 Spring Street; 646-613-1367; info@moma.org;
Hours: Mon–Sat 11–8, Sun 11–7; www.momastore.org;
Credit Cards: MC, Visa, AmEx, Discover, Diners;
Owner is the Museum of Modern Art

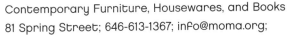

Price: 🪑🪑🪑 Personnel: 🪑🪑🪑🪑

Ambiance: 🪑🪑🪑🪑 Quality: 🪑🪑🪑🪑🪑

If you need to pick up a quick gift, stop in at MoMA Design Store. This not-to-be-missed busy shop specializes in everything for the home, including a nice book selection, kids' toys, furniture, accessories, and other unusual items. Most of the inventory isn't cheap, but there is something here for everyone spread out on two floors. The downstairs level has some wonderful pieces of furniture, mostly reproductions of Danish Modern classics, but also some contemporary styles. The other gallery is at the MoMA in Midtown. It is possible to shop online. Well worth a trip.

C.I.T.E.

Vintage and Contemporary Furniture
and Accessories; Interior Design
120 Wooster Street; 212-431-7272; citehome@cite-design.com;
Hours: Mon–Sat 11–7, Sun 12–6; www.cite-design.com;
Credit Cards: MC, Visa, AmEx; Owner is Caslyn Industries

Price: 🪑🪑🪑🪑 Personnel: 🪑🪑🪑

Ambiance: 🪑🪑🪑🪑 Quality: 🪑🪑🪑🪑

C.I.T.E. is a nice shop that is an offshoot of a design business. There are some unique pieces here along with some mid-20th-century accessories and a selection of lamps. One thing I found annoying was the signage plastered around the place asking people not to sit on the chairs, as if the designers did not make the chairs for people to actually use. The Web site has some pictures of inventory, descriptions, and prices.

KING'S ROAD HOME

Rustic, Contemporary Furniture
42 Wooster Street; 212-941-5011; Hours: Mon–Sat 11–7, Sun 12–6;
www.kingsroadhome.com; Credit Cards: MC, Visa, AmEx, Discover,
Diners; Owners are Christian Carlsen and John Palmer

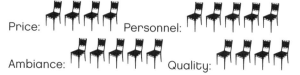

Price: Personnel: Ambiance: Quality:

King's Road Home is one of the few rustic shops in Soho. With bamboo chests and benches covered in cork, I would sum up the shop as "Rustic meets urban." It has some unusual pieces, and a range of prices. The space is large, and the upholstered goods are displayed well; they can be customized, too. One neat thing about the place is that its furniture is touted as being ecological. If you are concerned about the environment or prone to allergies and asthma, this could be a great place to check out. The owners have a flair for design and began their career in fashion. Designers get a 10% discount. The Web site is not fully up and running.

DISTANT ORIGIN

Art Deco and Deco-Style Furniture and Accessories
153 Mercer Street; 212-941-0024; info@distantorigin.com;
Hours: Mon, Tue, Wed, Fri 11–6:30, Thu, Sat 11–7, Sun 11:30–6;
www.distantorigin.com; Credit Cards: MC, Visa, AmEx;
Owners are Alex and Julio Hernandez

Price: Personnel: Ambiance: Quality:

If you like stores where exotic adventures in shopping await you in every nook and cranny, Distant Origin is a store I recommend you visit. With inventory from around the world, there are many wild and unique pieces, like ostrich-covered tables and tables with sharkskin or parchment coverings, and unusual accessories. I liked the side tables and fur blankets. There is also a large selection of Fortuny light fixtures from Italy. As a whole I found the inventory fabulous, especially the wonderful reproductions of Art Deco furniture. I don't feel that the prices are too high compared with other stores in the neighborhood. Designers receive a 10% discount on furniture. The Web site shows pictures of pieces with descriptions and also gives bios of all of their artists who design their furniture and accessories. Well worth a visit.

Brooklyn

Brooklyn is worth visiting if you are a New Yorker tired of paying Manhattan prices for home furnishings. I like the eclectic little shops along Atlantic Avenue, as well as some of the nice cafés and bakeries. I recommend the following shops: **City Foundry** (eclectic 20th-century furniture and accessories at great prices), **Darr**, and **Nest**. These are some of the cute neighborhood shops specializing in furniture and home décor.

NEW YORK AUCTION HOUSES

Up-to-date listings of upcoming auctions and antiques shows are published in each issue of *The New Yorker*

Christie's
20 Rockefeller Plaza
212-636-2000

William Doyle
175 East 87th Street
212-427-2730

Sotheby's
1334 York Avenue
212-606-7000

NEW YORK ANTIQUES SHOWS

Antiques at the Armory
January
69th Regiment Armory
Lexington Avenue at 26th Street
212-255-0020

Modernism: A Century of Art and Design
November
7th Regiment Armory
Park Avenue at 67th Street
212-777-5218

Gramercy Park Antiques Show
October
69th Regiment Armory
Lexington Avenue at 26th Street
212-255-0020

The Modern Show
February
69th Regiment Armory
Lexington Avenue at 26th Street
212-255-0020

The Pier Antiques Show
February
Passenger Ship Terminal Piers
48th to 55th Street and 12th Avenue
212-255-0020

Triple Pier Antiques Show

November
Passenger Hip Terminal Piers 88/90/92
12th Avenue between 48th and 55th Streets
212-255-0020

NEW YORK FLEA MARKETS

Chelsea Flea Market

Every weekend, outdoors
110 West 25th Street (6th Avenue)
212-929-0909

The Green Flea Market

Every Sunday
Schoolyard at Columbus Avenue and 77th Street
212-721-0900

CHAPTER 12

New Orleans

Steamy, sultry New Orleans, with its long and colorful history of French, English, Spanish, African, and Haitian influences, has evolved into an exciting cultural hotbed that seems more like its own exotic little country than just another city in the U.S. There is so much to see, taste, and smell in this city made famous by its Mardi Gras, famed French Quarter, world-renowned jazz clubs, fragrant jasmine blossoms, and fabulous cuisine, including the best in Creole and Cajun "cookin'." If your dream is to bring back a little flavor from this intoxicating place, you're in luck, because New Orleans is a wonderful furniture hot spot to explore.

New Orleans' best furniture districts, spilling over with a bounty of antique stores and only a few modern furniture stores, are quite compact. The best furniture finds (mostly French and English antiques) are located in two neighborhoods: the French Quarter and the Garden District. In the French Quarter, the furniture stores are concentrated on Royal Street and Chartres Street. The Garden District hot spot is Magazine Street, a long street with nearly 13 blocks of antiques stores scattered throughout the block. While walking the streets of the charming French Quarter is a wonderful way to spend a day, you will definitely need a car or taxi to cover the length of Magazine Street.

NEW ORLEANS RETAIL STORES

The French Quarter

The French Quarter, though very touristy, is home to famous Bourbon Street and some of the best jazz clubs and restaurants in the country. A charming neighborhood with colorfully painted buildings and a lot of action, The Quarter contains several antiques shops that are easy to visit on foot.

MOSS ANTIQUES, INC.

French and English Antiques

411 Royal Street; 504-522-3981; Hours: Mon–Sat 9–5;

Credit Cards: MC, Visa, AmEx; Owner is Keil Moss with others

Price: Personnel:

Ambiance: Quality:

    Moss Antiques, one of the oldest shops on Royal Street, is run by the fifth generation in the Moss family. This shop's history is far more interesting than the inventory, which, although not particularly unique, does have a nice selection of French and English pieces. The first generation of Moss who owned this store actually helped found many of the original shops of Royal Street. There are no set discounts here.

IDA MANHEIM ANTIQUES

English, French, and Dutch Antiques

409 Royal Street; 504-620-4114; ida@idamanheimantiques.com;

Hours: Mon–Sat 9–5; www.idamanheimantiques.com;

Credit Cards: MC, Visa, AmEx; Owner is Ida Manheim

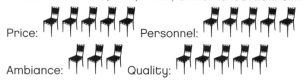

Price: Personnel:

Ambiance: Quality:

    A store that makes you feel a little like you are shopping in an expensive car dealership, Manheim Antiques is a large New Orleans establishment. As I browsed the shop alone, I felt intimidated by the help who seemed to be trying to determine if I were a serious buyer. The furniture is fancy and formal. The entire inventory comes from Europe, the specialty here being English, French, and Dutch furniture. Prices are extremely high here compared to other shops around the country with similar merchandise. The Web site has classical music in the background and fancy pictures but no prices. Now in its third generation, the business was founded by Ida Manheim's grandfather in 1919. Designers receive a 20% discount.

WALDHORN & ADLER

English and French Antiques/Jewelry
343 Royal Street; 504-581-6379 or 800-925-7912;
Hours: Mon–Sat 10–5; www.waldhornadlers.com;
Credit Cards: MC, Visa, AmEx; Owner is Coleman Adler

Price: 🪑🪑🪑🪑 Personnel: 🪑🪑🪑🪑🪑

Ambiance: 🪑🪑🪑🪑 Quality: 🪑🪑🪑

The service is wonderful at this well-established New Orleans antiques and jewelry store. The store is on two floors, and the furniture is mostly English and French Provincial antiques. If you are in the market for an armoire, this is the place to shop. Designers receive a 20% discount. The Web site is not finished yet. The entire inventory comes from Europe.

HURWITZ MINTZ

General Furniture Store
211 Royal Street; 504-568-9555; hmu@hurwitzmintz.com;
Hours: Mon, Wed 10–9, Tue, Thurs, Fri 10–6, Sat 10–8;
www.hurwitzmintz.com; Credit Cards: MC, Visa;
Owner is the Mintz Family

Price: 🪑🪑🪑 Personnel: 🪑🪑🪑🪑🪑

Ambiance: 🪑🪑🪑🪑 Quality: 🪑🪑🪑

At the end of Royal Street, Hurwitz Mintz has been in business 81 years. Like many of New Orleans' furniture shops, the store has an excellent reputation for service and most people in town have shopped here. Hurwitz Mintz sells decent reproduction furniture in a wide variety of furniture lines. The Mintz family has two locations in the French Quarter, the other store being Margaret Gregoire which specializes in contemporary furniture. Famous lines here at Hurwitz Mintz include Henredon, Drexel, Heritage and Century. Hurwitz Mintz ships worldwide. The Web site has a lot of pictures but no prices. You cannot purchase online.

FRENCH ANTIQUE SHOP, INC.

French Antiques and Chandeliers

225 Royal Street; 504-524-9861 or 866-524-9861;

info@gofrenchantiques.com; Hours: Mon–Fri 9–5, Sat 9–4:30;

www.gofrenchantiques.com; Credit Cards: MC, Visa, AmEx;

Owner is the Granet Family

Price: Personnel:

Ambiance: Quality:

Even though this shop is extremely expensive and the furniture a bit fancy, I love to come here and browse. Henry Granet, the owner, is always at the store and readily available to answer any questions. The store has a national reputation for carrying exquisite antique French furniture and has been in business since 1939. This being said, each of the several floors is painfully quiet, and to go up you need to be escorted by an employee in a large freight elevator. This can make even the most confident person feel a little nervous. Much of the furniture is gilded, and there are antique chandeliers everywhere. Designers receive a 25% discount. The Web site has many pictures and descriptions but no prices.

ROYAL ANTIQUES

English and French Antiques

309 Royal Street; 504-524-7033;

royalant@bellsouth.net; Hours: Mon–Sat 9–5;
www.royalantiques.com; Credit Cards: MC, Visa, AmEx;
Owner is the Shapiro Family

Price: Personnel:

Ambiance: Quality:

I love coming to Royal Antiques, one of my favorite shops in New Orleans. Nanette and Lester Shapiro have taken a 10,000-square-foot space and made it feel homey. Lester's claim to fame is that he was a world-class tennis player who competed in Wimbledon years ago. Their children, Neil and Leslee, are also very involved in this family business, which has been here since 1899. The merchandise is a nice mix of antiques, and the inventory is practical and simple, with many French Provincial pieces and 19th-century English. Royal Antiques also has a wonderful selection of antique jewelry. Prices are reasonable compared with other shops carrying similar inventory. Designers receive a 20% discount. The Web site is complete, but you cannot buy online.

KEIL'S ANTIQUES, INC.

European Antiques
325 Royal Street; 504-522-4552; Hours: Mon–Sat 9–5; Credit
Cards: MC, Visa, AmEx; Owner is a family (now a corporation)

Price: Personnel:

Ambiance: Quality:

Keil's is another Royal Street monument. The shop has been at the same location for over 100 years and has several floors, like many of the other stores on the block. The owners of Keil's and Royal Antiques are related but there is no business connection. Keil's probably has the most interesting selection of antique jewelry in New Orleans. Their furniture is traditional but not particularly unusual. The shop is big and can feel overwhelming when no help is around.

M.S. RAU ANTIQUES

European Antiques and Accessories
630 Royal Street; 504-523-5660 or 800-544-9440;
info@rauantiques.com; Hours: Mon–Sat 9–5;
www.rauantiques.com; Credit Cards: MC, Visa, AmEx, Diners Club,
Discover; Owner is William Rau

Price: 🪑🪑🪑🪑🪑🪑 Personnel: 🪑🪑🪑🪑

Ambiance: 🪑🪑🪑 Quality: 🪑🪑🪑🪑🪑

M.S. Rau is a touristy, old-line New Orleans antiques shop. Located next door to a psychic shop on Royal Street, a few blocks away from where the bulk of the antiques stores are. This store has been in business since 1912 and has stayed in the family. I was immediately greeted by a security guard upon entering, facing many cabinets of silver and other collectible objects. The shop has 30,000 square feet and 32 employees, making this store one of the largest establishments in New Orleans. Classical music plays in the background, and the store has a formal feel with many rooms. One drawback to shopping here is that price tags are hidden in various places on the furniture. You really must bend down, twist, and turn to find the price tag. This is done intentionally, and I am not sure why. In the back is a very fancy "private" room that you have to be escorted to, where they keep museum-quality pieces, including some that supposedly came from places like Windsor Castle, or so they say. Designers receive a 20% discount, and some discounting is available to the public. Prices are unbelievably high compared with those of other stores selling similar merchandise. The Web site is attractive and offers the chance to buy online.

WHISNANT GALLERIES

Unusual Eclectic Antique Furniture and Accessories
222 Chartres Street; 504-524-9766;
info@whisnantgalleries.com; Hours: Daily 9:30–5:30;
www.whisnantgalleries.com; Credit Cards: MC, Visa, AmEx;
Owner is the Whisnant Family

Price: Personnel: Ambiance: Quality:

Whisnant Galleries is a fun store to browse for those who are not looking for anything special but just want a wild shopping experience. I still can't figure out what Whisnant specializes in, but I like the fact that the owners like to stock whatever they see that interests them. Many of the items are conversation pieces; as I looked around, I'd think, "Where would I put this thing?" There is an impressive selection of tribal art, jewelry, animal objects, rifles, and oversized furniture pieces. I think the store is overpriced, but perhaps the high prices reflect the uniqueness of the inventory. You can browse their Web site and even see prices, but you can't buy online. Designers receive a 15–20% discount, depending on the piece. Others may also receive discounts sometimes. Excellent service and laid-back atmosphere make shopping here a worthwhile experience.

Garden District (Magazine Street)

Magazine Street has traditionally been known as an out-of-the-way place to find antiques without the high French Quarter prices. However, in the past five years, Magazine Street has become more expensive and its prices now closely match that of many of the stores in the French Quarter. Spanning over six miles, Magazine Street has many newly rehabbed homes and also boasts wonderful restaurants, many of which have opened in the past five years as the neighborhood has undergone a notable transformation. You will also, however, still see plenty of the traditional beauty of Magazine Street in its many older charming painted cottages and stunning plantation-style homes.

BUSH ANTIQUES
Antique Beds, Furniture, and Accessories
2109–2111 Magazine Street; 504-581-3518;
Hours: Mon–Sat 10–5; www.bushantiques.com;
Credit Cards: MC, Visa, AmEx, Discover; Owner is Allain Bush

Price: Personnel: Ambiance: Quality:

Bush Antiques stands apart from any store in this city. Allain Bush and her family, who have been in this business for over 30 years, acquire much of their inventory from France and some directly from homes in New Orleans. The store has a relaxed, rustic, shabby-chic atmosphere like much of the old city that you will love getting lost in. It specializes in beautiful French antique beds and has two floors devoted to a wide variety of Continental furniture, flea market finds (or so they appear to be), Christian art, unusual vintage lighting, and architectural ornaments. I enjoyed talking with Allain Bush, who is an extremely personable and friendly woman. Clearly she is very proud of her store and rightly so. Prices are not low, but you're sure to find some one-of-a-kind pieces. Most items cost over $1,000. Discounts vary and depend on the item.

KEVIN STONE ANTIQUES

European Antiques

3420 Magazine Street; 504-458-7043; ksantiquer@aol.com;

Hours: Mon–Sat 11–5; Credit Cards: MC, Visa, AmEx, Discover;

Owners are Mark Diamond and Kevin Stone

Price: Personnel: Ambiance: Quality:

Kevin Stone and Mark Diamond just opened this great store, once occupied by Empire Antiques. Specializing in eclectic European furniture, they have many unusual pieces. Most of their business is to the trade. Designers receive a 20% discount, and others can negotiate at times, too. These two owners are extremely friendly and helpful.

ST. GERTRUDE

French Antiques

3424 Magazine Street; 504-897-9258; jill@stgertrude.com;

Hours: Mon–Sat 10–5; www.stgertrude.com; Credit cards: MC, Visa, AmEx; Owner is Jill Stoutz

Price:  Personnel:

Ambiance: Quality:

St. Gertrude is a lovely store in an old house that used to be occupied by French Antiques. Most of the inventory is from France, and there is a small home accessories area in the back of the store. My general feeling about St. Gertrude is that the furniture is overpriced for what it is, but they do offer a 10% discount to designers. While they do not offer a large selection of furniture, the pieces they do have a quite pretty and definitely authentic. The Web site allows you to buy online and lists the prices.

MAISON de PROVENCE

French Antiques

3434 Magazine Street; 504-895-2301; Hours: Mon–Sat 10:30–4:30; www.maisondeprovence.com; Credit Cards: MC, Visa, AmEx; Owner is Terri Goldsmith

Price:  Personnel:

Ambiance: Quality:

I adored the lively French music I heard as I opened the door to this shop. Just as appealing as the music is the shop's calm atmosphere, along with its inventory of furniture which mostly resembles expensive shabby-chic French, Swedish, and Italian antiques with a rustic flair. I found the staff friendly and helpful. Prices are high, even though they offer a 15% designer discount. The Web site is user-friendly with pictures of their inventory, although prices are not disclosed.

P.W. ROSENTHAL ANTIQUES

Unusual French Antiques and Accessories

3506 Magazine Street; 504-899-2668; pwrantiques@4isp.net; Hours: Mon–Sat 10–5; Credit Cards: MC, Visa, Discover, AmEx; Owners are Sarah and Paul Rosenthal

Price: | Personnel: | Ambiance: | Quality:

This store overflows with a laid-back personality, from the owners to the help. I was pleasantly surprised by its most unusual selection of French antiques and accessories. High ceilings, rickety wooden floors, and rustic pieces personify Rosenthal Antiques. There are many rooms to browse in this pleasantly relaxed and warm atmosphere. Designers receive a 20% discount, and there may be some negotiating possible for those not in the trade.

SHABBY SLIPS

Danish, French, and Swedish Antiques
3522 Magazine Street; 504-897-897-5477
or 888-549-4637; cell 504-723-2409; shabslip@bellsouth.net;
Hours: Mon–Sat 10–5; Credit Cards: MC, Visa, AmEx;
Owner is Petricia Thompson

Price: | Personnel: | Ambiance: | Quality:

Shabby not! I both loved and admired this gutsy furniture store, one of my favorites in New Orleans. Not afraid to break out from the pack of French furniture shops here, Shabby Slips is anything but shabby or ordinary. Specializing in unique Danish, French, and fabulous 18th-century Swedish antiques, Shabby Slips also offers a slipcovering service. The name, Shabby Slips, refers to the slipcovering side of the business. With white walls, large but delicate chandeliers, and romantic French music playing in the background, the store has a pleasant atmosphere, and the owner, Petricia Thompson, is everything a store owner should be: friendly and helpful. Designers receive a 20% discount and 10% discount on slipcovers. All furniture comes from Europe. Prices are high, but the selection of 18th- and 19th-century furniture from Sweden, in particular, is unusual and carefully assembled in the store.

EMPIRE ANTIQUES

French Empire Antiques
3617 Magazine Street; 504-897-0252; empantiq@bellsouth.net;
Hours: Mon–Sat 10–4; www.empireantiques.net; Credit Cards: MC,
Visa; Owners are Nancy Napoli and Lois Comeaux

Price: Personnel:

Ambiance: Quality:

Empire Antiques, one of the oldest stores on Magazine Street, has moved to a new and much larger space after its original location was destroyed in a fire. If you are interested in period French furniture (18th and 19th century), you will have a field day at Empire Antiques. Note that prices are extremely high relative to other stores with similar merchandise, but designers are eligible for a 20% discount; discounts are also available periodically for the public. Service is fair compared with other shops in the neighborhood. The Web site is extremely user-friendly, giving descriptions, pictures, and prices.

CATHERINE COTTRELL

18th- and 19th-Century Antiques; Interior Design
3638 Magazine Street; 504-895-5511; ctccid@aol.com;
Hours: Mon–Sat 10–5; Credit Cards: MC, Visa;
Owner is Catherine Cottrell

Price: Personnel:

Ambiance: Quality:

Catherine Cottrell, a former New York City ballet dancer, has put her mark on everything in this lovely store, from the dramatic red-painted entry to its small collection of European antiques. Cottrell, who works mostly as an interior designer traveling between New York and New Orleans, carries many specialty painted furniture pieces from Europe in her shop. Designers receive a 20% discount on the expensive collection. I think the selection is nice, and there are some unique accessories here.

WIRTHMORE ANTIQUES

Mostly French Provincial Antiques

3727 Magazine Street (504-269-0660), 3900 Magazine Street (504-899-3811); wirthmore@mindspring.com; Hours: Mon–Sat 10–5; www.wirthmoreantiques.com; Credit Cards: MC, Visa, AmEx; Owner is Gay Wirth

Price: Personnel:

Ambiance: Quality:

I walked into this corner shop (3727 Magazine Street) and suddenly found myself transposed to a small shop in the countryside of France. The smell of wax is heavy in the air, and most furniture is French Provincial (turn of the 19th century), although I saw some Italian pieces, too. Prices are high, though discounts are available (the store clerk wouldn't reveal the actual discounts to the trade or public). There are two locations, with the other being just up the block on Magazine Street. The Web site has pictures of the inventory but no prices. I think service could be improved here.

UPTOWNER

18th–19th-Century French and Italian Antique Furniture and Accessories

3828 Magazine Street; 504-891-7700; uptowner@bellsouth.net; Hours: Mon–Sat 10–5; Credit Cards: MC, Visa; Owners are Roslyn and James Schneider

Price: Personnel:

Ambiance: Quality:

Uptowner is a charming store with a great mixture of formal and casual traditional furniture. On the day I visited, I noticed how carefully selected the inventory was, with service to match. Located in a large building with several rooms, the store has been in New Orleans for the past 10 years. The shop is as inviting as the classical music it plays, and provides a relaxing shopping experience. The owner spent a lot of time with me explaining how and where he gets his inventory (all of it comes from Italy and France). The Schneiders have another location up the street with similar merchandise. Discounts to designers and the public are possible.

BREMERMANN DESIGNS

European (Mostly French) Antiques; Interior Design
3943 Magazine Street; 504-891-7763;
bremdes@bellsouth.net; Hours: Mon–Fri 9:30–5, Sat 10–5;
www.bremermanndesigns.com; Credit Cards: MC, Visa, AmEx;
Owner is Gerrie Bremermann

Price: Personnel:

Ambiance: Quality:

I've had a love affair with Bremermann Designs since the time I first visited this store eight years ago. Located in an old white house with a beautifully landscaped small front garden, the store is welcoming. Pricey it is, and sometimes pricier than its competition, but the help is friendly and knowledgeable. I think an added bonus is the great artwork available. Much of the artwork is modern, blending well with all the antiques. There are some modern pieces of furniture here, too. There are four rooms off the hallway, each with a different motif. Designers receive a 20% discount on antiques and a 10% discount on new furniture and art-work. The Web site is attractive, and prices are listed.

MAC MAISON, LTD.

Italian, French, and Swedish Antiques and Accessories
3963 Magazine Street; 504-891-2863; macmaison@bellsouth.net;
Hours: Mon–Sat 10–5; Credit Cards: MC, Visa (3% surcharge
added to use credit cards); Owner is Michael Carbine

Price: Personnel:

Ambiance: Quality:

In business for over 12 years, Mac Maison is a household name in the New Orleans furniture district. The store is a big, dark, rather eerie-looking warehouse filled with unusual objects everywhere you look. There is a great supply of architectural elements and lighting. Not much has changed here over the past decade, but the inventory stays interesting. Designers receive a 20% discount, and the public may sometimes receive a discount, depending on the piece. The entire inventory comes from Europe.

KARLA KATZ

Unusual French and Italian Antiques
4017 Magazine Street; 504-897-0061;
karlakatzco@aol.com; Hours: Mon–Sat 10–5;
Credit Cards: MC, Visa, AmEx; Owner is Karla Katz

Price: Personnel:

Ambiance: Quality:

Light, airy, and newly expanded, Karla Katz is a French antiques store with a modern feel. I enjoy looking at the inventory, most of which is French and Italian. Karla, who has been at this location for nine years, is known around town for her flair for finding unusual pieces and her decorating talents. The majority of her time is spent designing large neighborhood homes. This shop also has an impressive selection of vintage light fixtures. All of the furniture comes directly from France and Italy. Prices are high, but the trade receives a 20–30% discount.

JON VACCARI DESIGN

Eclectic Antiques and 1940s Furniture
4858 Magazine Street; 504-899-7632;
info@jonvaccaridesign.com; Hours: Mon–Fri 10–5, Sat 11–5;
www.jonvaccaridesign.com; Credit Cards: MC, Visa, AmEx;
Owner is Jon Vaccari

Price: Personnel:

Ambiance: Quality:

Jon Vaccari, perhaps one of the most unique shops in New Orleans, carries an eclectic mix of furniture from the 18th and 19th centuries along with the most unusual 20th-century furniture collection from the 1940s. The result of mixing old with new in this treasure chest gives the shop a dynamic and elegant look that fits well with today's society. The store has been well received in both New Orleans and in the rest of the country. Designers receive a 10% discount. The Web site shows pictures of inventory and descriptions but no prices.

NEW ORLEANS AUCTION HOUSES

Neal
4038 Magazine Street
504-899-5329

New Orleans Auction Galleries
801 Magazine Street
504-566-1849
www.neworleansauction.com

NEW ORLEANS ANTIQUES SHOWS

Bayou Lafourche Antiques Show and Sale
September
Thibodaux Civic Center
310 North Canal Blvd.
985-446-3858

NEW ORLEANS FLEA MARKETS

French Market-Flea Market/Farmers Market
Every day from 8 to 6:30
1235 North Peters
504-522-2621

Chapter 13

Philadelphia

Philadelphia, home to the famous Liberty Bell which so eloquently expresses the freedoms our forefathers carved out for us, is a city loaded with American history. Although the essence of Early American style can still be seen in Philadelphia's architecture and many historic sites, unfortunately this genre no longer plays a major role in this city once known for manufacturing the best in Early American furniture. Because the demand for Early American furniture has decreased over time, some of the manufacturers have closed down. Others relocated to places outside Philadelphia where manufacturing is more cost-efficient.

While Philadelphia has developed into a formidable furniture hot spot, it is not as impressive as other large hot-spot cities in its furniture selection. The three principal areas within Philadelphia I reviewed for this book are Manayunk, Society Hill/Old City, and the Market Place Design Center. There are wonderful restaurants everywhere and I especially love the Italian food in Philadelphia. There are buses and taxis all around the city, and within neighborhoods, you can easily walk. If you want to travel to Manayunk you will need a car.

PHILADELPHIA RETAIL STORES

Society Hill and Old City

In the east part of Philadelphia, in the historic area near Independence Hall and Betsy Ross's home, are Society Hill and Old City. I strongly recommend visiting these areas to capture the true flavor of the history of this city and some of the fantastic little shops and chic eateries. "Antiques Row" consists of a few blocks in Society Hill on Pine Street, between 8th and 12th Streets. Only a few antiques shops are still on Pine Street (along with several new-furniture shops), but tourists and locals like walking up and down this street because there are beautiful Georgian-style vintage brownstones, churches, an old cemetery, and little parks nearby. Tour buses regularly go up and down this narrow street. For more information about this area, you can log on to www.antique-row.com. Near Society Hill is Old City, another updated historic neighborhood. I really like its urban feel, and especially the shops on 3rd Street, between Market and Arch Streets. For a quick bite to eat, there are lots of nice outdoor cafés located on Market Street between 2nd and 4th Streets.

MATTHEW IZZO SHOP

Contemporary 1950s-Inspired Furniture and Accessories
928 Pine Street; 215-922-2570, cell 215-266-9747;
matthewizzo@comcast.net; Hours: Mon–Sat 10:30–6:30,
Sun 12–5; www.matthewizzo.com; Credit Cards: MC, Visa, AmEx;
Owner is Denise Izzo

Price: Personnel:
Ambiance: Quality:

    This is a chic, lovely store that can't be missed with its electric blue signage outside. The furniture here is affordable and hip—a throwback to the '50s. The accessories are wonderful, too. I like the vases, lamps, picture frames, and other household accessories. There are some good vintage pieces here, and you can order handcrafted furniture, which takes about six weeks for delivery. Matthew Izzo, himself, designs many of the pieces. I found the service good. Designers receive a 10% discount. The Web site displays the inventory.

M. FINKEL & DAUGHTER

Early American Furniture (early 1800s)
936 Pine Street; 215-627-7797; mailbox@finkelantiques.com;
Hours: Mon–Fri 9:30–5:30, Sat, Sun by appointment;

www.finkelantiques.com; Credit Cards: MC, Visa, AmEx;
Owner is Amy Finkel

Price:  Personnel:

Ambiance: Quality:

Located in a little brown brick corner building that looks like it hasn't
been touched in 50 years, M. Finkel is a gem if you are interested in Early
American furniture. Not many American antiques shops are left in
Philadelphia, and this one is an old-timer. A family business now run by
Amy Finkel, this shop has been at this address since 1947. There are two
floors of furniture and knickknacks. I especially love the Early American
long benches, which I think make the perfect foyer piece for a New England
or English country-style home. Service is excellent but prices are high here.
The store does have a little bit of a run-down, shabby appearance. M. Finkel
has booths in many of the national antiques shows. Designers receive a
10–15% discount. I have a feeling that discounts may also be available to the
public who are interested in buying the more expensive pieces. The Web site
only shows samplers (needlepoints), and not furniture.

ACCENT ON DESIGN, INC.

European Antiques and Accessories/Consignments
1032 Pine Street; 215-733-0703; smitleyt@aol.com;
Hours: Mon 11–6, Tue–Sun 11–6; www.aod1032.com;
Credit Cards: MC, Visa, AmEx; Owner is Tom Smitley

Price: Personnel:

Ambiance: Quality:

To grandmother's house we go! Accent on Design is located in an old
brick building with a big red, white, and blue "Open" flag outside its front
door. Actually, if your grandma's house was anything like mine, chock full
of all kinds of hidden treasures, this place will take you on a virtual trip
down Memory Lane. The store's wide variety of merchandise makes this
place a lot like shopping at a nicer flea market. The atmosphere is relaxed,

and there is something for everyone. If you have antique furniture you can come here for furniture cleaning products. Designers can get discounts of between 15% and 20%. The owner does lots of antiques shows and also owns a large warehouse that you can visit if you make an appointment.

TWIST

Mid-Century Modern Furniture and Accessories
1134 Pine Street; 215-925-1242; www.twisthome.com;
Hours: Wed–Sat 11–6, Sun 12–4, Mon (appointment only); Credit Cards: MC, Visa, AmEx, Discover; Owners are Sharne Algotsson and Lisa Formica

Price: Personnel:
Ambiance: Quality:

I was crazy about this refreshingly simple, small store. A small space with shabby white-painted floors, Twist carries vintage furniture, mostly Mid-Century Modern, but also furniture spanning the period from the early 1920s to 1975. It also has beautiful accessories, like bowls, platters, and colorful artwork. The sign outside is colorful, and I really like the pretty flower planters in the front. There is not a lot of inventory, but it is obvious that this owner has spent a lot of time carefully selecting and displaying it. Twist is now carrying a custom sofa and chair line. You'll love the bold, colorful fabrics the owners use to cover the furniture. Designer discounts depend on the individual piece. The Web site is attractive but you cannot purchase online nor can you see prices.

MODERNE GALLERY

Art Deco Furniture, Accessories,
and Works by Furniture Designer George Nakashima
111 North 3rd Street; 215-923-8536; raibel@aol.com; Hours: Tue–Sat 11–6; www.modernegallery.com; Credit Cards: MC, Visa;
Owner is Robert Aibel

Price: Personnel:

Ambiance: ★★★★★ Quality: ★★★★★

This gallery is the most museum-like of all furniture shops I have seen in Philadelphia. Around the corner from the Betsy Ross's house and with a brown awning on the outside, this shop has four floors of well-displayed furniture. There are absolutely no price tags, and if you are in the mood to buy you need a salesperson to escort you through the entire building. I thought the owner and the saleswoman who I spoke with were extremely nice and helpful. There are no deals here, but for people who are interested in pieces made by well-known Deco designers this is a great place to shop. Designers receive a 10–20% discount. I especially love the chairs, mirrors, and garden pieces. The Nakashima pieces are made from beautifully carved wood and work well in many different home styles. Although Nakashima, a Japanese-American designer, is no longer alive, his rustic styles are still popular. The Web site has pictures and descriptions of pieces, some of which have been sold.

MINIMA

Italian Contemporary Furniture and Art
118 North 3rd Street; 215-922-2002; info@minima.com; Hours:
Tue–Sat 11–6; www.minima.com; Credit Cards: MC, Visa, AmEx;
Owner is Eugenie Perrett

Price: ★★★ Personnel: ★★★★★
Ambiance: ★★★★★ Quality: ★★★★★

This is an adorable showroom of two floors filled with mostly imported Italian furniture. The furniture is colorful, and many of the chairs are made from plastic—perfect for a kitchen with messy eaters! I think much of the furniture here caters to a younger audience. The artwork is colorful and interesting. Prices are very reasonable. Designers receive a discount depending on the size of the order.

FLOTSAM + JETSAM

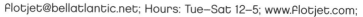

Eclectic Furniture and Accessories

149 North 3rd Street; 215-351-9914;

Flotjet@bellatlantic.net; Hours: Tue–Sat 12–5; www.flotjet.com;

Credit Cards: MC, Visa, AmEx; Owner is Meltem Birey

Price: Personnel:

Ambiance: Quality:

I was immediately welcomed by a large, mild-mannered dog when I entered the shop. This is a very eclectic antique and contemporary furniture shop with an artsy atmosphere. There are two floors in this beautiful space. The details are lovely; even the wooden floors have been beautifully stenciled. I loved the artwork, the mirrors, and one-of-a-kind Asian tables. There were also some beautiful vintage stone planters. There wasn't a lot of service available when I came here to browse. Designers receive a 10% discount. I like the Web site, which includes pictures, descriptions, prices, and even the ability to buy online.

WEXLER GALLERY

Art Gallery with Artist-Designed Furniture

201 North 3rd Street; 215-923-7030;

bobbieann@wexlergallery.com; Hours: Tue–Sat 10–6;

www.wexlergallery.com; Credit Cards: MC, Visa, AmEx;

Owner is Lewis Wexler

Price: Personnel:

Ambiance: Quality:

Mostly an art gallery in a large building with two floors, Wexler Gallery is worth a trip if you are in the area. Much of the furniture resembles Art Nouveau, and the woods used are interesting. All of the furniture is handmade and quite expensive. The gallery feels stark, and there wasn't a lot of service the day I visited. Designers usually receive a 10% discount. The Web site includes pictures and descriptions but no prices.

Center City

Located in the center of the city, hence the name, there are some beautiful old row houses and shops in this elegant little neighborhood. Center City feels more like a little neighborhood in Europe than part of downtown Philadelphia with all of the high-rise buildings surrounding it.

CALDERWOOD GALLERY

Furniture and Accessories from 1900 to 1950
1622 Spruce Street; 215-546-5357; Hours: Tue–Fri 11–5:30,
Sat 12–5:30; www.calderwoodgallery.com; Credit Cards:
MC, Visa, AmEx; Owners are Janet and Gary Calderwood

Price: Personnel:

Ambiance: Quality:

If you like Art Deco, early-20th-century furniture, or the 1950s, you have to cruise this shop. Very high-end, it feels like walking into a fancy row house on the Upper East Side in New York City. You wouldn't know this is a furniture store if you just walked by. It is very much like a private residence, with furniture suites located all around the building on a few floors. Most of the furniture was designed by important 20th-century designers. I was very impressed with the selection of elegant French 1940s iron tables. There is also a great collection of vintage black-and-white photographs of movie stars. Designers receive a discount that depends on the individual piece, but this is not the place to find a great deal. The Web site has wonderful pictures, but no prices.

Marketplace Design Center

Design Center with many showrooms; sells to the trade only
2400 Market Street; 215-561-5000; Mon–Fri 9–5;
www.marketplacedc.com

Philadelphia's Marketplace Design Center is a typical design center in a large city. Most of the showrooms represent lines that are well known, like Baker, Donghia, and Grange. Please be aware that if you try to enter this building without a designer, you will not be well received, even though the public is able to browse without a designer Monday–Friday from 10–5. Consequently, I was not even given a visitor's badge because I didn't have a so-called "designer's card." And because of this, the showrooms I visited generally had poor service. Even I was intimidated by the receptionist at the entrance, who seemed suspicious of my book and my reason for being there, so I just walked by her and kept on shopping!

Here are some interesting showrooms in the Marketplace:

INTERIUS

This is a new, small showroom that is primarily in the business of leasing 18th- and 19th-century Asian art and antiquities. The company is based in Delaware, with the showroom located here in the Design Center. The pieces are very interesting but expensive, and again, don't think of coming here if you are not in the trade.

THE MENAGERIE, LTD.

The Menagerie is located on the third floor of the Design Center. I found this to be one of the busiest showrooms I have shopped in any design center around the country. This is a full-service furniture showroom. The Menagerie reps lines like Bausman and Patina. Most of the furniture is traditional. There is also a large selection of lamps. There is a good cross-section between expensive and more moderately priced furniture. Although price tags were not on every piece of furniture, service was great and they even had a wonderful lunch buffet and desserts for people shopping in their showroom. I met with the owner, Gloria Leibovitz, a nice lady who was extremely busy the day I came here. She told me she has been in business for 27 years.

Manayunk

Only about a 15-minute drive from downtown Philadelphia, along the Schuylkill River, it's a worthwhile trip to Manayunk, a quaint, peaceful, and hip mountain town. Located on the west side of Philadelphia in what was once an industrial town, this is a neighborhood where many 20–40-year-olds now live. To get there, take 676 West to 76 West and exit on Lincoln Drive. Proceed straight to Main Street. The neighborhood is loaded with fun yuppie shops, great restaurants, ice cream parlors, and bakeries up and down the one mile or so of Main Street. Furniture and accessories chain shops along Main Street include Pottery Barn, Restoration Hardware, Somnia, and Ligne Roset.

PAUL DOWNS

Handmade, Custom Wood Furniture
100 Levering Street (just off Main Street); 610-639-8004;
pauldowns@pauldowns.com; Hours: Wed, Thu 1–8, Fri 12–8,
Sat 12–7, Sun 12–5; www.pauldowns.com; Credit Cards: MC,
Visa, AmEx, Discover; Owner is Paul Downs

Price: ... Personnel: ...
Ambiance: ... Quality: ...

If you have ever wanted to try your hand at designing unique functional cabinetry or furniture, you're in for an adventure. Paul Downs, the owner, likes to work one-on-one with the customer in achieving that personalized one-of-a-kind look. The quality is good, and I like the fact that this is a small operation so every detail is taken seriously. The look is casual or formal, whichever you prefer. You can see styles on the Web site . There are no discounts here.

MOON OVER MANAYUNK

Painted Cottage-Style Furniture and Accessories
4327 Main Street; 215-483-7255; moonovermanayunk@aol.com;
Hours: Mon 11–7, Tue, Wed 11–6, Thu 11–7, Sat 11–10; Credit Cards:
MC, Visa, AmEx, Discover; Owner is MaryLou Robertson

Price: ... Personnel: ...

Ambiance: Quality:

If you adore painted furniture as I do, this is a wonderful place to visit. The purple-painted façade of the Victorian-style house where this quaint Cottage-style store resides is every bit as colorful and charming as its painted inventory. Local artists paint much of what you see here. The owner was extremely friendly and passionate about her collection. The store has a feminine feel and is full of clever gift ideas. Discounts are available depending on the item.

OWEN PATRICK GALLERY

Modern Furniture and Housewares, Lighting
4345 Main Street; 215-482-9395; james@owenpatrick.com;
Hours: Tue, Thu 11–6, Wed, Fri, Sat 11–8, Sun 12–5;
www.owenpatrick.com; Credit Cards: MC, Visa, AmEx, Diners Club;
Owners are James Gilroy and Gary Pelkey

Price: Personnel:

Ambiance: Quality:

This is a very customer-friendly store with great service. Owen Patrick has been here for 15 years, a great accomplishment these days with the rise and fall of many furniture stores carrying this kind of unique and not-so-unique inventory. Just doubled in size, the store carries wonderful, simple contemporary, mostly Italian furniture. I love the lighting, storage systems, housewares, and pillows. This is the place to go to buy someone the perfect house gift if they have contemporary taste. The owners are passionate about their inventory. One of them was sure he had recognized me from "The Apprentice"! Check out their inventory online. Designers and others can receive discounts of usually between 15% and 25%.

BELLE MAISON

Mostly French Provincial-Style Furniture
and Eclectic French Accessories
4340 Main Street; 215-482-6222; Hours: Mon–Sat 11–7,

Wed, Fri 11–9, Sun 12–6; www.bellemaisononline.com;
Credit Cards: MC, Visa, AmEx, Discover; Owners are
Michelle F. Keating and Bernadette M. Krakovitz

Price: 🪑🪑🪑 Personnel: 🪑🪑🪑🪑🪑

Ambiance: 🪑🪑🪑🪑🪑🪑 Quality: 🪑🪑🪑🪑

Located in a large, beautifully painted yellow Southern-style building in a duplex space, the store is well designed with furniture in the mostly French Provincial style. Most of the inventory is new, but they have used some salvaged iron pieces to make some of the furniture. There is bedroom, dining, and outdoor furniture, along with beautiful linens for entertaining and some sinfully luxurious bath towels. The place has great French signage. I went especially mad over a vintage tea cart I spotted the day I shopped here. I really admire the owners for delivering such positive enthusiasm and good service in this most busy shop. Designers receive a discount of 20% or more. Their Web site will be up soon.

PHILADELPHIA AUCTION HOUSES

Freeman's Auction Company
1808 Chestnut Street
215-563-9275
www.freemansauction.com

Barry S. Slosberg, Inc.
2501 Ontario Street
215-425-7030 or 888-476-0888

PHILADELPHIA ANTIQUES SHOWS

The Philadelphia Antiques Show
April
33rd St. Armory
215-387-3500
Email: contact@PhilaAntiques.com

Antiques At the Center

(Formerly known as Philadelphia's Navy Pier Antiques Show)

April

Barn Star Productions

Pennsylvania Convention Center

1 Convention Center Place

1101 Arch Street

Philadelphia

215-418-5500

CHAPTER 14

San Francisco

After visiting San Francisco, you will, as in the song made famous by Tony Bennett, lose your heart to the place. The 750,000 lucky people who live in this sprawling upscale, avant-garde urban metropolis seem to have it all. There is a free-spirited liberalism in the air in San Francisco that nurtures the many colorful cultures that thrive here including its young hipsters, wealthy yuppies, and large gay communities. Hop aboard one of San Francisco's charming cable cars (three main routes traverse back and forth to the various parts of the city), and cruise elegant palm-tree-lined, hilly streets to historic Fisherman's Wharf where you can indulge in some of the greatest fresh seafood in the world. If you're the romantic type, then head down to the Pacific Ocean beach and experience one of San Francisco's mystic sunrises through the fog, or perhaps visit nearby Napa Valley, the womb of California winemaking. If all this doesn't make you want to stay in San Francisco forever, the furniture shopping here surely will.

As in many large cities, the neighborhoods in San Francisco may only be several blocks long, so basically all the stores are conveniently located within a few miles' radius. Note that because rent is so high in San Francisco, many stores with a large inventory will opt to house much of their inventory in warehouses. Always remember to ask the dealers if they have a warehouse where you can see more of their selection.

If your furniture shopping excursions have whetted your appetite, don't forget that food and wine are a real part of the San Francisco culture. Bon appetit! Check out SF's many great wine-tasting bars, including Nectar and Bacar.

SAN FRANCISCO RETAIL STORES

San Francisco Design District

The San Francisco Design District is a four-square-block area that houses the Design Center along with stores that cater to designers. Generally only designers get discounts (at least that is the party line in this part of the city). Most of the places I encountered focus exclusively on the trade, and that's too bad because overall I found the neighborhood to be absolutely awe-inspiring. In one of the shops, a designer asked me why I was taking notes and when I told her I was writing this book, she urged me not to because that would hurt her ability to control pricing with her clients. In fact, she yelled at me in front of everybody in the store. Case in point. Go figure.

HOLMES-SAMSEL ANTIQUES

European Antiques/Garden Furniture
Corner of Kansas and 16th Streets; 415-864-7300;
Hours: Mon–Fri 10–5; www.sanfranciscoantiquedealers.com;
Credit Cards: MC, Visa; Owners are Bernadette Holmes
and Adam Samsel

Price: | Personnel:

Ambiance: | Quality:

Holmes-Samsel is in one of the prettiest buildings in the Design District. The outside of the building is graced with the most gorgeous vintage and contemporary garden furniture set to a backdrop of an equally beautiful and colorful lush little garden area. I found the inside just as quaint. The place boasted several generous and intriguing roomfuls of a sizable variety of 18th–20th-century European furniture. Most of the pieces are French, but there is also a plentiful collection of Russian and Italian furniture that is as impressive as the service here. Don't be surprised if the inventory looks familiar, as you may have spotted some of it at Saks Fifth Avenue in downtown San Francisco. Holmes-Samsel

Antiques is well known in San Francisco. There is a nice selection of antique and vintage beds, and many of the vintage pieces here are reasonably priced. Designers receive a 20% discount. Although 90% of their business is to designers, unlike most dealers in this neighborhood the owners treat the general public well and will often offer a discount to them. The Web site doesn't show individual pieces or prices.

BENJAMIN STORCK, LTD.

20th-Century Furniture and Decorative Arts
295 Kansas Street; 415-863-1777; Hours: Mon–Fri 11–5;
www.benjaminstorckltd.com; Credit Cards: MC, Visa, AmEx;
Owner is Benjamin Storck

Price: 　　　　 Personnel: 　　　
Ambiance: 　　　　 Quality: 　　　　

Benjamin Storck opened this location recently after being in business in LA (the store there is called Modern One) for 18 years. The furniture here is wonderful; many well-known furniture designers and artists from the first half of the 20th century (many of whom were French) are represented. There are many other stores with furniture of the same period whose prices are considerably less, but the furniture at Storck is amazing. Although the sales help here weren't as available to answer questions as I would have liked, I would be willing to give this place a second chance because of the quality of the inventory. The Web site is worth exploring. There are pictures, prices, and dimensions. Designers receive a 20% discount.

THERIEN & CO. INCORPORATED

17th- and 18th-Century Continental Furniture
411 Vermont Street; 415-956-8850; Hours: Mon–Fri 9–5:30;
www.therien.com; Owners are Robert Garcia, Bruce Tremayne,
Phillip Steitz, and Walter Zolezz

Price: 　　　　 Personnel:

Ambiance: Quality:

Shopping at Therien is a bit like shopping at a Rolls-Royce or other high-priced dealership where we might sense the staff looking us over as though trying to determine if we can afford the merchandise. Such was the case at Therien. The salespeople seemed to size me over as though they were estimating a price on a vintage car set for auction. God forbid you should attempt to touch the merchandise! With most of the pieces priced at more than $20,000, who can blame them. All of the business here comes from designers, and discounts depend on each piece. Although expensive, the inventory is wonderful and unique, much of it museum quality. Many of these pieces are highly unusual and carefully selected, coming from Spain, Portugal, Germany, Italy, and France. I found it curious that so much of this expensive inventory was refinished or repainted, which can alter the value of the piece. Therien will provide a condition report. The Web site offers some pictures but no prices. There is also a location in Los Angeles.

ED HARDY SAN FRANCISCO

18th–20th-Century Furniture from All over the World
188 Henry Adams Street; 415-626-6300; ehardy@edhardysf.com;
Hours: Mon–Fri 9–5; www.edhardysf.com; Credit Cards: MC, Visa,
AmEx, Discover; Owner is Ed Hardy

Price: Personnel:

Ambiance: Quality:

Ed Hardy is a must-see store in San Francisco. The showroom is located in a rambling, fortress-like, beige stone compound accented by a warm selection of inviting garden furniture out front and in back. All the furniture is from Europe, every item uniquely designed: unusual and heavy Baroque Italian and Portuguese pieces, massive ornate cabinets and armoires, and a rare assortment of antique European chandeliers, just to name a few. That said, I felt the inside of the store was rather intimidating. There were many people working in the store, yet I couldn't seem to get help for several minutes. The owner would not even speak with me, saying he was too busy. Considering the prices being asked (many of the pieces cost over $20,000), I felt I deserved some attention and courtesy. I still recommend seeing the fascinating inventory. Designers receive a 20% discount on accessories and a 30% discount on furniture. The Web site is excellent with good pictures, descriptions, and prices.

GARDEN COURT ANTIQUES

17th–20th-Century Continental Antiques
5 Henry Adams Street; 415-355-1690;
jim@gardencourtantiques.com; Hours: Mon–Fri 9–5;
Credit Cards: MC, Visa; Owner is Sue Coleman

Price: Personnel:

Ambiance: Quality:

Garden Court Design is part of the San Francisco Design Center. I love the inventory here in what is probably one of the most romantic and charming spaces in the neighborhood. There is a wide variety of delightful furniture from the 17th through 20th century; much of it is so unique and rare that you will be hard pressed to find it anywhere else. The furniture is very expensive. Many pieces cost over $10,000, and some of the inventory is overpriced. Trying to find out the designer discount here was a little like trying to extract teeth from a Great White. When I posed the forbidden "designer discount" question to the store manager, the interior designer standing next to him announced that she would be very angry if he disclosed that information to me. Off with my head! Needless to say, I find the atmosphere a "little" too stiff and uncomfortable if you're not the trade. There is no Web site.

EPOCA

19th- and 20th-Century Antiques
300 Kansas Street, Suite 103; 415-864-6895; eric@epocasf.com;
Hours: Mon–Fri 10–5; www.epocasf.com; Credit Cards: MC, Visa,
AmEx; Owner is Eric Petsinger

Price: Personnel: Ambiance: Quality:

Epoca has been open for one year and based on the good service I received here, I'm betting this store will be around for a long time. While many of the dealers in this location treat the public badly because they are not designers, Eric Petsinger is affable and knowledgeable about his merchandise and couldn't have tried harder to be helpful. The furniture is nice, and there are some good-looking Continental pieces from the 19th and 20th centuries. There is a variety of well-selected, traditional inventory from Europe, most of which is made from wood. Designers receive a 20% discount here. The Web site includes prices and descriptions of much of the inventory.

HEATHER & COMPANY

18th–20th-Century Furniture and Consignments
212 Utah Street; 415-551-0011;
heatherandcompany@sbcglobal.net; Hours: Mon–Fri 10–6;
www.heatherandcompany.1stdibs.com; Credit Cards: MC, Visa, AmEx; Owner is Heather Dipteral

Price: Personnel: Ambiance: Quality:

Heather & Company feels a little like going to a really nice, high-end flea market or local auction. The inventory is quite diverse in this industrial-looking building located in the San Francisco Design District. I like the relaxed atmosphere, which is unique for shops in the district. Although I thought prices seemed a little high, Heather is very proud of her space and inventory, much of which is purchased locally. Designers receive a 20% discount, and the Web site is really nicely done, with pictures, descriptions, and prices. An unusually public-friendly store in what can be an intimidating for-the-trade-only neighborhood.

AMBIANCE ANTIQUES

French Provincial Antiques

135 Rhode Island Street; 550 15th Street, Suite 1; 415-255-9006;

Hours: Mon–Fri 10–5; www.ambianceantiques.com;

Credit Cards: MC, Visa; Owners are Teresa and Steven Beltrami

Price: Personnel: Ambiance: Quality:

Ambiance Antiques, a 30-year-old business, will only sell to the trade (I don't know their discount; they wouldn't tell me), but is worth a visit nonetheless. The name is apropos—the place does have a lot of ambiance and has the look of a European castle on the inside. The inventory is French Provincial and most of the designs are classic, nothing particularly unusual but there is a market for this kind of furniture, their specialty. The Web site shows pictures, prices, and dimensions along with brief descriptions. There is another location a few blocks from here, in the same neighborhood.

JRM INTERNATIONAL

Asian and European Antiques, Reproductions,

and Contemporary Furniture

340 Kansas Street; 415-864-8118; jrm@jrminternational.net;

Hours: Mon–Fri 9–5; Credit Cards: MC, Visa, AmEx;

Owner is John Robert Martin

Price: Personnel: Ambiance: Quality:

JRM International is a fabulous place to come for rustic furniture from Asia and beyond. The owner, a Berkeley design graduate, produces some of the furniture designs, and much of the inventory comes from around the world—France, Italy, Greece, Spain, Indonesia, and Thailand. Most of the pieces have exquisite lines. The furniture here is extremely expensive. My impression is that if you are not in the trade, you won't receive attention. Designers receive a 30% discount here, and there is no Web site. Because of the high prices, I would only shop here if I were in the trade.

San Francisco Design Center (SFDC)

Two Design Centers with many showrooms; sells to the trade only
2 Henry Adams and 101 Henry Adams; 415-490-5800; Mon–Fri 9–5;
www.sfdesigncenter.com

The San Francisco Design Center is a busy place for designers to shop in San Francisco. Located in two main buildings diagonally across from each other, the center's hours are Monday through Friday, 9 to 5. The SFDC has a casual feel, unlike many design centers around the country. While its 100 showrooms claim their policies of dealing with the public vary from showroom to showroom, most of them will sell only to the trade. If you've left your decorator back home, no sweat—the SFDC will refer you to at least five professional in-house buying services located right in the building for hire to the public, at a 25–40% markup over the net price, or the price the designer pays to the showroom. Unfortunately, in many of these places service is only so-so at best if you are not a designer or even if you are with a designer. All of the well-known showrooms are here, including Baker, Donghia, McGuire, along with some of my personal favorites like Enid Ford, De Sousa Hughes, and Lx Rossi. Plan to eat lunch here. SFDC has the best food I have eaten in any design center around the country.

Mission Bay Area

LIMN

Large Contemporary Furniture Store
290 Townsend Street; 415-543-5466;
dan.friedlander@limn.com; Hours: Mon–Fri 9:30–6, Sat, Sun 11–6;
www.limn.com; Credit Cards: MC, Visa, AmEx;
Owner is Dan Friedlander

Price: | Personnel:

Ambiance: | Quality:

You could easily drive by Limn, a San Francisco hot spot, so look out for the big red heart in front of the building. I highly recommend visiting Limn, if for no other reason than to just see their unusual and fun selection of contemporary furniture. Compared with other contemporary furniture stores in the country, I think Limn is clearly one of the best. Some 80% of the inventory is from Italy and has a pronounced artistic flair. Some of the furniture can be purchased off the floor; otherwise furniture takes five to six months to receive if ordered. There is a large upstairs, too, with a roof-top garden containing a nice selection of outdoor furniture. About 2,000 manufacturers are represented here, including Capellini, Cassina, Armani Casa, and B&B Italia. I especially love the interesting selection of chairs. I think the service is exceptional for a large, very expensive contemporary furniture store. Limn has been in business 23 years, 13 years at this location. Designer discounts don't really apply here. Everyone receives the net prices. The Web site shows inventory but no prices or dimensions. Well worth a trip.

Union Square

Union Square is in a commercial, downtown business district neighborhood. It is unusual to find furniture stores in this type of corporate atmosphere. There are, however, a few stores worth visiting in this neighborhood. Parking is limited to meters, which are sometimes hard to find.

FUMIKI SAN FRANCISCO
Contemporary and Antique Asian Furniture
272 Sutter Street; 415-362-6677; frank@fumiki.com;
Hours: Mon–Sat 10–6; www.fumiki.com; Credit Cards: MC, Visa,
AmEx; Owner is a Japanese company

Price: | Personnel:
Ambiance: | Quality:

Fumiki is a storefront in the business district. Take a peek inside, though, and you'll discover some interesting pieces of Asian furniture. I especially like the hand-carved wooden tables and stools. Prices are steep for some of these handcrafted wooden pieces, like the stools priced at over $1,000 each. There are two stories in this narrow space. The lower level has large selection of antique Asian chests. There are nice housewares, including some beautiful bowls that would make unusual house gifts. Most of the staff is Asian and bilingual. The music is classical and the atmosphere is serious. There is not a lot of ambiance here. Designers receive a 10% discount. The Web site shows pictures, dimensions, and prices.

BIG PAGODA COMPANY
Asian Furniture
310 Sutter Street; 415-296-8881; info@bigpagoda.com;
Hours: Mon–Sat 10–6; www.bigpagoda.com; Credit Cards: MC,
Visa, AmEx; Owner is Kurt Silver

Price: Personnel:

Ambiance: Quality:

Big Pagoda is a store that has created its own contemporary line of Asian-inspired furniture. I like the vibrant colors used on the furniture. There are some unique, more expensive pieces as well as affordable accessories for the home. Furniture prices, though, are steep. With a factory in China, Big Pagoda has done well in the hotel business, selling its line to hotels like The W and The Four Seasons. Designers receive a 20% discount. The Web site shows pictures, dimensions, and prices.

South of Market

HUGHLIN IMPORTS & THE ASIAN COLLECTION
Asian Antique Furniture and Decorative Arts
566 Folsom Street; heinrich@hughlin.com;
Hours: Tue–Sat 11–5; www.hughlin.com; Credit Cards: MC, Visa;
Owners are James Bastable and Hugh Coughlin

Price: | Personnel: | Ambiance: | Quality:

With its bright orange façade, this store is hard to miss and that's good, because the place is a treasure. I think this is one of the most special Asian decorative arts stores in the country. I was greeted by the manager who is German and extremely nice, helpful, and informative. Although there isn't a lot of furniture per se, I think the selection is unexpected and extremely interesting. The business began 25 years ago with Korean furniture. I particularly like the impressive, intricately carved wood over-doors that frame the hallways. They seem reasonably priced at roughly $2,000 for a large overhang that is hundreds of years old—a bargain compared with other stores selling Asian artifacts around the country. Designers receive a 10% discount. The Web site, though, needs improvement; there are a few pictures, no prices, and little information. Worth a trip.

Jackson Square

Jackson Square is a six-block square right next to Chinatown, just a couple of blocks from the downtown area; its boundaries are Columbus, Battery, Pacific, and Washington. This is a very walkable neighborhood, with some cute restaurants—and, of course, Chinatown is a food hot spot in this city. Jackson Square has been hyped as being "the place to buy antiques," but in my opinion its shops are overpriced, touristy, and the inventory is not particularly special. Most of these shops, because of their urban location, have doorbells for entry. The atmosphere is a little stiff for the antiques novice. There are, however, some noteworthy shops. Design Within Reach and Kartell are located in this neighborhood.

HEDGE

Vintage and Custom Furniture
in the Style of the French 1940s–'70s
48 Gold Street; 415-357-1102; Hours: Mon–Fri 10–5;

www.hedgegallery.com; Credit Cards: N/A;
Owners are Roth Martin and Steven Volpe

Price: Personnel:

Ambiance: Quality:

For those who like the sophistication of French 1940s–'70s furniture, Hedge is a great place to see. It is the only store of its kind in San Francisco. The owners, architects and designers of furniture, spend a great deal of time creating designs from the past while adding their own unique touch. They offer a luscious array of colors for lacquering. The Web site is nice, showing the vintage and contemporary collections, listing prices and dimensions. I thought the service here was excellent. This is a new location for these hip shop owners with exquisite taste. Designers receive a discount of approximately 15%.

DANIEL STEIN ANTIQUES

Mostly English Antiques
458 Jackson Street; 415-956-5620; info@danielsteinantiques.com;
Hours: Mon–Fri 9:30–5, Sat 11–4; www.danielsteinantiques.com;
Credit Cards: MC, Visa, AmEx, Discover; Owner is Daniel Stein

Price: Personnel:

Ambiance: Quality:

Daniel Stein Antiques is housed in a beautiful, elegant white stone building with a gated entry. The store is a good place to go to buy high-end English antiques. Some of the inventory is rare and unusual, but most of the furniture consists of traditional English classics that never go out of style. Designers receive a 20% discount. The Web site shows pictures, prices, and descriptions of the pieces.

REBUFFEL ANTIQUES

Continental Antiques
441 Jackson Street; 415-835-2455; info@rebuffelantiques.com;

Hours: Mon–Fri 10–5, Sat 11–4; www.rebuffelantiques.com;
Credit Cards: MC, Visa, AmEx, Discover;
Owner is Laurent Rebuffel

Price: Personnel: Ambiance: Quality:

Rebuffel Antiques is a great shop with unusual inventory from all over Europe. I especially liked the interesting antique stone statuary and English bookcases I saw on my visit. If you want to see more of Rebuffel's inventory, check out their warehouse in South of Market. Personally, I felt that the prices, as in many shops in Jackson Square, are inflated. Designers receive a 30% discount here. The Web site includes pictures, prices, and descriptions.

Russian Hill

The Russian Hill section of San Francisco is worth a visit. There are many hip and eclectic stores and restaurants in this busy little neighborhood.

SWALLOWTAIL INTERIORS

Eclectic Mix of Antiques and Contemporary Furniture;
Interior Design Services
2217 Polk Street; 415-567-1555; info@swallowtailhome.com;
Hours: Daily 12–6; www.swallowtailhome.com;
Credit Cards: MC, Visa, AmEx, Discover; Owner is Sheri Sheridan

Price: Personnel: Ambiance: Quality:

Swallowtail Interiors has received a lot of acclaim in San Francisco for carrying some extremely unique pieces. The store is a little cramped but fascinating to walk around. There is a nice selection of antiques, modern furniture, funky lamps, Lucite pieces, garden accessories, and light fixtures. There is also a great selection of interesting chairs and artifacts. Wall hangings are everywhere and in a wide variety of prices. This is truly the busiest shop I visited in San Francisco. Designers receive a 10–20% discount. There is another location 20 miles from here in Oakland. The owner told me that her view of the store is "urban chic meets 19th-century naturalist." She won Best Designer Under 40 in San Francisco. The Web site includes pictures and prices but is a little haphazard in its layout.

JOHN WHEATMAN & ASSOCIATES, INC.

Asian-Influenced Contemporary Furniture
and Some Antiques; Interior Design
1933 Union Street; 415-346-8300; Hours: Mon–Fri 10–5,
Sat 10–4:30; Credit Cards: MC, Visa, AmEx;
Owner is John Wheatman

Price: _____ Personnel: _____
Ambiance: _____ Quality: _____

John Wheatman is an interior designer who also has a small two-story gallery in a pretty space. My service experience here was unimpressive, but I like the selection of nice wooden pieces of contemporary, Asian-inspired furniture. Most of the furniture is very simple. John Wheatman has designed several of the pieces in the store. No discounts are available. There are several cute stores and restaurants in the neighborhood and a fabulous bakery across the way.

PAST PERFECT

Vintage Antiques Mall
2224–30 Union Street; 415-929-7651; Hours: Daily 11:30–7;
Credit Cards: MC, Visa; Owner is Melanie Shane

Price: _____ Personnel: _____
Ambiance: _____ Quality: _____

Past Perfect is an attractive antiques mall with a bold black-and-white-striped awning on popular Union Street, selling vintage classic furniture and accessories. There is also vintage clothing here. The furniture is well-displayed, and the store seems very busy. Most of the furniture is post-1950s. Designers receive a 10% discount.

Western Addition

My favorite street in this neighborhood is Hayes Street. This is a youthful neighborhood with many cute stores and restaurants. There is a lot of action in this part of town. Definitely a San Francisco hot spot!

EVELYN'S ANTIQUES
Antique Chinese Furniture
381 Hayes Street; 415-255-1815; et@evelynantique.com;
Hours: Mon–Sat 10:30–6:30; www.evelynantique.com;
Credit Cards: MC, Visa, AmEx; Owner is Evelyn Tam

Price: Personnel:

Ambiance: Quality:

I highly recommend visiting Evelyn's Antiques, if only to see the largest collection of Chinese antiques in the country. What a find this place is! The store feels like a warehouse and though Hayes Street seems an unlikely location for the sophisticated shop, locals come here regularly to see the newest inventory. Custom furniture is available and repairs are done on the premises. Designers receive a 20% discount. Don't expect the best service here; on the other hand, you can feel free to browse at your leisure. The Web site gives pictures and dimensions but no prices or detailed explanations of the pieces.

FRIEND
Contemporary, Fun Furniture and Housewares
401 Hayes Street; 415-552-1717; info@friend-sf.com;
Hours: Daily 11–7; Credit Cards: MC, Visa, AmEx, Discover; Owners are Jacqueline and Mark Lenox

Price: Personnel:

Ambiance:  Quality:

Friend is located on the busy corner of Gough and Hayes. There is an amazing selection of Kartell, along with some great housewares and vibrant-colored paintings.

PROPELLER

Contemporary Furniture and Accessories
555 Hayes Street; 415-701-7767; lorn@propeller-sf.com;
Hours: Tue–Sat 11–7, Sun 12–5; Credit Cards: MC, Visa, AmEx;
Owner is Lorn Dittfeild

Price:  Personnel:

Ambiance:  Quality:

Propeller, a small shop on Hayes, has had a lot of hype here in San Francisco. I was excited to see the store, which is far from stuffy. Propeller is hip and fun, and emphasizes work by not necessarily well-known designers. There are one-of-a-kind contemporary chairs, lamps, rugs, and blankets, along with some great pottery displayed against a hot-pink wall. I highly recommend coming here to browse. The materials, colors, and objects are really wonderful. Designer discounts depend on quantity purchases.

ART DECO COLLECTION

Art Deco Furniture and Accessories
1632 Market Street; 415-255-1902; info@artdecocollection.com;
Hours: Wed–Fri 12–7, Sat, Sun 12–5; www.artdecocollection.com;
Credit Cards: MC, Visa, AmEx; Owner is Richard Fishman

Price: Personnel:

Ambiance: Quality:

Art Deco Collection just opened here on busy Market Street. The space feels like a car dealership, but look around and you will see an impressive selection of Deco furniture and accessories. Most notably, this place has a large selection of Art Deco bars and liquor carts. There are also some great salon suites in a lacquered finish. I also liked the extensive and beautiful selection of side tables. The business has been going strong for 15 years in its other location in Oakland and now in this location. The inventory comes from Europe. The store has a stiff feel, with lots of "Do not sit on furniture" signs. I personally think that if you are running a furniture store and not a museum, customers should be allowed to sit on their prospective purchases; after all, that's half the fun of furniture shopping. The Web site is nice, with pictures and descriptions but no prices. Designer discounts vary.

NEW DEAL

Contemporary Furniture
1632B Market Street; 415-552-6208; newdeal@newdealhome.com;
Hours: Mon–Fri 11–7, Sat, Sun 11–5; www.newdealhome.com;
Credit Cards: MC, Visa, AmEx; Owners are Terje Arnesen and Albert Downs

Price: [chairs] Personnel: [chairs]

Ambiance: [chairs] Quality: [chairs]

New Deal is a store you can't miss, with its bright yellow façade. Now in its 11th year of business, this shop has created a nice following. Most of the furniture is made in Los Angeles, and there are some unusual, fun couches, painted pieces, and a nice selection of lamps. The space is small, but there is a good sampling of inventory. Many pieces can be customized. Designers receive a 10% discount. The atmosphere is relaxed and friendly. The Web site has some pictures and prices for some but not all items.

Other Places to Shop in the San Francisco Area

If you happen to be passing through Berkeley, I recommend taking a stroll down 4th Street and visiting a store called Traditions for the Home. This is a large furniture store with lines like Henredon, Harden, and Ralph

Lauren as well as some antique pieces. The look here is rustic, and there are mostly reproductions. Service is excellent (I got a one-hour tour by a very enthusiastic store manager). The time to come here is when there is an annual sale where most of the merchandise is discounted by 50% to 80%.

If you love great independent bookstores, check out Cody's Books next door. Also nearby, at 1823 Eastshore, check out The Magazine, which specializes in remakes of classic modern furniture. The look here is great, but prices are high.

About 20 minutes outside of San Francisco, San Anselmo has a large selection of antiques shops, but most of them sell overpriced Victorian furniture. The town of San Anselmo is cute, though, and worth a nice sightseeing trip.

SAN FRANCISCO AUCTION HOUSES

Bonham's and Butterfield's
220 San Bruno Avenue
415-861-7500

Cambridge Auction House
1513 Arbuckle Court
Santa Clara
408-970-3201

Christie's
400 Montgomery Street
415-982-0982

Sotheby's
214 Grant Avenue
415-772-9028

SAN FRANCISCO ANTIQUES SHOWS

Antiques Fair in the Park
November
San Francisco County Fair Building
Lincoln Way and 9th Avenue
Golden Gate Park
415-465-2475

Marin County Antiques Fair
December
Marin Civic Center
3501 Civic Center Drive
San Rafael
415-383-2252

SAN FRANCISCO FLEA MARKETS

Antique and Artisan Market
Every Thursday and Friday
United Nations Plaza
Market and 7th Streets
415-255-1923

Berkeley Flea Market
Every Saturday and Sunday
Ashby Avenue at Martin Luther King Jr. Way
Berkeley
510-644-0744
20 miles outside of San Francisco

CHAPTER 15

Seattle

Surrounded by the magnificent icy blue Pacific and majestic cascading mountains, this beautiful city is known not just for its love of art and nice furniture, but as a lively cultural melting pot. Seattle is a liberal, "happening" place filled with tourists and transplants from all over the United States and the world doing "their thing," including some hippie holdovers. Close to Victoria and Vancouver, Seattle is also the Pacific Northwest gateway for many Canadians, Europeans, and Asians. There are many side trips possible from Seattle by boat.

As for furniture, Seattle has some of the finest Asian antiques stores I have ever seen. Bring your walking shoes, because even though most of the city's furniture stores are centrally located in a small downtown area just a few minutes apart from each other, the steep, hilly streets, like those in San Francisco, make walking a challenge here. Unfortunately, the economy has hit this furniture hot spot hard in the last couple of years, causing quite a turnover among retail furniture stores. Many of these stores have been forced to close, although I am glad to say the stores I reviewed are the survivors.

SEATTLE RETAIL STORES

Belltown

Belltown is the downtown of Seattle and the spot right along the ocean. There are many apartment buildings and some quaint shops in the neighborhood. Most of Belltown's residents are young and upwardly mobile. There are some unique home furnishing stores in the neighborhood worth visiting.

EGBERT'S

Contemporary European Furniture and Housewares
2231 1st Avenue; 206-728-5682; egberts@mindspring.com;
Hours: Tue–Sat 9:30–6; Credit Cards: MC, Visa, AmEx;
Owner is Jim Egbert

Price: | Personnel: | Ambiance: | Quality:

A longtime (27 years) favorite of Seattle residents, Egbert's has something for everyone. Importing contemporary furniture from all over Europe, Jim Egbert specializes in Mid-Century classics with a Scandinavian bent. The store is comfortable, with three large rooms and a relaxed sales staff. Being the Hermès nut that I am, I was swept head-over-heels by some Hermès-looking chairs made from saddle leather. There is a wide range of prices and inventory. If you're a gift giver or are into entertaining at home, stock up on the wonderful and exotic offerings of housewares and gift items priced at $25 and up. To name a few: unique and brilliantly colored glass bowls of varying sizes and shapes from Germany, fabulous costume jewelry pieces, books, exotic wooden salad bowls from Africa, one-of-a-kind serving dishes. This is a busy store that attracts a chic clientele who appreciate Egbert's diverse selection. Also noteworthy are the wonderful lamps and light fixtures. Designers receive a 15% discount.

CHARTREUSE INTERNATIONAL

Mid-Century Modern
2609 1st Avenue; 206-328-4844; sales@modchartreuse.com;
Hours: Wed–Sat 11:30–6:30, Sun 12–5; www.modchartreuse.com;
Credit Cards: MC, Visa; Owner is Mari Franke

Price: | Personnel: | Ambiance: | Quality:

Chartreuse International is an amusing, quirky shop to browse. Service here is superb. When I walked in, I was shocked when a man who was repairing some furniture dropped what he was doing and offered to give me a complete tour of the store. All of the vintage classics are here, with a concentration on furniture from the 1950s to '70s. Some of the well-known designers here are Bertoia, Eames, and Saarinen. There is a big selection of vintage furniture along with contemporary reproductions that are well priced. Some of the inventory is good, some is great, and some is absolutely wild. All worth a look, including some great Mid-Century light fixtures. Designers (and even the public) can receive a 10% discount. Another perk about shopping here is that they offer free shipping on everything over $100 (what a deal!). The Web site has some nice pictures, descriptions, and prices, but it is not yet possible to buy online.

Pike's Market

If you're new to Seattle, Pike's Market, an indoor and outdoor shopping area, is a good place to start your furniture shopping expedition. Located in downtown Seattle, this amazing nine-acre, dense shopping bazaar is filled with all kinds of restaurants and shops, including some good furniture shopping. The main entrance is on Pike Street and the water. Some of the building has open walls and tourists come from all over the world to see this large market. Pike's Market is near the Seattle Art Museum and is located right in the heart of the city. Though established nearly a century ago, the place is still often described as "the soul of Seattle" and plays a vital role in this city's economy and culture. Experiencing Pike's Market and its many marvelous shops should be a "to do" on your list.

PORTER DAVIS ANTIQUES
English and French Antiques
103 University; 206-622-5310; Hours: Mon–Fri 10–5:30,
Sat 10:30–5; Credit Cards: MC, Visa, AmEx, Discover;
Owner is Jenkins "Jenks" Henslee

Price: Personnel: Ambiance: Quality:

Across the way from the Seattle Art Museum (SAM) Porter Davis is a well-known antiques shop. Although the furniture is of a good quality, and there are many classic pieces in this very old shop, the inventory is very expensive and seems overpriced; however, this is a touristy neighborhood, and many tourists will pay Jenks Henslee's prices. Service could have been better. Mr. Henslee wouldn't tell me the designer discount policy.

Capitol Hill

Capitol Hill is one of Seattle's more colorful and artsy areas. There is a sizable gay community here, along with many college-aged kids and older people. This fun, trendy neighborhood has some of Seattle's must-try upscale restaurants, as well as some hot furniture shops.

AREA 51

Mid-Century-Style Furniture
401 East Pine Street; 206-568-4782; Hours: Mon–Sat 11–7,
Sun 12–6; Credit Cards: MC, Visa, AmEx;
Owners are Jason Hollman and Daniel Metzler

Price: Personnel: Ambiance: Quality:

I was totally infatuated with this store. Area 51 is in a big industrial warehouse building with stark white floors and walls. While the furniture has all the great contemporary style and fun flair of an IKEA (reviewed below), the quality is a notch above IKEA. I found many pieces of furniture for under $300 that I really liked. Much of the furniture at Area 51 copies the expensive stuff but is chic, attractive, and serviceable. I found the service to be excellent. The salesperson I worked with made a great effort to show me around the store and point out unusual pieces. Designers receive a 10% discount, and some discounts are available to the public. The store began as a vintage shop and still has that influence, apparent in a few of the great vintage pieces you can still find here. There is also some great glass and plastic accessory pieces.

STANDARD HOME

Mid-Century Modern Furniture
1108 Pike Street; 206-464-0850;
laura@standardhomeseattle.com; Hours: Wed–Sun 12–6;
www.standardhomeseattle.com; Credit Cards: MC, Visa;
Owner is Laura Michalek

Price: 🪑🪑🪑 Personnel: 🪑🪑🪑🪑🪑

Ambiance: 🪑🪑🪑🪑🪑 Quality: 🪑🪑🪑🪑

Standard Home is a fabulous find. Its simple façade matches the inventory inside. If you like Mid-Century Modern furniture designed by Eames, Herman Miller, and others of this period, you will love the many carefully selected pieces here. Laura Michalek is a character, very nice, bubbly, outgoing, and hands-on, and clearly passionate about her merchandise. There isn't a lot of wiggle room here, and the atmosphere is not the best, but the furniture is great. Most pieces cost less than $1,000. While visiting, I especially fell in love with an ostrich table and Lucite chairs. Some of the furniture, though, looks like flea market finds. Designers receive a 10% discount. Neither inventory nor prices are online. Laura also provides auctioneer services for individuals.

DAVID WEATHERFORD ANTIQUES & INTERIORS

English and French Antiques and Interior Design
133 14th Avenue East; 206-329-6533; Hours: Mon–Fri 9–5, Sat 10–5;
www.davidweatherford.com; Credit Cards: MC, Visa, AmEx;
Owner is David Weatherford

Price: 🪑🪑🪑🪑🪑🪑 Personnel: 🪑🪑🪑

Ambiance: 🪑🪑🪑🪑🪑 Quality: 🪑🪑🪑🪑

David Weatherford is a well-known shop in Seattle. With another shop located a few miles away in the downtown area, this one is in a beautiful Colonial-style house that has a lot of charm. The furniture sold here is classic European antiques, with an emphasis on French and

English furniture. I found the service to be a little cold and intimidating, but it is a nice store to browse and so is the neighborhood. David Weatherford designs some interesting spaces, including hotels and homes all around the country. The Web site is very well designed and offers pictures, prices, and the ability to buy online. Designers receive a 10% discount.

Pioneer Square

Pioneer Square is the historic section of Seattle. When much of Seattle burned down at the turn of the 19th century, Pioneer Square was one of the few neighborhoods left mostly intact. I like all of the cute shops and cafés here.

ELLIOTT BAY ANTIQUES

Asian Antiques

165 South Jackson Street; 206-340-0770;

eba@nwlink.com; Hours: Mon–Sat 10–5:30;

www.chinese-antique-furniture.com; Credit Cards: MC, Visa, AmEx; Owners are Susan and Stephen Croft

Price: ♦♦♦♦♦ Personnel: ♦♦♦♦♦♦

Ambiance: ♦♦♦♦♦♦ Quality: ♦♦♦♦♦

Located in a large, loft-like space, Elliott Bay Antiques is a wonderful store carrying a selective variety of Asian antiques. Much of the furniture is from China, but there are several pieces from other parts of Asia as well. Its owner, Stephen Croft, an ex–New Orleans son and very charming gentleman, gave me the royal treatment, making the time and effort to educate me on his inventory (without knowing I was writing this book). I especially loved his selection of Chinese Art Deco club chairs. The lines were most unusual. Prices are fair for this most unusual selection. The Web site shows the entire collection and gives descriptions but no prices. This shop is worth the trip. Designers receive a 20% discount.

JEAN WILLIAMS ANTIQUES

English and French Antiques/Reproductions
115 South Jackson Street; 206-622-1110;
wwwantique@msn.com; Hours: Mon–Sat 10–5:30;
www.jeanwilliamsantiques.com; Credit Cards: MC, Visa, AmEx;
Owners are Jean and Brad Williams

Price: 🪑🪑🪑🪑🪑 Personnel: 🪑🪑🪑🪑🪑

Ambiance: 🪑🪑🪑🪑🪑 Quality: 🪑🪑🪑🪑🪑

Jean Williams has been at this location for many years. I loved shopping here because of the cheerful décor (mustard yellow walls) and informal setting. I also found Brad Williams to be extremely knowledgeable and friendly. Most of the furniture is 19th-century French, but the Williamses also make reproductions that I think look unbelievably real. The reproductions are even made to scale, based on the size and proportions of French Provincial furniture from the early 19th century. The upside with buying reproductions here is that they are much less expensive than the period pieces. I also like the fact that they have posted a large sign saying there are payment options, which is unique for an upscale antiques store. There is one sale each year, and designers get a 20% discount. Their Web site shows inventory, but does not state prices.

Downtown

The downtown area in Seattle is made up of a few streets surrounding the Fairmont Olympic Hotel on University Street. This area has all of the chain stores and restaurants you would expect to see in the commercial district of any large city. You can walk here; there is no need for a car. Cabs are in generally good supply.

WALKER-POINSETT

European Antiques
1405 Fifth Avenue; 206-624-4973;
info@walker-poinsett.com; Hours: Mon–Sat 9–5, Sun 10–2;

www.walker-poinsett.com; Credit Cards: MC, Visa, AmEx; Owners are Charles Walker and Joel Poinsett

Price: Personnel: Ambiance: Quality:

Previously located in the lower level of the Fairmont Olympic Hotel, Walker-Poinsett has recently moved and doubled its space. Walker-Poinsett is a well-known Seattle antiques store carrying very high-end, mostly English furniture. Many dealers referred me to this shop. Charles Walker said they have been in business for 25 years and it seems as though their honest reputation has earned them repeat business. It can be an intimidating place to shop if you don't know anything about antiques. The furniture is authentic and the owners are very knowledgeable. The Web site is well designed and shows pictures and descriptions of the pieces. Prices are also included. Designers get a 20% discount.

Western Avenue (aka Furniture Row)

Stretching several blocks in downtown Seattle, Western Avenue is really the big street to shop for furniture. If you only have time to visit one neighborhood to see furniture stores, Western Avenue is the place. The street has a very industrial feel and there isn't much charm here, but the stores are terrific. There is a good mix of antiques and contemporary furniture. There are a few national stores in the neighborhood, like Ligne Roset and Mitchell Gold at House, which attract a large following.

KASALA

Contemporary Furniture
1505 Western Avenue; 203-623-7795 or 800-kasala1;
seastore@kasala.com; Hours: Mon–Sat 10–6, Sun 12–5;
www.kasala.com; Credit Cards: MC, Visa, AmEx, Discover;
Owner is Dan Flickinger

Price: Personnel:

Ambiance: Quality:

Kasala is a great place to shop for a young single person. There is a big selection here and lots of vivid colors. I think Kasala is a cross between Danish Modern and Italian leather. When I came here, there was a big sale taking place. Kasala has another store in Bellevue, a suburb of Seattle. I found the quality and service to be good. I think there are some good values here, like the functional, attractive storage units (assembly required), also the leather furniture. Kasala has been here for 17 years—no small feat for a Seattle furniture store. Designers receive a 10% discount. Although there is a Web site, the furniture collection is not shown.

DIVA

Contemporary European Furniture
1300 Western Avenue; 206-287-9992; s.ammor@divafurniture.com;
Hours: Mon–Fri 9:30–6, Sat 11–6, Sun 12–5; www.divafurniture.com;
Credit Cards: MC, Visa, AmEx; Owners are Phillippe Rousselin and Stephanie de Oliveira

Price: Personnel:

Ambiance: Quality:

If you are looking for sleek and contemporary Italian (B&B Italia, Maxalto, etc.) and other contemporary European-styled furniture, this is a perfect place to shop. This is a starkly modern, loft-like showroom with white walls. Diva has an impressive selection of lighting, many of the fixtures made by Fontana, and ranges from $250 to $4,000. There are no price tags, because with many fabric and finish options the price can fluctuate greatly. Service is very good here, but be prepared for the high prices. Designers receive a 15% discount. The Web site shows pictures, but no prices. It is not possible to buy online.

INFORM

Contemporary European Furniture

1220 Western Avenue; 206-622-1608; Allison@informseattle.com;

Hours: Mon–Sat 10–6, Sun 12–5; www.informseattle.com; Credit

Cards: MC, Visa, AmEx; Owners are Nancy and Niels Bendtsen

Price: Personnel:

Ambiance: Quality:

Inform, a company based in Vancouver for 25 years, has recently opened a showroom in Seattle. I found furniture designs by Knoll, Herman Miller, and Kartell, to name a few. While there were many interesting pieces here, including some unusual bentwood chairs and benches, I found many of the square-shaped sofas to be uncomfortable and expensive relative to that of the competition. Fabrics are decent, but I wouldn't necessarily come here for the fabrics. Designers receive a 15–20% discount depending on the manufacturer. Service is good. The Web site lists manufacturers but shows no pictures.

McKINNON FURNITURE

Handmade Arts & Crafts–Style Furniture

1201 Western Avenue; 206-622-6474 or 800-532-5461;

showroom@mckinnonfurniture.com; Hours: Mon–Fri 10–6,

Sat 10–5, Sun 12–5; www.mckinnonfurniture.com;

Credit Cards: MC, Visa, AmEx, Discover;

Owners are Sheila McKinnon and Theresa Schneider

Price: Personnel:

Ambiance: Quality:

If you like quality handmade furniture, McKinnon Furniture is one store you should visit. It's a busy place that seems to attract a fair share of customers. When I came here, I waited for several minutes before the saleswoman was finished with all of her clients and could help me. Service was ultimately very good, though, and I felt that I got a lot of attention.

McKinnon specializes in handmade furniture representative of Stickley/Arts & Crafts furniture. What I admire about this store, aside from the fact that its furniture is all handmade, is that the finishing is well done. You can even select your own finishes. There are no designer discounts, but there are volume discounts offered for purchases over $2,500 of 10–15%. The Web site is excellent, showing images, variations, and prices. They even include a map and directions to their showroom. You can't buy online.

DEEP INTERIOR

Contemporary, Rustic Furniture and Accessories
1006 Western Avenue; 206-621-1380; Hours: Mon–Fri 10–6,
Sat 10–5, Sun 12–5; www.deepinterior.com; Credit Cards: MC, Visa,
AmEx; Owner is Kevin Kurbs

Price: Personnel:

Ambiance: Quality:

Deep Interior has some nice rattan chairs, great candlesticks, and notable leather classics. Prices seem high here in this crowded space. One nice feature about Deep Interior is that if you buy furniture here, they will not charge a decorating fee. Decorating services include window covering, carpeting, and general interior decorating. Discounts to designers usually start at $5,000 and the discounts vary. The Web site shows pictures and prices, but you cannot buy online.

CURRENT

Contemporary Italian Furniture
629 Western Avenue; 206-622-2433;
info@currentonline.com; Hours: Mon–Sat 10–6, Sun 12–5;
www.currentonline.com; Credit Cards: MC, Visa, AmEx;
Owner is Ron Gawith

Price: Personnel:

Ambiance: Quality:

I thoroughly enjoyed shopping at Current. Ron Gawith, a 23-year veteran, was very helpful and showed his passion for the business by giving me a tour of his entire showroom, pointing out many of his designers' pieces. I thought that the variety of furniture was spectacular and well displayed, and I particularly liked the housewares and lighting. Much of the furniture is upholstered in primary colors. Designers can receive a discount depending on each manufacturer, but there is also a sale once a year. Well-known manufacturers whose lines are sold here include: Minotti, Armani Casa, Cassina, and Desalto.

ANTIQUE IMPORTERS

English Country Furniture
620 Alaskan Way (Entrance is also on Western Avenue);
206-628-8905; Hours: Mon–Thu 9:30–6, Fri, Sat 9:30–7;
Credit Cards: MC, Visa, AmEx, Discover; Owner is Chris Kappler

Price: | Personnel:
Ambiance: | Quality:

Chris Kappler has had this big warehouse for 22 years. He is very friendly, and the store has a relaxed atmosphere for those of you who don't want to be bugged. I couldn't get over the vast selection of antique pine furniture. Designers can get discounts; there is no set discount.

Lake Union

Lake Union is a busy part of town right near the downtown. Up until recently, there wasn't much here except for big warehouses. The neighborhood has been gentrified and there are a number of interesting restaurants and shops. I would advise driving a car in this part of town.

GLENN RICHARDS

Asian Antiques and Contemporary Asian Furniture
964 Denny Way; 206-287-1877; john@glennrichards.com;

Hours: Tue–Sat 10–6; www.glennrichards.com;
Credit Cards: MC, Visa, AmEx; Owners are Laurie and John Fairman

Price:  Personnel: Ambiance: Quality:

Located on a busy street, this store has a dull façade that may prompt you to keep on going when passing by in your car, but I strongly recommend a visit here if you're at all interested in Asian. Glenn Richards has the largest selection of Asian furniture I have ever seen. I received excellent service, and the saleswoman walked me around the huge showroom. The warehouse-like space is divided into rooms according to country, so it is easy to find the specific inventory you want if searching for items from a particular area. If nothing else, it is a great place to learn about furniture and artifacts from all over Asia. The owners also own the famous upscale Seattle Asian antiques store, Honeychurch, around the corner. The Web site shows inventory, but not prices. It is not possible to buy online. Designers receive a 20% discount.

HONEYCHURCH ANTIQUES

Fine Asian Antiques and Art
411 Westlake Avenue North; 206-622-1225;
john@honeychurch.com; Hours: Tue–Sat 11–5;
www.honeychurch.com; Credit Cards: MC, Visa, AmEx;
Owners are Laurie and John Fairman

Price:  Personnel: Ambiance: Quality:

Honeychurch is one of the best-known quality Asian antiques stores in the country. Containing a museum collection of art and antiques, this fascinating shop has a national reputation that is well deserved. John Fairman walked me around the store, pointing out many never-before-seen pieces. His explanation of this complex subject matter was very relaxed and understandable. Even the façade of the brown-painted building is Asian-looking. The business has been around for 30 years. Designers receive a discount of 20%. The owners travel to Asia four to five times each year to replenish their inventory. The Web site offers some pictures and descriptions but no prices. Well worth a trip.

DAVID SMITH & CO.

Asian Furniture/Antiques

334 Boren Avenue North; 206-223-1598; sales@davidsmithco.com; Hours: Daily 11–6; www.davidsmithco.com; Credit Cards: MC, Visa, AmEx, Discover; Owner is David Smith

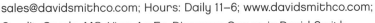 

Price: Personnel:

Ambiance: Quality:

David Smith is one of my favorite stores anywhere. A local Seattle woman I ran into gave me the heads-up on this wonderful place. I drove by several times before realizing I had the right address. With big green nylon umbrellas in front as markers, this is one of the most unusual furniture stores in the country. The inside of the shop has just as many surprises as the outside. In business for 15 years, David Smith has a laid-back shop on one square block. The warehouse is so much fun to browse, you might want to set aside an afternoon. He wholesales to dealers as well. Much of the furniture is from Indonesia and is made from teak and bamboo. Other furniture is from China, Thailand, and Java where David manufactures much of his own line of furniture. Noteworthy is the garden furniture; I found a great plantation chaise for only $200. Many pieces cost less than $200. The furniture is highly unusual and sophisticated, yet affordable. Designers receive a 20% discount. The Web site has wonderful pictures and explanations of inventory but no prices.

Fremont

Fremont is a fun neighborhood with cute restaurants, bars and shops. This is a popular place for twenty-somethings to hang out.

DELUXE JUNK

Flea Market Finds
3518 Fremont Place North; 206-634-2733;
deluxejunk@comcast.net; Hours: Wed–Sun 11:30–5:30;
Credit Cards: MC, Visa, AmEx, Discover; Owner is David Marzullo

Price: Personnel: Ambiance: Quality:

If you like going to flea markets, Deluxe Junk is ideal. I liked coming here, not so much because the inventory is so fabulous, but because the lively, happening atmosphere feels like being at a flea market with chic 20-year-olds. There is a little bit of everything, with a bent toward retro styles. Most of the customers are young people, and the store is always packed. In one corner you'll find vintage toasters; in another, vintage sunglasses, books, and clothes. This is a well-known Seattle shop that has been in business for 25 years.

Seattle Design Center

Design Center with many showrooms; sells to the trade only
5701 Sixth Avenue South; 206-762-1200; Mon–Fri 9–5;
www.seattledesigncenter.com

The Seattle Design Center, located in Georgetown, just three miles south of the Safeco stadium where the Mariners play, is like most of the rest of the design centers in this country, and is reserved for designers and their clients. Like the Design Center of the Americas (DCOTA) in Miami, the Seattle Design Center (SDC) requires you to have a designer to shop, but if you don't have one they will provide you a list of designers who will be able to help you (for a fee, of course). These designers work on call Monday through Friday, 12 to 5. I got a little lost getting there—keep in mind, it is in an industrial neighborhood adjacent to several highways. The building, partitioned off into two buildings under one roof, has about 150 national and local furniture manufacturers represented here with approximately 65 showrooms. Among the national heavyweights are Beacon Hill, Scalamandre, and Ebanista (I like this showroom very much). Local showrooms worth noting are Elinor & Verve, RL Finer, Terris Draheim, and Ralph Hays. The Center is on two floors and there is a little eatery in the middle of the building. List prices are shown, from which a designer receives a discount. No net prices are disclosed if you are not a designer.

Renton

Renton is a suburb of Seattle with many shopping centers and restaurants. I drove there just to see Seattle's well-known IKEA.

IKEA *(see also appendix)*
600 SW 43rd Street; 425-656-2980;
Hours: Mon–Fri 10–9:30, Sat 10–9, Sun 10–8

People in Seattle can't seem to get enough of IKEA. In fact, so heavy is its influence on the Seattle community, many locals are now referring to the "IKEA-ization of Seattle." Like a self-contained city in itself, the place is so humongous you can easily get lost in it. Both you and your kids will love the daycare center set up so they can play while you shop. There is even a large cafeteria with kid food on the menu. I have to say, this particular Seattle chain store location is pretty amazing in that it has creative displays of fun, happening, chic, contemporary furniture that seem to go on forever. The furniture may be a little rickety, but no one seems to care. The low prices here make these exceptionally well-styled pieces a good value when compared to the high prices of other retailers. I think the best values are in sofas, storage units, children's furniture, and desk lamps. Other products I like are the kitchen chairs and tables. It is hard getting someone to help you here, so you need to be self-sufficient. The Web site offers pictures, descriptions, and prices. Many pieces can be ordered online. I think this is a very easy Web site to shop.

SEATTLE AUCTION HOUSES

Hamilton Auction Gallery
6305 6th Avenue
Tacoma
253-534-4445

Seattle Auction House
5931 4th Avenue South
206-764-4444

SEATTLE FLEA MARKETS

Fremont Sunday Market
600 North 34th Street
206-282-5706

CHAPTER 16

Washington, DC

Aside from being America's great political stronghold, Washington, DC is a cultural and social force as powerful as anywhere in the country. World-renowned performances at the Kennedy Center for the Performing Arts, black-tie events, official state dinners, and elegant private parties in the Georgetown circuit that read like a "who's who" of world leaders are an everyday way of life here.

Likewise, the city where our government hangs its hat also offers many wonderful furniture shopping possibilities. As diverse as its inhabitants, there is a wide selection of furniture here, old and new, expensive and modest. Many of the Washington stores I visited were proud to share with me the list of well-known celebrities and political bigwigs that frequent the shops here, including Laura Bush.

You don't need a car around here because everything is in close proximity within neighborhoods. I would recommend bringing your walking shoes because certain areas, like Georgetown, are hilly. Public transportation is available with buses and trains. Taxis are usually easy to catch. For a nice afternoon, you may also wish to visit Alexandria, Virginia, and Bethesda, Maryland. These towns are no more than thirty minutes outside of Washington. If you only have one day to spend furniture shopping in DC, I would recommend taking a stroll along Wisconsin Avenue in Georgetown, beginning in the 1200 block or so and walking up a few miles. You'll find this to be not only a fun shopping experience, but an enlightening and educational one as well. Many of the furniture stores that are located in attractive row houses have rich historical pasts to share. There are also great eateries in the neighborhood and on the little side streets!

If you are interested in some wonderful sightseeing excursions in the DC area, I highly recommend taking tours of the following: The State Department, Hillwood (home of Marjorie Merriwether Post), The Kreeger (former home of the past Chairman of Geico Insurance), and Tudor Place (home to Martha Washington's granddaughter). I found these tours to be interesting and the homes really fun to browse.

DC RETAIL STORES

Georgetown Area

Georgetown is one of the most charming neighborhoods in America. The neighborhood has some of the oldest houses in the country and they are worth seeing. I like the energy and cosmopolitan feel in Georgetown, not to mention some great restaurants and ice cream parlors.

RH 1300

20th- and 21st-Century Furniture and Accessories
1300 Wisconsin Avenue; 202-464-7400;
RH1300@randomharvestinc.com; Hours: Mon–Thu 11–6, Fri 11–8,
Sat 11–6, Sun 12–6; Credit Cards: MC, Visa, AmEx;
Owner is Beth Aberg

Price: 🪑🪑🪑   Personnel: 🪑🪑🪑🪑🪑
Ambiance: 🪑🪑🪑🪑🪑   Quality: 🪑🪑🪑🪑🪑

RH 1300 is one of my favorite stores in DC. I found this small store specializing in mid-20th- and 21st-century furniture to be as chic and fresh as the great jazz music that greeted me; a refreshing departure from many of the more conservative and traditional furniture stores in the Georgetown area. Newly opened and located in a charming grayish building on the corner of Wisconsin and 13th, this very hip store is frequented by a mostly young crowd (probably between 20 and 40 years old). I was left to peruse the store myself, which suited me fine. Prices are extremely fair, with most items costing under $1,000. Designers receive a 10% discount for items off the floor, or 20% off special orders after spending $10,000. When asked if any famous people have been in the store, the clerk told me that Laura Bush had visited. The same owner has another Georgetown store, the popular Random Harvest, whose furniture doesn't at all resemble that of RH 1300.

RANDOM HARVEST

English and French Country, Rustic Antiques and Reproductions
1313 Wisconsin Avenue; 202-333-5569;
RH1300@randomharvestinc.com; Hours: Mon–Thu 11–6, Fri 11–8,
Sat 11–6, Sun 12–6; Credit Cards: MC, Visa, AmEx;
Owner is Beth Aberg

Price: | | | | | | Personnel: | | | | | |
Ambiance: | | | | | | Quality: | | | | | |

Random Harvest's inventory is ordinary compared to its upbeat sister store, RH 1300. To its favor, though, Random Harvest's furniture is practical and functional—perfect for a family. When I walked in to this large, rustic mom-and-pop space painted an invitingly pretty celadon green, I was immediately greeted by the scent of newly waxed furniture. Many of the pieces are reproductions of French Provincial and 19th-century English. There are many fabrics available, and the store offers upholstery service. Prices seem fair for the quality. Most items are between $1,000 and $2,000. Returns are offered as store credit only within 14 days of purchase. This is a busy store, and you may have to wait for assistance. There are no designer discounts.

DARRELL DEAN ANTIQUES AND DECORATIVE ARTS

Eclectic European Antiques and Accessories
1524 Wisconsin Avenue; 202-333-6330;
Darrell@darrelldeanantiques.com; Hours: Tue–Sat 10:30–5:30;
www.darrelldeanantiques.com; Credit Cards: MC, Visa, Discover;
Owner is Darrell Dean

Price: Personnel:

Ambiance: Quality:

Don't let the rickety old chairs outside the entrance fool you—Darrell Dean is an uncommon mix of sophisticated and funky. This most unusual "cocktail" is spread out on two floors of a row house with a pale gray façade. Darrell Dean prides himself on not getting stuck on one period of furniture. The day I came to the shop there was a collection of hand sculptures, cool bar stools, a big Chinese root wood chair (very wild), and other things that would capture anyone's attention. Darrell, a mild-mannered guy who dresses casually in blue jeans, gives the shop an overall pleasant, comfortable atmosphere. I felt very much at ease browsing around this shop. Prices are high, though 15–20% discounts are given to designers (and sometimes customers). Local and national celebrities have come to shop here, and on the day I shopped, I met a client who was married to a well-known, high-profile journalist. The store has an attractive Web site, with pictures and prices of inventory.

JOHN ROSSELLI

English Antiques and Reproductions, Fabrics
1515 Wisconsin Avenue, NW; 202-337-7676; Hours: Mon–Fri 10-5,
Sat 11–4; Credit Cards: MC, Visa, AmEx; Owner is John Rosselli

Price: Personnel:

Ambiance: Quality:

This store, which sells mostly period traditional English furniture, is so quiet you might think it closed when entering. Customer service is definitely not the priority here; in fact, the staff was so stoic, I felt nervous about asking questions. The store is worth a visit, however, for the many painted pieces and pretty light fixtures which John Rosselli produces. Their workroom is in New York, and they represent a nice variety of fabrics from many traditional fabric designers. They ship all around the country. Prices are very high, and discounts are only given to designers who show their business cards.

GORE * DEAN ON DESIGNER'S ROW

European Antiques and Accessories

1525–1529 Wisconsin Avenue, NW; 202-625-9199;
goredeanantiques@aol.com; Hours: Mon–Fri 9:30–5, Sat 11–6;
www.gore-dean.com; Credit Cards: MC, Visa, AmEx;
Owner is Deborah Gore Dean

Price: 🪑🪑🪑🪑🪑 Personnel: 🪑🪑🪑🪑🪑

Ambiance: 🪑🪑🪑🪑🪑 Quality: 🪑🪑🪑🪑🪑

I liked visiting this well-known Georgetown store. The atmosphere is as mellow as the quiet jazz playing in the background. There are beautiful linens, many of them handmade, and a host of European antiques and reproduction furniture. This store has beautiful light fixtures, and there is a second floor for more browsing, where other dealers are located. I especially loved the old wide-planked floors which really add character to the shop. There are many upholstery fabrics by J. Robert Scott to choose from. Prices are steep (higher than most shops in the neighborhood); designers, who represent most of the business, get a 15% discount on antiques. Even with a discount, there are no bargains here. There is no return policy. The Web site includes pictures and prices.

D. STRICKLIN ANTIQUES

Eclectic European Antiques
1653 Wisconsin Avenue, NW; 202-333-1653;
Hours: Hit or miss or by appointment;
Owner is Debe Stricklin (pronounced "Debbie")

Price: 🪑🪑🪑🪑🪑 Personnel: 🪑🪑🪑🪑🪑

Ambiance: 🪑🪑🪑🪑🪑 Quality: 🪑🪑🪑🪑🪑

With no sign in front, no business cards, no price tags, and no real store hours, shopping at this store is a challenge! You may be wondering, then, why it rates five chairs plus a chair of distinction. Despite the hit-or-miss nature of the place, I was completely won over by both the endearing, eccentric owner, Debe, and her store from the minute I entered the shop. D. Stricklin has the most unusual European antiques and architectural objects. On the day of my visit, I saw some huge gates from a home in Europe that were spectacular, and all kinds of crazy-looking tables and lamps. I especially liked an incredible light fixture hanging off a tree, not something you see every day! Debe buys throughout Europe, and it shows. All I could think when I saw the store is that a theater company would die to have these pieces as props. What truly makes this place unique is the woman who owns it, a nonconformist, high-spirited character who was fun meeting. Although there are no price tags, Debe insists she quotes the same price to everybody. Designers get a 20% discount. I am not so sure it is easy to negotiate here.

SIXTEEN FIFTY-NINE ANTIQUES/INTERIORS

Mid-Century Modern Furniture and Accessories/Art

1659 Wisconsin Avenue, NW; 202-333-1480; sixteenfiftynine@hotmail.com; Hours: Tue–Sat 11–5; www.sixteenfiftynine.com; Credit Cards: MC and Visa; Owner is Mike Johnson

Price: Personnel: Ambiance: Quality:

With a gracious walk-up entrance set back a little from the street, this chic new store offers mostly Mid-Century Modern furniture. Practical sums up the inventory here. One curious note about the owner is that Mike Johnson, an avid collector of this Mid-Century Modern furniture with a background in the construction business, decided to pursue his interest by opening the store. What a 360-degree turnaround, from hard hats and concrete to stylish Mid-Century! An incredibly friendly and knowledgeable guy, Mike spent much time answering my questions. Prices are quite attractive here—most items sell for under $1,000. In my opinion the prices are very fair, given the craze for 20th-century furniture. Returns are allowed only as store credit.

A MANO

Home Accessories

1677 Wisconsin Avenue, NW; 202-298-7200;

Hours: Mon–Sat 10–6, Sun 12–5; amanoinc@aol.com;

Credit Cards: MC, Visa, AmEx; Owner is Adam Mahr

Price: Personnel: Ambiance: Quality:

If you are spending any time in Georgetown, definitely stop here for a shopping treat! A Mano, also located in Naples, Florida, feels like you are visiting a beautiful villa in the countryside of Italy. This store has a collection of the most unusual rustic and formal dishes, serving pieces, and unique accessories made by a myriad of designers from all around the world. As busy as the store was when I went inside, I was greeted by the most gracious woman (she had no clue I was writing this book!) who took the time to explain the background and merchandise of the store. I was pleasantly surprised to see a beautiful terrace in the back which houses a collection of luscious-colored and unusually shaped planter boxes made in all sizes. Whether you are accessorizing your home or your garden, A Mano is a must-see.

MILLER & ARNEY ANTIQUES

European Antiques

1737 Wisconsin Avenue, NW; 202-338-2369;

antiques@millerarney.com; Hours: Mon–Sat 9:30–5;

www.millerarney.com; Credit Cards: MC, Visa, AmEx;

Owner is Joe Miller

Price: Personnel: Ambiance: Quality:

This store has been around for 30 years, making it one of the longest-running antiques stores in DC. The same owner is still there and from the looks of it, not much has changed. The outside is a blond brick two-story building that you might just as soon pass up, but if you're a fan of period European furniture, I encourage you to stop here. I felt like I was inside a Draconian boardroom at a bank when I entered, intimidated by the dark furniture and dim lighting that surrounded me. Joe Miller, a man who looks like a politician himself, has a lot of interesting stories to tell about famous politicians and celebrities who have shopped in his store, including Elton John, Tom Daschle, Hillary Clinton, and others. Prices are fair for the merchandise he is selling, and some negotiating is possible. "Everyone wants to feel as if they have gotten a good deal these days," says Joe Miller. Returns are allowed for a full refund. Most items are over $2,000. You'll enjoy both the owner's stories and the inventory! The Web site contains only a few pictures and no prices.

SARAH WESSEL DESIGNS

Upholstery, French Antiques, and Accessories
3214 O Street NW; 202-337-1910; Hours: Tue–Sat 11–5:30;
sarwessel@hotmail.com; Credit Cards: MC, Visa;
Owner is Sarah Wessel

Price: Personnel:

Ambiance: Quality:

Just around the corner from Wisconsin Avenue in the heart of Georgetown is this cute little antiques shop next to the well-known antiques store, Susquehanna Antique Company. The first things I noticed in this shop were the lovely chairs and sofas. Much of the store is a design shop, catering to designers and homeowners looking for upholstery, fabrics, wall coverings, and flooring. Other charming accessories include pillows, linens, and handbags. There is also a small selection of vintage garden furniture. I wouldn't necessarily send someone out of their way to shop here, but it is a cute neighborhood shop with good service.

SUSQUEHANNA ANTIQUE COMPANY, INC.

European and American Antiques and Art
3216 O Street, NW; 202-333-1511; davidf15x@aol.com;

Hours: Mon–Sat 10–6; www.susquehannaantiques.com;
Credit Cards: MC, Visa, AmEx; Owner is David Friedman

Price: Personnel: Ambiance: Quality:

Probably the oldest surviving antiques store in DC, Susquehanna is now operated by the family's third generation. This is a must-see store that really captures the flavor of the traditional DC area. It is a large store with a relaxing feel if you just want to browse. Everything here is period. Most of the inventory is English, but there is also a good supply of American and French. Even the breed of the store's mascot, an adorable little Cavalier King Charles Spaniel dog named Pups, is from dogs seen in early paintings. Now located in a brick building just off Wisconsin Avenue, Susquehanna has moved a few times in its 100 years of business. Unlike many of its competitors, Susquehanna allows you to actually shop and buy online. David Friedman is enthusiastic about his merchandise, and prices are very fair for the merchandise relative to other dealers selling the same quality. Discounts of 10–15% are standard for designers, but sometimes more is given. An online newsletter will be created soon. Worth the trip! The Web site includes pictures, prices, and extensive descriptions of inventory.

JUDE KISSINGER

18th- and 19th-Century French Furniture
3148 Dumbarton Street, NW; 202-298-8444; Hours: Mon–Sat 11–5;
Owner is Jude Kissinger

Price: Personnel: Ambiance: Quality:

What you first notice about this store, located in a brownstone just off Wisconsin Avenue on a mostly residential street, are the big, ugly orange chairs out in front to attract walkers-by. But don't let these funky chairs fool you. Inside, Jude Kissinger is a store with some special and classic 19th-century French furniture. Most of the stuff is simple, covered in white canvas cloth. Only here for two years, Jude was previously in LA. This is one of the few DC stores specializing in French antiques. Discounts to designers are between 15% and20%.

GOOD EYE INTERIORS

Mid-Century Modern
4918 Wisconsin Avenue, NW; 202-244-8516;
travis@goodeyeonline.com; Hours: Fri 12–7, Sat 11–7, Sun 12–5;
www.goodeyeonline.com; Credit Cards: MC, Visa, Discover;
Owner is Travis Smith

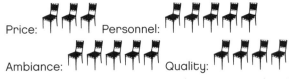

Price: Personnel:
Ambiance: Quality:

Up a distance on Wisconsin Avenue, in an electric-orange-painted small building on a busy section of the street, is Good Eye Interiors. You may be inclined not to stop here, where there aren't any other furniture stores, but if you are a retro furniture fan you will miss the boat if you don't explore this great, nationally well known store. Travis Smith has been in this business for 20 years and devotes his life to finding the best inventory. The furniture here is Mid-Century Modern. There's no telling what wonderful finds await you among two full floors of furnishings (one being the basement). Inventory changes constantly. Prices are affordable, most items being $500 or less. Designers get a 10% discount, and there are periodic sales. Many sales are from outside DC, and lots of designers come here from New York City to buy furniture here. Great service and a fun shopping experience. They have a very creative Web site that includes pictures of inventory, room layouts, and vignettes showing furniture in a room so shoppers can have an easier time decorating their home. Prices are posted on the Web site , and it is possible to buy online.

BO CONCEPT

Contemporary Furniture
3342 M Street NW; 202-333-5656;
georgetown@boconceptusa.com; Hours: Mon–Sat 10–7, Sun 12–5;

www.boconcept.com; Credit Cards: MC, Visa, AmEx;
Owned by a Danish corporation

Price: Personnel: Ambiance: Quality:

I am completely infatuated with Bo Concept. This well-known international furniture store now has locations around the world. Like many other contemporary furniture designers, Bo Concept appeals to a younger, hip crowd that wants both fashion and functionality. The furniture here is a step up from the stuff at IKEA, and the service is impressive. This store has such wonderful designs, and I was impressed not only by the low prices, but also by the surprisingly good craftsmanship relative to the prices. I especially liked all of the storage systems made in a variety of colors and materials with flexible sizing. I found the staff to be extremely knowledgeable about the merchandise and very friendly. You will love the fun monochromatic fabrics. Bo Concept is also a great source for affordable lighting. The Web site includes pictures and prices, but it is not possible to buy online.

HOLLIS & KNIGHT, LTD.

General Furniture Store
3320 M Street NW; 202-333-6999; mail@hollisandknight.com;
Hours: Tue–Sat 10–6, Sun, Mon 12–5; www.hollisandknight.com;
Credit Cards: MC and Visa; Owner is Wendell Barrett

Price: Personnel: Ambiance: Quality:

Many DC dwellers come here to do one-stop shopping for their homes. Next to Cady's Alley, a small building with few furniture stores but a great lighting store (and soon-to-arrive restaurants), is Hollis & Knight's big two-floor showroom. The store has a large selection of mostly reproduction and some contemporary pieces, but most of the furniture has a traditional feel. Many of the pieces are made under their own private label. There is a complete selection of fabrics, rugs, and carpeting. Discounts to decorators depend on the individual lines of furniture. There is a three-day return policy. The Web site includes pictures, but discloses prices only for a few items.

Adams Neighborhood/14th and U Street Corridor

These neighborhoods feel more like the real "city." Both neighborhoods are right near the downtown and have some trendy, but not really fancy, shops and restaurants.

THE BRASS KNOB

Restored Hardware, Garden Accessories,
Architectural Ornaments
2311 18th Street; 202-332-3370; bk@thebrassknob.com;
Hours: Mon–Sat 10:30–6, Sun 12–5; www.thebrassknob.com;
Owners are Donetta George and Ron Allan

Price: 🪑🪑🪑🪑 Personnel: 🪑🪑🪑🪑🪑

Ambiance: 🪑🪑🪑🪑🪑 Quality: 🪑🪑🪑🪑🪑

In the Adams neighborhood is The Brass Knob, a great hardware source for people who wish to add a little vintage character to their homes. Having been in business for 23 years, this place has every kind of restored hardware, knobs, garden pieces, and lighting you can imagine. You could spend hours perusing the inventory. Unfortunately, such stores are a dying breed because antique hardware is so rare these days. The Web site includes pictures and pricing.

GOODWOOD

American Furniture and Decorative Arts
1428 U Street; 202-986-3640; danandanna@verizon.net;
Hours: Thu 5–9, Fri, Sat 11–7, Sun 11–5; Credit Cards: MC, Visa;
Owners are Anna and Daniel Kahoe

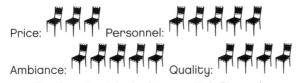

Price: Personnel:

Ambiance: Quality:

Goodwood might be better called Green Acres, as in the old TV series. Look for a large brown sign on a very large, gray warehouse-looking building that looks like a barn . . . quite a departure for the urban city slickers in this town. Located in the 14th and U Street corridor, this store is a really fun shopping experience. There are interesting things to look at in every corner, kind of like shopping at a great flea market. Most of the furniture is Early American, but there are also lots of great architectural artifacts and accessories. Feel free to browse at your own leisure. The store has friendly staff and fair prices. Designers receive a 15% discount, and occasionally the public receives a discount.

Washington Design Center

Design Center with many showrooms; sells to the trade and in the lower level, some showrooms sell to the public, too
300 D Street SW; 202-554-5053; Hours: Mon–Fri 9-5 Sat 10–3 open in lower level to the public; www.kitchenbathcenter.com

Housed near many federal buildings, the Washington Design Center is a sprawling facility with eight floors. Most showrooms are only open to designers, yet all the showrooms allowed me to browse freely without checking for an ID. Favorite national showrooms located here include: Holly Hunt, Hines, Baker, Brunschwig & Fils, Nancy Corzine, Kirk Brummel, Swedish Country, and Donghia. Other showrooms I liked that are only located in DC include Pugrant and DSA Associates. Pricing here shows a list price, but designers do not pay list because they receive a discount not offered to the public. Most furniture here is expensive, discount or no discount, and many of the pieces need to be custom-ordered.

DC AREA AUCTION HOUSES

Sloan's and Kenyon
301-634-2330
4605 Bradley Boulevard
Bethesda, MD 20815
www.sloansandkenyon.com

Weschler's
800-331-1430 or 202-628-1281
909 East Street, NW
Washington, DC 20004
www.weschlers.com

DC AREA ANTIQUES SHOWS

Baltimore Summer Antiques Fair
September
Downtown at Inner Harbor
West Pratt Entrance
Baltimore, MD
310-933-6994 or 410-649-7396 (during the show)

Spring Antiques Show
March
The DC Armory
301-933-9433

Washington Antiques Show
January
The Omni Shore Hotel
202-965-0640

DC AREA FLEA MARKETS

Georgetown Flea Market
Wisconsin Avenue, Washington, DC (Just North of S. Street);
202-775-FLEA; sussman@georgetownfleamarket.com;
Managers are Bill Millstead and Butch Finch
Every Sunday, 9–5, all year long

CHAPTER 17

High Point, North Carolina

In a book like this covering mostly major cities, it may be hard for you to understand how High Point fits into the furniture store equation. Well, High Point is not only the furniture capital of the U.S., but also the place where many furniture store owners from around the country get their inventory during "Market," a trade show which occurs twice each year in April and October. The entire area surrounding and including High Point is centered on the furniture industry. Manufacturers of all kinds of furniture (mostly the big names) have factories and outlets in this town and surrounding communities. Greensboro is next to High Point and a great airport to commute from when coming here. High Point is small and not a particularly pretty town. It feels industrial and commercial, and of course, everything is all about furniture here.

High Point During Market

There have not been many books written about High Point, and the few that were published have actually added to the confusion surrounding what actually goes on in our nation's furniture capital. Hopefully, the following will help lessen some of that confusion.

As in the fashion industry, where fashion designers convene in Paris/New York to introduce their new lines for the year and take orders from buyers, High Point is where dealers come from around the world to display their furnishings twice a year so furniture store buyers can make their buying decisions six months in advance. *Market* is the country's major trade show where buyers and furniture industry leaders not only get a feel for what furniture trends are today but also where the industry is going. Lots of the furniture styles displayed here are not even seen in other parts of the country, but the majority of American consumers are familiar with and buy furniture from the many lines sold in High Point. There are three main buildings in High Point for buyers at Market. In these buildings, buyers are carefully screened before being allowed inside to keep the public out. Market is not open to the public, unless you come with a designer. Only buyers and designers are eligible for the wholesale prices charged at this trade-only show. Visiting High Point during Market, I had a very difficult time getting into the booths at the show because I was considered to be the "press," and not a store owner.

During Market, the town is packed with people, and shuttle buses take buyers to and from the surrounding areas into the furniture area (where Main Street and Commerce intersect).

When Market is not taking place, the buildings are used for other purposes like community events, shows, benefits, etc. There are, however, 70 outlet stores in the surrounding area and they provide shoppers with year-round furniture shopping possibilities.

What Does High Point Have for the Public?

Capitalizing on High Point's draw as a furniture capital, local furniture manufacturers who have plants in High Point, Hickory, and surrounding neighborhoods have eagerly opened showrooms to the public. The furniture shown in these outlet stores is largely mainstream and appeals to most Americans. Many showrooms are for the trade only, but those open to the public have become popular spots for people from around the world looking for typically medium-priced, mostly traditional furniture, sometimes at a discount. Some showrooms also sell samples or furniture that has been discontinued.

Planning a Trip to High Point

If you want to know what is going on in High Point, go to www.highpoint.org. This Web site tells what is taking place and will refer you to other Web sites for more information. There is also a wonderful book called *Shopping the North Carolina Furniture Outlets* by Ellen R. Shapiro, (Three Rivers Press, April 2003), which tells you the layout of the town and the major design buildings that are showrooms during Market, and recommends places to stay, eat, and visit. Another perk of this book is that it tells you how to ship your purchases home at the best rates.

Hotels in the neighborhood charge high prices during Market. Staying in Greensboro instead of High Point may get you a better deal and still allow you to take the shuttle to High Point, which is just 15 minutes away. Flying into High Point during the show can be a challenge—flights for Market book early. There are good airfare deals, though, and the overnight expenses will pay off in the long run. You can fly into Charlotte, North Carolina, and then drive about two hours to High Point, or you can fly into Greensboro, which is right next to High Point.

Shopping at Market with a Designer

This next statement is a bit controversial, and I'm certain that the designers will feel overwhelmed and overly challenged at this suggestion, but I strongly recommend going with your designer to High Point during Market when the goods are at least half off what you would pay at a retail store in your neighborhood. Prices are lower during Market because shop owners from around the country are here to shop the selection, buying at wholesale prices. The low prices will be an incentive to pay a designer's commission so that you won't have to figure out where to go when you get there. Let the designer do the legwork for you and navigate you around the town and into all the showrooms. Your designer can shop with you at all of the showrooms you're interested in within this 11-million-square-foot neighborhood.

Shopping on Your Own

You may prefer to avoid the congestion of Market and shop High Point's year-round showrooms and outlets on your own, looking for good furniture at discounted prices. The first misconception about High Point is that it's an easy place to shop. People think that they can just stop there for a day and find everything in one spot. False! There are virtually hundreds of stores and showrooms here spread out over several miles. If you have never been to High Point, figuring out where to go could be challenging. Many compare a trip to High Point with going on a huge scavenger hunt. I recommend not trying to see it all in one trip—you will confuse yourself.

For your first visit to High Point, I recommend spending the day at a place called **Furnitureland South.** This is the world's largest home furnishings store, with 1 million square feet of furniture, so get ready to spend some time here! Don't worry about wasting away; they have a café on the premises.

At Furnitureland South you can either walk the showroom by yourself, (and feel totally overwhelmed), or you can choose to have a salesperson give you a personal tour. Most of the salespeople are also ASID designers, so they are able to help you design a room. You can get lost, but I was advised to walk in the same direction as the tracks for the lighting. If you are wandering the store by yourself and feel confused, you can go to one of the nearby kiosks and type in questions and receive answers immediately. I wish all stores had this kiosk feature; it would save us all a lot of time.

Unlike many showrooms in High Point, Furnitureland South doesn't manufacture anything.

Because the store is so large, representing more than 450 manufacturers, it has buying power that allows it to give consumers discounts they may otherwise not get at another retailer. As is the case in all of High Point, customers can expect to get 40% off the retail price, but sometimes the store has sales or special markdowns. (Designers do not receive discounts different from that of the public.) There is even a separate building on the premises that houses discontinued or damaged merchandise. Most of the furniture here is traditional (although there is a modern section) and in the medium-priced category. Even if you don't see something on the floor that you are interested in purchasing, and want a piece from particular furniture lines, your salesperson will be able to get it from the factory.

Owned by the Harris family, Furnitureland South has been in business for 35 years.

The service is exceptional, and the general public feels comfortable shopping here. Hours are Monday through Saturday, 8:30 to 5:30; on Thursday and Friday the store is open until 8:30 p.m.

If you are unable to travel to High Point, check out Furnitureland South's Web site at www.furniturelandsouth.com. This is an easy and comprehensive Web site to shop. You need to call the store for prices, but you can see the selection and comparison-shop on the Web site. Famous brands include: Lexington, Century, Bernhardt, Karastan, Drexel Heritage, Anichini Linens, Lane, Hichory White, and Leathercraft. There is a large selection of children's and garden furniture, too. Shipping usually takes 8–12 weeks. The showroom will store furniture for up to one year for no additional charge.

Comparison-Shopping the Nation's Chain Stores

BO CONCEPT

www.boconcept.com; 1-480-443-0900; Shipping Cost - $50 local shipping; Warranty - 1-year warranty on furniture, 14 days for returns

Bo Concept is a wonderful store from Europe that specializes in clean-lined contemporary furniture. The stores, mostly on the East Coast, cater to a younger, hip crowd that wants fashion and functionality. The furniture is a good value for the money. Flexible sizing is an option on some items. Lighting is contemporary, cute, and inexpensive. It is not possible to buy online.

BOMBAY COMPANY

www.bombaycompany.com; 1-888-2BOMBAY; Shipping Cost - Based on purchase price ($1000.01–$1,200 = $144.95); Warranty - 30 days for return/refund

Bombay is well liked throughout the country. The pieces, surprisingly decent reproductions of English and French antiques, are durable and there is an amazing selection, including all different kinds of home décor items and even a kid's line. Most popular pieces are tables, chests, mirrors, and lamps. The furniture is reasonably priced, costing less than $500; many tables and chests cost less than $200. Shopping here is fun and easy for a consumer. If you open a Bombay charge account, you get an additional 10% discount on any purchase. Delivery is usually 7–10 days. The return policy is liberal. All the pieces come with a lifetime free-from-manufacturer's-defect warranty, so keep the receipt. The inventory in the stores is usually the same as on the Web. Online Web purchases can be exchanged directly at any store site; bring along the packing slip.

CB2

www.cb2.com; 1-800-606-6252; Shipping Cost - Local charges begin at $60, up to $225 for over $5,000 worth of merchandise; national begins at $175 for up to $800 of merchandise, up to $550 for over $8,000 worth of merchandise; Warranty - Returns for defects should be made within 7 days of receiving item. Have liberal return policy; say they stand behind items.

CB2 is a popular furniture store only in Chicago right now, catering to the young population looking for hip furniture in colorful finishes. Part of Crate & Barrel, CB2 has a great assortment of furniture and accessories, and nothing costs more than about $500. There are lots of options for less than $100. I especially like the tables, vases, and chests.

COST PLUS

www.costplus.com; 1-510-893-7300; Shipping Cost - Products available in store for take-home purchases; Warranty - Warranties are offered from individual manufacturers whose products are at Cost Plus. Take returns at any time; need original receipt for money back. If pay by check or debit card, store credit issued only. Need receipt for bedding, window coverings, and shower curtains for credit.

Cost Plus has an impressive selection of rustic, dark wood furniture. One bonus is that the furniture is ecological and the woods are grown in designated forests. Prices are low and there are always good sales. Most pieces cost less than $500 for larger-scale furniture.

COSTCO HOME

www.costco.com; 1-800-955-2292; Shipping Cost - Dependent upon manufacturer; Warranty - Take returns at any time for quality concerns.

Based in Kirkland, Washington, Costco Home has recently opened a second location in Tempe, Arizona. The store feels just like shopping in Costco. Costco sells furniture lines from hundreds of manufacturers. There is a little of everything here. I think the children's furniture is a good value and nicely designed. Don't expect the best service—they cut corners to keep overhead low. The quality is hit or miss.

CRATE & BARREL

www.crateandbarrel.com; 1-800967-6696; Shipping Cost - Over $200, 10%, local charges begin at $60; Warranty - 30 days for return/refund, but no written warranty. Defective merchandise handled on per-case basis.

Crate & Barrel is one of the most popular places to shop in the country. Filled with transitional styles that can work in the country or city, Crate & Barrel is a medium-priced store that occasionally has some good sales. I think the quality is fair for the prices. There are other stores that have this look for less money, but Crate & Barrel's best asset is that they know how to display their furniture and they have good signage and lighting. Service, when you can actually find someone available, is usually very good. While the return policy is quite liberal, there is no written warranty extended to the customer. This troubles me. Recently I tried to review furniture at Crate & Barrel for *Consumers Digest* magazine but was told I couldn't review the furniture because Crate & Barrel has no written warranty. The Crate & Barrel outlets are great and there are always good deals to find. The Web site has the same merchandise as in the store. Brands sold here include Mitchell Gold, Shenandoah, American Leather, and Richter. Furniture delivery time is between 2 and 20 weeks. I love their new hip store, CB2. There are only two stores in the country so far, both in Chicago.

DESIGN WITHIN REACH

www.dwr.com; 1-800-944-2233; Shipping Cost - Automatically calculated based on weight of order; Warranty - No written warranty. Return policy is usually 1 year, and the policy is handled on a case-by-case basis.

Design Within Reach has contemporary furniture based on classic modern designs. They tout themselves as selling the hottest iconic designs of the 20th century because they buy merchandise strictly from the best and most-sought-after designers. Prices here are often jokingly referred to as "Design Out of Reach." Despite the higher prices, service is good and the furniture is a decent value.

EDDIE BAUER

www.eddiebauer.com; 1-800-625-7935; Shipping Cost - Over $160, 10%; Warranty - 30 days for return/refund, after 30 days repair/replace for defects only

Eddie Bauer has come up with some good furniture that is traditional and resembles styles from the 18th and 19th centuries. It is not possible to buy online, but you can see the collection online. The furniture is well built and comes in a variety of prices.

EQ3

www.eq3.com; 415-552-2626; Shipping Cost - Local transport charges $65 which covers up to 3 items, plus $15 for each additional piece. Covers a 20-mile radius, or $3 charge for each additional mile. Shipping across the country is calculated by weight and size; Warranty - Most case goods have a 1-year warranty; upholstered goods have a 5-year warranty on the frame and 1 year on the upholstery. Leather upholstery has a 5-year warranty. Returns are allowed for up to 14 days in original packaging except for custom upholstery.

EQ3 is a relatively new division of Palliser, based in Canada. There are new stores all around the country. As at CB2, the furniture here resembles both a bit of retro and contemporary and appeals to a younger clientele. The prices are low, most pieces selling for less than $500, many for less than $200. This store reminds me of IKEA in its quality, prices, and look. I think the furniture is a good value, and I like the designs. You can't buy online. Prices vary from store to store because EQ3 is a franchise.

ETHAN ALLEN

www.ethanallen.com; 1-888-EAHELP; Shipping Cost - No delivery charges if ordered in your area; Warranty - Wood furniture, 5-

year warranty; frames and springs, 7-year warranty. Case goods have a 5-year warranty.

Ethan Allen has come a long way from the stodgy Early American furniture look it once had. The furniture is now more contemporary in feel, although more of a transitional look and the furniture is still made in a variety of wood finishes. There is something here for everyone, and the well-trained and professional staff is able to answer just about any questions. The stores can't always display their entire inventory, but the rest is on their Web site. Instead of having sales, Ethan Allen now has everyday "low" pricing, which is fairer and less confusing to the consumer. There is discounting, however, for floor samples that have been discontinued. Most of the 300+ stores today are now corporately owned. Delivery time for case goods is 6–10 weeks and for upholstered goods, 10–12 weeks. It is not possible to buy online. I think the upholstered pieces are an excellent value.

HOLD EVERYTHING

www.holdeverything.com; 1-800-421-2264; Shipping Cost - Over $150, 11%; Warranty - 30-day return/refund; items warranted against damage, defects, or quality concerns for life

I love the office furniture here. Prices are low, and the selection offers something for everyone. The catalog is expanding to offer more options in the near future.

IKEA

www.ikea-usa.com; 1-800-434-IKEA; Shipping Cost - Varies by state, calculated based on weight/volume, destination of freight, and cost of merchandise; Warranty - 45 days return/refund

IKEA furniture features contemporary and functional designs, and a selection of colors and fabrics that suits a large percentage of the population. Quality varies, but the look, chic style, and reasonable prices win over the customers. I love the inexpensive lamps and the good deals on the couches.

LIGNE ROSET

www.ligne-roset-usa.com; 1-800-BYROSET; Shipping Cost - Priced per item; Warranty - 5-year written warranty on all furniture

Ligne Roset is a popular furniture shop based in France that is rapidly expanding in the U.S. The furniture is not inexpensive, but the designs are simple, classic contemporary, and the upholstered pieces are extremely comfortable. There is a lot of cotton and knit upholstery that comes in an assortment of solid colors.

PIER 1 IMPORTS

www.pier1.com; 1-800-245-4595; Shipping Cost - $200–$299.99, $30; $300–$399.99, $40; $400–$499.99, $50; $500 & up, $60; Warranty - 6 months for return/refund, 25-year limited frame warranty

Pier 1 Imports is a store where everyone can shop. There is something here for people of all ages and for all styles of homes. Much of the furniture is decent quality, manufactured abroad, and costs under $500. The look is rustic, and there is always a strong exotic candle scent wafting through the air. There are nice housewares and fair prices. Pier 1 just began a higher-end catalog-only business called Special Finds. Designers even get a 20% discount here. Service is sometimes slow because the stores are usually very busy.

POTTERY BARN

www.potterybarn.com; 1-888-779-5176; Shipping Cost - Over $200, 10%; Warranty - 30 days for return/refund, 1 year against defects

Pottery Barn has a mostly rustic, traditional look with some transitional pieces mixed in with the bunch. There is a wide range of prices, but most of the inventory is medium priced. Its catalog and Web site have the same inventory or more than the stores. The quality is very good. Pottery Barn stores are usually very busy and sometimes it is hard finding someone to help you. The service is usually good once you have a salesperson helping you. Delivery time is anywhere from 5 days to 8 weeks. Popular manufacturers here include Mitchell Gold, Bernhardt, and Hyatt. Pottery Barn also owns the increasingly popular West Elm (see below), which is considered more chic and less expensive than Pottery Barn.

RESTORATION HARDWARE

www.restorationhardware.com; 1-800-762-1005; Shipping Cost - Over $200, 10%; over $10,000, 5%; Warranty - 30 days for return/refund; after 30 days replace/refund for manufacturer defects only

Restoration Hardware's name can mislead the consumer who doesn't realize that there are some great pieces of furniture here. The prices are high, but I like the selection of leather-upholstered furniture that is classic and clubby in feel. The stores also sell bathroom accessories and window treatments. The quality is good, and the service is excellent and very personal.

ROCHE-BOBOIS

www.roche-bobois.com; 1-888-779-5176; Shipping Cost - No delivery charges; Warranty - 10-year warranty against manufacturer defects; custom orders not subject to cancellation

Roche-Bobois sells expensive furniture from France and Italy. The look is simple, and the pieces here are well-built and classic in feel. The couches are extremely comfortable and the leather quality is excellent. Service is good, and there are occasional sales.

ROOM AND BOARD

www.roomandboard.com; 1-800-486-6554; Shipping Cost - Local delivery $55, elsewhere $155–$195 for unlimited number of items; Warranty - Full refund for items in current stock

Room and Board has nine locations across the country and sells mostly classic contemporary lines from a variety of manufacturers. Service is excellent, and the stores have a comfortable feel. Room and Board appeals to usually an urban person who wants to do one-stop shopping. Prices range.

TARGET HOME

www.target.com; 1-800-591-3869; Shipping Cost - $4.50 plus $0.49 per pound of order; calculated at time of order; Warranty - Return/refund for 90 days, after which will not replace defective merchandise

Worth checking out is the recently established Target Home, who sells furniture only through their Web site at this time. For students and couples looking for that cute, inexpensive extra piece of furniture, Target Home is a good route to shop. Carrying everything for the home, the furniture is really well designed at a great price.

URBAN OUTFITTERS

www.urbanoutfitters.com; 1-800-282-2200; Shipping Cost - Under $100, $5.95; over $100, no shipping charge unless noted on item; Warranty - 30 days for return/refund; after 30 days replace/refund for manufacturer defects only

Urban Outfitters is an interesting place to buy a little of everything. Besides selling clothing, games, books, and odds and ends, Urban Outfitters has just come out with a furniture catalog. The furniture is mostly classic mid-19th-century copies at an unbelievably low price. Many pieces sell for $300–$500. I am not sure about the long-term durability, but this line has been popular. In some of the stores you can even find some vintage pieces that have been restored. Hip, fun, and worth a visit.

WEST ELM

www.westelm.com; 1-866-WESTELM; Shipping Cost - Over $200, 10%; Warranty - 30 days for return/refund, after 30 days replace/refund for manufacturer defects only

West Elm is Pottery Barn's less expensive, more contemporary furniture line. The furniture is a great value. The look is classic and simple, and the prices are fair. Most pieces cost less than $500. Along with their easy-to-shop catalog, West Elm has four stores currently—one each in New York and Chicago, two in San Francisco. The Web site is easy to use.

WILLIAMS–SONOMA HOME

www.wshome.com; 1-888-922-4108; Shipping Cost - Over $400, 9%; Warranty - Custom-upholstered in fabric shown can be returned for full refund for 30 days; in fabric other than shown, must be cancelled within 24 hours of purchase; full refund for defects for 30 days including shipping, after 30 days just cost of product and taxes. Written warranty on case pieces/tables, 1 year; cushions, beds, mechanisms, 7 years; upholstery and slipcovers, 1 year.

Williams-Sonoma Home is Williams-Sonoma's first furniture catalog ever. Making promises of guaranteed upholstered goods coming in 45 days or less has caused people to take notice of this new catalog. Have not reviewed yet because it is a new business.

Z GALLERIE
www.zgallerie.com; 1-800-358-8288; Shipping Cost - Over $200, 10%; Warranty - 30 days for return/refund

Z Gallerie is popping up all over the country. Its look is traditional, comfortable, and a little dressy. Noteworthy because of the look and price is its nice, large art gallery with great art at extremely affordable prices (all pieces mostly under $100). Much of the art is already framed. I recommend visiting the store if only for the art. There are also some great gift selections like picture frames, books, mirrors, and candles. As at many large chain stores, they are at times short-staffed, but the atmosphere is relaxing and the neutral colors make the store inviting. There is also a large selection of holiday accessories. There is no catalog, but the inventory online is the same as in the store. The lines sold here include Bernhardt, Southern, and Rowe. Delivery times vary.

Successful Auction Shopping

Absentee Bid

An absentee bid refers to an auction bidder who submits a bid before the auction. This bid reflects the upper limit the bidder is willing to pay.

American Federal

This era encompasses the late 18th to the mid-19th centuries. Its look incorporates mahogany wood and the use of caned seats and seat backs. Many of the pieces reflect Americans' fascination with Greek and Roman motifs. Look for lyres, curved feet and cornucopias carved into the pieces. The principal American designer during this period was Duncan Phyfe.

Art Deco

Beginning in France, this popular early 20th Century style of furniture is characterized by the bold use of colors, luxurious fabrics, exotic woods and geometric designs. This sophisticated style incorporated steel and glass into many of the pieces of furniture. Le Corbusier was a leading designer during this period. Other famous Art Deco designers include Adnet, Arbus, Dufet, Boulle, Gray, Leleu, and Prou.

Art Moderne

The design period between the years 1925–1940. This period is characterized by geometric furniture design. Angles are emphasized.

Art Nouveau

This design style flourished in the late 19th and early 20th centuries.

Furniture from this period is characterized by asymmetrical flowing lines. Many of the pieces are painted and a strong Asian influence is present. Flowers and nature are prominent symbols used in the pieces. Tiffany and Galle were two of the major designers during this period.

Arts & Crafts

This period began in the 1860s in England. Look for straight lines and flat surfaces. Exposed hardware is also a common feature. William Morris and Charles Eastlake were the leading designers of Arts and Crafts, which advocated handmade pieces as opposed to the cheap mass-produced factory pieces that began appearing during this time.

Biedermeier

Named after a cartoon character in a German newspaper, Biedermeier was a popular style that is highly collectible today. The Biedermeier style originated in Germany but many of its pieces were made in Austria. The production period was short—1815 to 1830. The style is characterized by simple lines with functional designs. Legs are straight or tapered. The most common wood grains from this period include maple, birch, ash and other fruitwoods. Biedermeier has a very contemporary feel. It was briefly reproduced by the Swedes in the late 1800s.

Chinese Chippendale

This design period extended from 1750–1800. English merchant fleets were traveling the globe and the Chinese influence is seen in the wooden pieces produced during this time. Extensive lattice work on chairs and elaborate carving on legs and back cutouts are characteristic of this style. Thomas Chippendale made this style famous and it is still famous today.

Colonial

Sometimes dubbed "Early American," the Colonial style began in the 17th century and continued to dominate through a large part of the 18th century. Much of the style resembles English designs of the time— chests and trestle tables. As the period progressed, the influence of

Queen Anne, Chippendale and Empire styles can be seen. The Windsor chair is characteristic of this period.

English Regency

This period spans the late 18th century and early 19th. George IV was the monarch at the time and tended to favor pieces which were similar to the French Directoire and Empire periods. The furnishings were simpler and smaller in scale than those produced during the earlier Georgian period. Chinese and Egyptian motifs were used.

French Kings

Louis XIV

This period of design takes its name from one of the most famous of all French monarchs, Louis XIV, the "Sun King" who constructed the elaborate chateau outside of Paris known as Versailles. The period began in the mid-17th century and sometimes is termed the "Baroque Period." The designs are characterized by straight lines, high back chairs with carving, the use of upholstery, marble-top console tables, gilding, oak and walnut woods.

Louis XV

This period began in the mid-18th century and is characterized by ornate furniture styles. Most of the designs were feminine in style due to the influence of two of the king's mistresses of the period, Madame de Pomadour and Madame du Barry. The furniture has lots of curves, bombe chests, cabriole legs and an abundant use of gilding.

Louis XVI

This period began in the latter quarter of the 18th century and includes the violent political upheaval caused by the French Revolution which began in 1789. The design lines are straighter, the styles simpler and the furniture motifs are somewhat more classical.

French Empire

The Empire period approximates the time span when Napoleon was Emperor of France, from 1804–1815. Many of the styles take their cue from Napoleon's military campaigns in Greece and especially in Egypt. Carvings of lions, sphinxes, eagles and the letter "N" are seen on the furniture pieces. The Emperor's first wife, Josephine heavily influenced the designers of the time. The pieces are fancy but also serious. The tabletops are marble with metal feet. Rosewood and mahogany woods are featured.

French Provincial

Today this term has an entirely new meaning for many Americans buying furniture. Technically, the term refers to those styles of the late 17th and early 18th centuries. The majority of the pieces were peasant-made furniture created in the French countryside—farm tables, ladder-back chairs with straw seats. Native woods such as oak, walnut, ash and fruitwood are used.

Georgian

This period is large, covering most of the 18th century in English furniture design. The name is derived from the three British monarchs of this era, George I, George II, and George III. George III was the English monarch who occupied the throne during the time of the American Revolution. The era is full of famous furniture designers whose names have become household words—Robert Adam, Thomas Chippendale, George Hepplewhite and Thomas Sheraton. Mahogany was the principal wood used. The Georgian period is also well known for its use of the sideboard and cabriole legs on chairs and tables.

List Price

The list price is the price that many showrooms put on their price tags. This price is what a buyer would pay without having a designer. Designers get a discount off this price.

Lot Number

The lot number is the property identification number in an auction.

Net Price

The net price is the price that a designer pays for a piece of furniture. This reflects a discount off the list price.

Queen Anne

The American version of the Queen Anne style remains popular today. The American pieces were sturdier than their European counterparts so more of them survived. Less emphasis was placed on decoration. Rather, designers concentrated on form—the cabriole leg added strength. In the U.S., classical and oriental motifs characterized this style. The high boy chest and Queen Anne chair were the two most popular pieces. This furniture was usually made with walnut, but a few pieces were done in mahogany. The shell motif is incorporated into many Queen Anne pieces.

Reserve Price

In the auction business, the reserve price is the lowest price for which a seller is willing to sell his property.

Sale Price

The sale price is the final bidding price for an item at auction.

Shaker

The Shaker era was uniquely American. It existed in the late 18th century through the early 19th century. It was created by an American religious group living in small villages up and down the East coast of North America. All of the pieces were handmade. Machine manufacturing was frowned upon. The Shakers placed a lot of emphasis on function—swivel stools and chairs. Most items were constructed from pine and bear a strong resemblance to French Provincial furniture.

To the Trade

Stores owners often have policies restricting the public from shopping at their stores. This term refers to interior designers or those in the architectural or construction trade.

Trade Discount

Trade discounts are discounts given only to members of the trade. Some antiques stores and boutiques give substantial discounts to interior designers and other members of the trade. Trade discounts are common in design centers.

Victorian

Named after the reign of Britain's Queen Victoria who reigned from 1830–1900, Victorian styles were heavily influenced by the Industrial Revolution and the use of machinery to manufacture pieces in factory settings. The style is characterized by heavy frames, extensive use of red velvet upholstery and the introduction of metal springs in sofas and chairs. Mahogany and walnut are the most common woods used and most seat backs are oval shaped and upholstered.

William and Mary

The William and Mary style from roughly 1690–1720 brought a more delicate shape to furniture pieces of the time. This was primarily an American style. Legs are shaped, thinner and more spindly. Decoration is applied rather than carved. Veneers are used and painted dark to resemble more expensive ebony pieces.